REFLECTIVE HIST

Barbara Finkelstein and William J

The Failed Promise of
the American High School,
1890–1995

David L. Angus and Jeffrey E. Mirel

TEACHERS
COLLEGE
PRESS

Teachers College, Columbia University
New York and London

Published by Teachers College Press, 1234 Amsterdam Avenue, New York, NY 10027

Library of Congress Cataloging-in-Publication Data

Angus, David L.
    The failed promise of the American high school, 1890–1995 / David
L. Angus and Jeffrey E. Mirel.
        p.   cm. — (Reflective history series)
    Includes bibliographical references and index.
    ISBN 0-8077-3843-3 (cloth : alk. paper). — ISBN 0-8077-3842-5
(pbk. : alk. paper)
    1. High schools—United States—History.   2. Education, Secondary—
United States—Curricula—History.   3. Educational change—United
States—History.   I. Mirel, Jeffrey, 1948–   . II. Title.
III. Series.
    LA222.A543   1999
    373.73—dc21   99-17345

ISBN 0-8077-3842-5 (paper)
ISBN 0-8077-3843-3 (cloth)

Printed on acid-free paper
Manufactured in the United States of America

06 05 04 03 02 01 00 99   8 7 6 5 4 3 2 1

To the memory of Albert Shanker (1928–1997)
a man of courage and wisdom
whose commitment to democracy and education
continues to be an inspiration

Contents

Acknowledgments

In the late 1980s, amid a lively national debate about the nature and direction of public education, the two of us began exploring the history of the American high school. Our hope was that by illuminating that history we could not only shed light on how the institution developed but also help educators and educational policy makers develop policies and practices that would enable high schools to realize their heretofore failed promise of providing equal educational opportunity.

In the course of our researching and writing, we have been aided by many organizations and individuals, and we are delighted to have this opportunity to thank them for the support they gave us. The Spencer Foundation, through its Small Grants program, enabled us to complete a crucial part of our data gathering on curriculum and coursetaking in the 1930s and 1940s. The Social Science Research Institute (SSRI) of Northern Illinois University provided Jeff with a two-year fellowship that allowed him to make considerable progress on the research and writing of the book. Jeff would like to thank Harvey Smith, Director of SSRI, for his support. In addition, he would like to thank Dean Jerrold Zar of the Northern Illinois University Graduate School and the Graduate Committee for Research and Artistry which awarded him a summer research grant to work on this project.

We also are deeply grateful to Gordon Olson and the other archivists of the Grand Rapids Historical Society, who were unfailingly helpful in guiding us to materials and sources during our many visits to that city. In addition, we wish to thank staff members from the central office of the Grand Rapids public schools and each of the high schools that we visited for aiding us in our research efforts. C. Phillip Kearney, former Director of the Bureau of School Services at the University of Michigan, provided access to the Bureau's files, from which we assembled our data on the Detroit high schools. William Bushaw allowed us to use the records of the North Central Association, from which we assembled data on high schools in the state of Michigan.

A number of friends and colleagues have been especially supportive of our efforts, offering criticism and insights at every stage of the process. Mary Ann Dzuback, Valerie Lee, Edward McCellan, Liz McPike, and Bella Rosenberg have read and commented on either essays directly related to the book or specific chapters from it. They have influenced our interpretations in numerous ways, compelling us to refine and sharpen our arguments. Barbara Finkelstein, Diane Ravitch, William Reese, John Rury, and Maris Vinovskis have read and critiqued the entire manuscript. Painful as their advice occasionally has been, the book is much better for their suggestions. All of these friends and colleagues have helped us improve the manuscript; none is responsible for its errors or inaccuracies. Finally, we'd like to thank our editor, Brian Ellerbeck, for his support and encouragement.

For the love and devotion of our families, both of us are deeply grateful. David would like to thank Anna, whose quiet patience and sense of proportion has made the last two years seem worth living and, thus, the book worth finishing. Jeff's children, Josh, Lisa, and Diana, were high school students during most of the time that he was working on the book. Their experiences in those years helped influence his ideas about high schools, but he is quite sure that his ideas rarely influenced them. Nevertheless, they are continuing sources of joy and pride. Jeff's wife, Barbara, provided careful and insightful analysis of every section of this book. Her love and strength are the guiding stars of his life.

The book is dedicated to the memory of Albert Shanker.

Introduction

IN SEPTEMBER 1989, President George Bush and the nation's governors (led by then-governor of Arkansas Bill Clinton) met in Charlottesville, Virginia, and committed themselves to revitalizing American public education by establishing "clear national performance goals, goals that will make us internationally competitive" (Weinraub, 1989, p. A10). Two of these goals specifically focused on changing patterns of curriculum and coursetaking. Goal 3 declared that "American students will leave grades four, eight, and twelve having demonstrated competency in challenging subject matter including English, mathematics, science, history and geography; and every school in America will ensure that all students learn to use their minds well, so they may be prepared for responsible citizenship, further learning, and productive employment." Goal 4 called for U.S. students to be "first in the world in science and math achievement" (U.S. Department of Education, 1991, p. 3). In March 1994, President Clinton continued the process begun in Charlottesville by signing the "Goals 2000: Educate America Act." The act pledged $400 million annually in grants for states and school districts that committed themselves to establishing "high standards for curriculum content and student performance" (Pitsch, 1994, p. 1).

Although these efforts received bipartisan support, they nevertheless set off a storm of controversy. In congressional debates and subsequent discussions, supporters of Goals 2000 argued that these measures will help ensure equal educational opportunity for all American students. Critics, by contrast, claimed that the new measures will have precisely the opposite effect, actually increasing educational *in*equality (see, for example, Eisner, 1994; Maehr & Maehr, 1996; Ravitch, 1995; Shanker, 1994a, 1994b). How can thoughtful analysts of American education see the same policies in so radically different terms? What assumptions and beliefs do these analysts bring to the debate that leads to their divergent projections about the outcomes of these initiatives? What historical trends and developments in American education give credence to these disparate views?

This book examines these questions. We see the current controversy over goals and standards as the latest manifestation of a century-old debate about the meaning and methods of achieving equal educational opportunity. Yet we also believe that the current controversy marks a dramatic change in the nature of that

1

debate. Underlying the call for national goals are the beliefs that high and demanding standards are essential for educational improvement, that academic subjects must have priority in the curriculum, and that all American students can and must perform at substantially higher levels than in the past. In asserting these beliefs, supporters of national goals and rigorous educational standards are presenting the first sustained challenge to the philosophy and structure of schooling that have dominated public education for most of this century.

To explore these developments we analyze the history of the comprehensive high school, the institution that embodies that philosophy and structure more clearly than any other component of the American educational enterprise. At the heart of the prevailing American conception of what constitutes a good high school education are three fundamental beliefs: first, that the curriculum should be differentiated with respect to the backgrounds, plans, aspirations, and interests of students; second, that such differentiation is the key to universalizing high school attendance; and third, that, unlike in many European nations, these differentiated curricula should be offered by and within a single institutional setting.

Americans have long expressed great confidence and pride in this vision of "secondary education for all." Comprehensive high schools are at once democratic, efficient, practical, and supportive of Americans' belief in individuality. The early history of public secondary education throughout the world seemed to bear this out. America led the world in making secondary education, and eventually higher education, open and available to increasingly larger proportions of the population. Indeed, due to these successes, following World War II, some European nations sought to reform their secondary schools along American lines.

Recently, however, a number of nations that after World War II rejected the American model of differentiated high school curricula began to approach and eventually overtake the United States in progress toward universal high school attendance. By 1982, Japan, for example, had achieved higher rates of high school attendance than the United States and had done so while offering a high school curriculum that had few curricular options and was heavy on academic courses. Furthermore, international comparisons revealed that students from some of these nations also were outperforming Americans on standardized tests of basic skills (National Center for Education Statistics [NCES], 1987, 1992).[1] By the early 1980s, many Americans began questioning whether the comprehensive high school was still serving the best interests of our young people and our nation.

Indeed, in 1983, *A Nation at Risk* identified American high schools as a major contributor to the rising tide of educational mediocrity. The report argued that "[a]verage achievement of high school students on most standardized tests is now lower than 26 years ago," that Scholastic Aptitude Test scores have been in "virtually unbroken decline" for 2 decades, and that "science achievement scores of U.S. 17 year olds" have fallen since 1969 (National Commission on Excellence in Education, 1983, pp. 18–19). *A Nation at Risk* attributed many of these problems to the "cafeteria-style curriculum" in high schools and to the "extensive" range of programs and courses available to students. To correct those problems, the report advocated a program of "New Basics," a required core of academic courses for all students that would reduce the number of curricular options. In rejecting the differentiated curriculum and its wide range of electives, *A Nation at Risk* demanded not only a major reassessment of curricular structures and course offerings, but reassessment of our ideas about equal educational opportunity as well.

This call for a core curriculum of academic subjects stood in stark contrast to the findings of a similarly urgent assessment of the American high school in the 1950s. Responding to the launch of Sputnik and the growing threat of Soviet Communism, James Bryant Conant declared in *The American High School Today* (1959) that because of the differentiated curriculum the comprehensive high school was an institution that embodied the best in the American democratic spirit. "I think it is safe to say," he wrote, "that the comprehensive high school is characteristic of our society and further that it has come into being because of our economic history and our devotion to the ideals of equality of opportunity and equality of status" (Conant, 1959, p. 40).

The unifying theme of the current controversy about Goals 2000 and the positions articulated in *A Nation at Risk* and *The American High School Today* is the conviction that equal educational opportunity is a primary goal of high schools and that the crucial educational decision for achieving that goal concerns the degree of curricular differentiation. Many educational historians have analyzed these issues either by examining the intellectual exchanges among curriculum theorists, educational policy makers, and practicing educators or by investigating the actual impact of specific curriculum policy changes on the educational experiences of high school students. Despite some superb studies in both these areas (see, for example, Herbst, 1996; Kantor, 1988; Kliebard, 1986; Krug, 1964, 1972; Labaree, 1988; Perlmann, 1988; Reese, 1995; Rury, 1991) we believe this previous work is insufficient. Generally, it rests on two questionable assumptions about the history of the twentieth-century high school. First, virtually all those who have explored the history of the high school assume that the main curriculum debates centered around whether high schools should be primarily academic, vocational, or a mixture of the two. Second, most scholars assume that by 1930 the fundamental nature of the institution had been set and that future developments were merely variations on themes established during the Progressive Era.

Our research challenges both assumptions. We find that in addition to the academic and vocational aspects of high schools a third, perhaps even more important aspect, a custodial mission, has profoundly shaped the modern history of the institution and its quest for equal educational opportunity. Other historians have noted the growing custodial role of the high school in the first part of this century, but most generally downplay its significance, seeing it simply as an expansion of the movement toward curricular differentiation that began in the Progressive Era.[2] We see the shift to custodialism as a fundamental change in the social and economic function of the high school that consequently transformed the nature of the institution.

To explain this process of change that we believe is central to the modern development of the American high school, we bring together elements of the two dominant methodological approaches that historians have used to explore the history of this institution. While we reinterpret what people said about high schools, we also analyze new sources of quantitative data that reveal students' coursetaking experiences within schools. These data enable us to assess the degree to which the policy debates actually influenced school practice and the degree to which the coursetaking experiences of students coincided with the plans and expectations of educational policy makers.

Our data come from several different sources that allow us to present a "nested" picture of student coursetaking for most of this century. The data include a series of U.S. Office of Education surveys conducted in 1928, 1934, 1949, 1961, and 1973 that provide increasingly detailed and trustworthy snapshots of high school course enrollments. In addition, researchers under contract to the National Center for Education Statistics gathered similar data in 1982, 1987, 1990, and 1994, usually from student transcripts, which we link to the earlier studies (Greer & Harbeck, 1962; NCES, 1993, 1997; Ostendorf & Horn, 1976; U.S. Office of Education, 1930, 1938, 1951; West, Diodata, & Sandberg, 1984; Wright, 1965).

Next we examine school-level data gathered by the Bureau of School Services at the University of Michigan, which accredited high schools in the state from 1897 to 1992. These data enable us to analyze coursetaking trends in all high schools in Michigan from 1928 to 1990. Michigan is an especially good site for such analysis because of the great diversity of its population and economic regions, including large industrial centers and vast areas of the state devoted to agriculture and extraction industries.

We also examine course offerings and student coursetaking in Detroit, focusing on school-level data from the late 1920s to the 1990s. Detroit is also a good site for such analysis because during much of this century it was a national leader in such areas as the implementation of differentiated high school curricula (Mirel, 1993). Finally, we link these data with our analysis of 1,445 individual records of high school students who attended school between 1900 and 1940 in Grand Rapids, Michigan, a representative, midwestern city that was a showcase for innovative vocational programs during the Progressive Era (Spring, 1972; Violas, 1978).

Drawing on these national-, state-, school-, and student-level data, we present a new interpretation of the role of high schools in the quest for equal educational opportunity. This quest has been marked by great controversy about conflicting definitions of educational equality, and radically changing aims and goals of the institution. Invariably these controversies, including the current debate over national goals and standards, have transformed the nature and function of the high school and forced repeated revisions of its curriculum.

In presenting this history, it is important to be clear about what we have and have not examined in our analysis. In our reinterpretation of what educational theorists have said about high school curricula, our focus is mainly on the debate between advocates of uniform academic programs and supporters of curricular differentiation. While we briefly discuss other topics that relate to this debate, we do so only to the degree that they illuminate aspects of that larger controversy. Similarly, in our quantitative analyses, we concentrate mainly on the trends in coursetaking by public high school students. Occasionally we discuss the content of those courses, but as with our examination of the theoretical debates we do so only when the evidence provides additional insight into the larger questions that we are pursuing. Our book is not a study of course *content* in American high schools but rather a study of the changing nature and function of public secondary education as revealed by our reinterpretation of the national debates and our analysis of coursetaking trends.

NOTES

1. In 1970, 86% of secondary school–age children in Japan were in school compared with 92% in the United States. Twelve years later Japanese enrollments exceeded those in the United States, 95 to 92% (National Center for Education Statistics, 1987).

2. An important exception is the work of Norton Grubb and Marvin Lazerson (1982), who have discussed the "warehousing" function of high schools.

1

The Professionalization of
Curriculum Planning

DURING THE LATTER HALF of the nineteenth century, the public high school gradually replaced the private academy as the dominant form of secondary education in America. This happened first in the large cities in the 1850s, followed by the smaller cities and towns in the 1860s and 1870s and in villages and rural areas still later (Reese, 1995). This development was not without conflict. In many cities the legitimacy of the high school was questioned and occasionally its existence was threatened, largely because urban school boards were unable to build primary and grammar schools fast enough to keep up with their growing cities. Overcrowded schools, half-day sessions, the use of inappropriate rented facilities, and children being turned away at the schoolhouse door were common occurrences. Critics claimed that it was poor public policy to provide expensive secondary education for a few students when primary schooling could not be provided for all. Further, they often claimed that the students who attended the high school were drawn solely from those classes that could afford to send their children to private schools. In this climate, the high school was forced to justify its purposes, curriculum, and even the social composition of its student population (Angus, 1981, 1988; Burrell & Eckelberry, 1934; Mirel, 1981).

As recent scholarship has shown, almost from their beginnings the vast majority of public high schools were dual purpose institutions, serving both those who intended to go on to college and those who, in the phrase of the day, planned to enter business, professional, and mechanical pursuits. The college-bound, overwhelmingly boys until the 1880s, followed the classical course, consisting largely of classical languages, history, and some mathematics, while the majority of students, both boys and girls, followed the English course, which included modern languages and literature, mathematics, the natural sciences, history, geography, and so on. The students represented a wide range of social strata, although very few were foreign born or from the lowest occupations. Total enrollments were low since only a few children completed the 6 or 7 years of primary and grammar school and passed the examination required for high school entry (Angus, 1988; Herbst, 1996; Reese, 1995).

As the high school matured in the last quarter of the century, enrollments rose, often doubling in a decade, and the courses of study multiplied. Those planning for college could choose from several curricula, linked to the expanding number of different degrees offered in American colleges and universities. Students preparing for immediate occupation also faced choices, commercial courses for those heading for the business world, normal courses for those planning to teach, manual training, mechanical drawing, and surveying for those looking toward "mechanical pursuits." Elective and after-school courses in music, physical education, and art were also common. Not only was there a great expansion in the number and range of subject fields offered, but there was a good deal of experimentation with the arrangement of subjects into coherent courses of study, their placement in the grades, and their time allotments. With respect to these matters, no two high schools were alike; there were no "norms," no standard practice, no clear leaders and followers.

The main reason for this was that throughout the century, curriculum decisions, as well as virtually all other decisions, were made by locally elected boards of education, not by career educators. Not surprisingly, curriculum decisions were political decisions in the broad sense, and boards showed considerable responsiveness to ongoing local concerns (Lawson, 1940; Tyack & Hansot, 1982). While superintendents and high school principals often were asked for their recommendations on curriculum matters, these recommendations might be deferred, adopted in whole or in part, or ignored altogether. Carrying equal or greater weight in curriculum decisions were such factors as pressure from parents or from ethnic voting blocks and demographic or fiscal crises.

This is not to say that there were no national trends in the latter half of the century. Two such trends worth noting were the movement for a more practical curriculum, called the manual training movement, and a drive to alter the relationship between high schools and colleges, both stretching from the 1870s into the 1890s. The first of these was moderately successful in establishing manual training high schools, manual training courses in existing high schools, or single offerings in high schools and even some grammar schools in many cities around the country. But the movement was led by the same "amateurs" who made up the local boards of education and the struggle for these changes was fought out there. Educational "professionals" were split on the question, some arguing that manual training allowed public schools to train young people for a broader range of occupations than just the professions, and others seeing it as too narrow or outside the scope of legitimate public interest.

The second movement, linking high schools to colleges, was, we believe, even less successful. Although many historians have argued that the nineteenth-century high school was dominated by the colleges, we see their influence as modest and limited to those courses of study that led directly to admission to one or another college course. As a rule, colleges and universities did not add subjects as admission requirements that were not already being offered in public high schools (Broome, 1903). Local boards may have rearranged subjects within courses of study to conform to shifts in college requirements, especially after the acceptance of the "diploma system" of admission pioneered by the University of Michigan in 1871,[1] but they did not look to the colleges for guidance in the matter of curriculum more broadly conceived. In fact, it was precisely this lack of response to what career educators saw as their expert knowledge on curriculum that led to the single most important educational document of the nineteenth century, the Report of the Committee of Ten on Secondary School Subjects (Angus & Mirel, 1994). In the last quarter of the nineteenth century, urban school superintendents, high school principals, and college and university faculty increasingly turned to professional status as a means for gaining greater influence and control over educational policy and practice in relation to colleges and local school boards.

THE COMMITTEE OF TEN

In the summer of 1892, the National Council of Education, an elite group of 60 members of the National Educational Association (NEA), appointed a committee of 10 members to prepare a report on the uniformity of high school programs and the requirements for admission to college. Chaired by Charles W. Eliot, President of Harvard University, the committee included President James B. Angell of the University of Michigan, President James Taylor of Vassar College, President Richard Jesse of the University of Missouri, and President James Baker of the University of Colorado, who had just resigned his position as principal of Denver High School and who also served as chair of the National Council of Education. Besides the university presidents, the committee included W. T. Harris, U.S. Commissioner of Education; Professor Henry King of Oberlin College; John Tetlow, headmaster of Girls' High School in Boston; and James Mackenzie, headmaster of Lawrenceville School in New Jersey. Only one "high school man," Principal Oscar Robinson of Albany, represented public secondary schools.

In addition to the original committee, nine subcommittees (called "conferences") also were set up, each with 10 members. These conferences made recommendations on the teaching of nine carefully selected subject areas: Latin; Greek; English; modern languages; mathematics; physics, astronomy, and chemistry; natural history (biology, including botany, zoology, and physiology); history, civil government, and political economy; and geography (physical geography, geology, and meteorology). The main committee distilled the recommendations from the conferences into its final report.

At the time of its release, the report of the Committee of Ten was the most important educational document ever issued in the United States, and no account of the history of education in America is complete without some discussion of it (Broome, 1903; Cremin, 1961; Cubberly, 1919; Hawkins, 1972; Herbst, 1996;

Kliebard, 1986; Krug, 1964; Powell, 1980; Sizer, 1964). We agree that the report was a watershed document but not for the reasons historians traditionally have given, namely, that it shaped high school curriculum for a generation or more and that it highlighted the domination of colleges over high schools. Rather, we see the report as a crucial first step toward the professionalization of curriculum planning and as a direct assault on the control of high school curricula by lay boards of education (Angus, 1993).

In brief, the substance of the report rested on three interrelated principles. The first had to do with the question of differentiation. The committee had asked the subject conferences to decide whether their subject "should be treated differently for pupils who are going to college, for those who are going to a scientific school, and for those who, presumably, are going to neither." Based on their responses, the committee concluded that "every subject which is taught at all in a secondary school should be taught in the same way and to the same extent to every pupil as long as he pursues it, no matter what the probable destination of the pupil may be, or at what point his education is to cease" (NEA, 1894, p. 17). The second principle dealt with the question of election of studies. Since it was clear to the committee that individual students could never be expected to do all the work in all the subjects recommended by the conferences and that not all high schools would be able to offer all the subjects recommended, an elective option was needed. This led to a sort of "twin" principle of election in which individual high schools would choose the subset of subjects they could offer and arrange them into courses of study, while individual students would choose from these courses of study. However, this was to be no "shopping mall high school" (Powell, Farrar, & Cohen, 1985). The committee maintained that schools should not deviate far from the recommendations of the conferences and should arrange the subjects to reflect equal "seriousness, dignity, and efficacy," while students should be allowed to make only a "carefully guided choice among a limited number of subjects" (NEA, 1894, pp. 39–40). This recommendation led to the third principle, that of equivalence, the only one having to do with college admission requirements. The committee argued that if a high school followed the first two principles, then every college and university should accept the school's arrangements as adequate for admission to at least one of its degree programs (NEA, 1894).

The committee was well aware that the nine "core" subjects represented by the conferences was a short list compared with all the subjects then offered in the nation's high schools, and it tried to show flexibility with regard to some of these courses, recommending that students be permitted to substitute bookkeeping and business arithmetic for algebra, and industrial subjects for science in grade 11 or 12. But, predictably, these compromises failed to satisfy those who advocated entire high schools organized around such courses, and this became the basis for one of the lines of attack on the "elitism" of the committee's report.

These critics (and a host of later historians) argued that the committee was unconcerned with the vast majority of boys and girls then crowding into the nation's high schools who, it was assumed, would drop out of school because of boredom with the curriculum. But the committee had indeed acknowledged these students and their majority status in the high schools of the day; it merely took a very different view of what they should study in high school. In an often cited passage, the committee declared:

> The secondary schools of the United States, taken as a whole, do not exist for the purpose of preparing boys and girls for the colleges. Only an insignificant percentage of the graduates of these schools go to colleges or scientific schools. . . . A secondary school programme intended for national use must therefore be made for those children whose education is not to be pursued beyond the secondary school. The preparation of a few pupils for college or scientific school should in the ordinary secondary school be the incidental, not the principal object. (NEA, 1894, pp. 51–52)

Nevertheless, because the committee argued strongly that all students should follow essentially similar "academic" courses of study, critics of the report later distorted that idea by reducing it to an aphorism, "fitting for college is essentially the same as fitting for life." Indeed, these critics often cited this aphorism to represent, or rather misrepresent, the whole report (Kliebard, 1986).

Actually, the report called for two efforts to bring greater "uniformity" to the programs of high school students. It called on high schools to stop adding more and more short "informational" courses to the curriculum, since these were crowding out the more time-honored subjects. In addition, it called on colleges and universities to stop the proliferation of new admission requirements each time they added new bachelor's degrees, and for those colleges and universities that were committed to the examination method of admission, to come to some common agreements about what subjects and levels would be tested. The committee held firmly to the principle that all students should take a core of rigorous, "academic" courses.

In sum, the report of the Committee of Ten was both the first clarion call for the high school curriculum to be designed by career educators instead of lay boards and the first call for a national curriculum. It was an attempt to end the proliferation of subjects, courses, college entrance requirements, and specialized high schools that characterized the late nineteenth century. Moreover, it was the first, and only, "back-to-basics" movement led by professional educators.

THE RISE OF THE EDUCATION PROFESSIONS

If the Committee of Ten was an attempt to more sharply draw a line between career educators and lay boards of education and to claim the territory of the high school curriculum for the professionals, it also set off a protracted struggle for hegemony *within* the emergent profession. Beginning around the turn of the century, a deepening alliance of big city superintendents, high school principals, and professors of education within universities attempted to wrest control over secondary school affairs from the college presidents and liberal arts faculty members who had dominated the Committee of Ten. This development coincided with and supported the founding and expansion of schools of education within universities and eventually helped to define an educational professional as one who had been trained in such institutions.

One arena of this power struggle was the NEA itself. The membership of committees subsequent to the Committee of Ten revealed the increasing power of the "educationist" alliance within the organization. For example, the 12-member Committee on College Entrance Requirements, appointed to recommend ways to implement the earlier report, included six "high school men" and four professors of education. No college presidents served on the committee. The Committee of Fifteen was dominated by urban superintendents, and its subcommittee on the organization of city school systems led the struggle to free school systems from the heavy hand of lay board control by proposing a "corporate model" of school governance that limited the board's oversight to policy and fiscal matters, while leaving all educational matters in the hands of the superintendent.

As school administrators increasingly sought professional status, they adopted this corporate model of school governance as a prime article of faith. In 1896, the NEA created the Department of School Administration to advance the new idea and to provide a home within the organization for school board members who accepted this philosophy. A board member from Aurora, Illinois, speaking at the first meeting, declared, "The relation of a board of education to its superintendent should not differ in theory or in fact from the relation which the board of directors of an incorporated manufacturing or other commercial enterprise sustains to its superintendent" (NEA, 1896, p. 980). An early textbook on school administration took the argument a step further: "A superintendent of schools cannot properly be considered a subordinate of a board of education; even less is he a subordinate of any board member. A professional man cannot be a subordinate of one who in respect to his profession is a layman" (Chancellor, 1908, p. 10).

At the same time that school superintendents were campaigning for greater control over all aspects of the educational process in their school systems, an important shift was occurring in terms of who spoke for colleges in their interactions with high schools. In the 1890s, it was the presidents or the most prestigious professors who represented the interests of the colleges, but in the next century, the universities were increasingly represented by professors of education who made a specialty of these relations. When the North Central Association of Colleges and Secondary Schools (NCA) was founded in 1895, four college presidents were in attendance and three of them subsequently served as president of the association. However, by 1904, when the NCA had established a Commission on Accredited

Schools and a Board of Inspectors to inspect the high school members, the universities were represented not by their presidents but by faculty members in the emerging subprofession of secondary education. These high school inspectors employed by the universities or by state departments of education quickly formed what would be a long-lasting alliance with the high school principals they were hired to inspect. After 1916, when the NCA divided into a Commission on Secondary Schools and a Commission on Institutions of Higher Education meeting separately, the *only* university people who consistently attended the high school commission meetings were faculty from the departments and schools of education and those involved in high school inspection (Davis, 1945; Grinnell, 1935).

Within the universities, there were also tensions developing between faculty in the older liberal arts departments and the new faculties of education, tensions that would have profound implications for the development of high schools (Clifford & Guthrie, 1988). While connection with the university served the interests of superintendents by providing them the cloak of scientific expertise in their struggle for greater control over urban school systems (Tyack & Hansot, 1982), the university's demands for research productivity and academic respectability from the education faculty often clashed with the demands for "practicality" coming from these superintendents and others in elementary and secondary schools. This tension between practical demands and research actually mirrored the situation of the high school, caught between local demands for a more practical curriculum and the demands of the colleges for a broader and more stringent preparatory curriculum. The new schools of education attempted to relieve this tension by creating research- and theory-oriented graduate programs and isolating these from their teacher education function. Consequently, the education faculty increasingly recommended that the high schools follow the same strategy by devising curricula that sharply differentiated the two functions of the institution, "fitting for life and fitting for college."

By 1910, all the elements contributing to the growth of a profession of education were in place. Increasingly important professional associations such as the NEA were able to project their authority with reports and studies that attracted national attention. These organizations routinely asserted that professional educators should have the same control over their areas of expertise as professionals in other fields. At the same time, colleges and universities were playing ever larger roles in education both as the training grounds for these new education professionals and through the process of inspecting and certifying high school curricula and programs. And, perhaps most important, universities increasingly placed control over professional educational training and high school inspection and certification in the hands of the emerging schools and colleges of education rather than in academic departments. But if university-based education professors, in alliance with superintendents and high school principals, were poised to assert control over the high schools and in particular their curricula, what ideas about the goals and purposes of the high schools would they attempt to implement?

COMMON IDEAS OF THE PROFESSIONAL
CURRICULUM PLANNERS

Much has been written about the fundamental differences and disagreements among the major curriculum theorists of the twentieth century. Lawrence Cremin's classic work, *The Transformation of the School* (1961), began this tradition by dividing progressive educational leaders into "romantic," "radical," and "scientific" schools of thought, stressing the battles among these points of view. Krug (1964) also featured the theme of intellectual conflict, particularly in such chapters as "Harris, Hall, and the Herbartians" and "Social Efficiency Triumphant." If anything, Herbert Kliebard's (1986) book on the development of curriculum theory in America stresses even more the idea of different schools of thought "struggling" over the curriculum. What has been largely overlooked in this approach is just how many ideas these people shared, in terms of not only what a "modern" high school should be and do, but also the underlying principles and values that they took for granted. These taken-for-granted aspects of their thinking have had such a profound effect on the practices and legitimations of practices in our high schools that they still influence our thinking about secondary education.

These ideas are: (1) nineteenth-century high schools were bastions of elite, college preparatory training that were largely irrelevant to the lives of most young Americans; (2) in order to make high schools more democratic, to ensure what these leaders believed was truly "equal educational opportunity," professional educators had to greatly expand the high school curriculum; (3) this curriculum expansion had to include the introduction of new courses (especially practical courses), new subjects, new arrangements of access to courses, new graduation requirements, and new college entrance requirements; (4) in contrast to the lay boards of education that attempted to design high schools to meet the needs of their various communities, the new educational leaders believed that the new courses and programs should be designed with the "needs" of individual students, or at least large groupings of students, in mind; and (5) while there was considerable disagreement about just how these needs should be determined, how the groupings of students should be made, all these educational leaders agreed that these decisions should be made by professionals, not by lay boards of education. Taken together, these new educational leaders called for an entirely new order in secondary education.[2]

As is often the case with those who think of themselves as on the threshold of a new order, these reformers sought to distance themselves as much as possible from the past. They did this by presenting a distorted history of the nine-teenth-century high school and by uniformly rejecting the report of the Commit-tee of Ten as a relic of the past. Secondary education textbooks of the first 3 de-cades of the twentieth century routinely included short sections on the history of American high schools, describing them as mainly or strictly academic institu-tions, enrolling a small elite of wealthy or intellectually talented youngsters for the sole purpose of "fitting" them for college.

In addition, these reformers presupposed a definition of equality of educa-tional opportunity that was strikingly at odds with that of the Committee of Ten. Whereas the committee had stressed the idea that high school students should study mainly the same subjects in the same amounts and in the same ways, regardless of their "probable destinies," the new educational professionals argued that this was a *denial* of equal opportunity. In their minds, equal opportunity meant an equal chance to prepare for a future consistent with one's interests, abilities, and home situation. This required a much more elaborate curriculum and a system to differ-entiate students into separate programs of studies. The reformers truly believed that this approach would provide greater equality because more students would find something valuable in the high school and would remain in school longer (NEA, 1908).

Given their portrayal of the nineteenth-century high school as an elite, col-lege preparatory school, it is not surprising that the new education professionals sought to expand the vocational offerings of the high school, railed against the colleges and universities for setting admission requirements too high and for re-quiring subjects of little use to the average student, and pressured local boards to lower and broaden high school graduation requirements to make "room" in the curriculum for the new courses. While they were moderately successful in such efforts early in the twentieth century, it was not until 1918 that they produced a document on a par with the report of the Committee of Ten that gave voice to the reform consensus among professionals and set the stage for a more vigorous as-sault on past practice.

THE CARDINAL PRINCIPLES OF SECONDARY EDUCATION

The manifesto that codified the curriculum reform consensus we have been de-scribing was *Cardinal Principles of Secondary Education*, issued by the Com-mission on the Reorganization of Secondary Education (CRSE), a commission co-sponsored by the NEA and the U.S. Bureau of Education. The CRSE was similar to the Committee of Ten in that its work began with a set of committees working on separate subject fields in the high school curriculum and a 26-member over-sight committee to review these reports and summarize them as a set of general principles. But when the work of the subject committees stretched into several years, the reviewing committee decided to draw up a general statement separate from the subject committees. In 1918, this document was issued as *Cardinal Principles* (Krug, 1964).

Although its method of investigating the problems of secondary education was similar to that taken by the Committee of Ten, virtually everything else about the CRSE and *Cardinal Principles* was different, beginning with the composition of the commission. While the Committee of Ten had been dominated by the presidents of research universities and headmasters of private schools, the CRSE embodied the emerging alliance of professors of education, educational administrators, and representatives of high schools. The commission included six professors of education, three representatives from normal schools, three people from the U.S. Bureau of Education, three local school administrators, two public high school teachers, two state high school supervisors, and one college president who had formerly been a professor of education. There were no representatives from academic departments (CRSE, 1918; Krug, 1964).

Also unlike the report of the Committee of Ten, *Cardinal Principles* made no reference to subjects or their arrangement into curricula. Indeed, the CRSE seemed to utterly repudiate the position of the Committee of Ten regarding the importance of subject matter as a basis for high school curriculum development. Instead of core subjects or subject areas, the CRSE identified seven "objectives" for secondary education: "1. Health. 2. Command of fundamental processes. 3. Worthy home-membership. 4. Vocation. 5. Citizenship. 6. Worthy use of leisure. 7. Ethical character" (CRSE, 1918, pp. 10–11). Closely related to this neglect of subject areas and subject matter was the repudiation of the vision of equal educational opportunity contained in the report of the Committee of Ten. Echoing the position that differentiation was the key to equal educational opportunity, the CRSE declared:

> Secondary education in the past has met the needs of only a few groups. The growing recognition that progress in our American democracy depends in no small measure upon adequate provision for specialization in many fields is the chief cause leading to the present reorganization of secondary education. Only through attention to the needs of various groups of individuals as shown by aptitudes, abilities, and aspirations can the secondary school secure from each pupil his best effort. (CRSE, 1918, p. 21)

In order to achieve these goals, the CRSE recommended that schools greatly increase "the range of subjects," expand programs in "exploration and guidance," adapt "content and methods" to students' capacities and interests, introduce greater flexibility in terms of the "election" of courses and programs, and, above all, differentiate the curriculum. "The work of the senior high school should be organized into differentiated curriculums," the CRSE declared. "The basis of differentiation should be in the broad sense of the term, vocational, thus justifying the names commonly given, such as agricultural, business, clerical, industrial, fine-arts, and household-arts curriculums." Almost as an afterthought, the commission added that "[p]rovision should be made also for those having distinctly academic interests and needs" (pp. 21–22).

Professional educators hailed *Cardinal Principles* because it succinctly expressed the emerging conventional wisdom on the high school and because it steered a course around the main shoals of the curriculum debates of the times. It favored differentiation, but not early differentiation; it favored vocational education, but not highly specialized vocational education; it called for the comprehensive high school in preference to specialized vocational high schools; it favored multiple curricula in the high schools but did not argue that every subject had to justify its existence by virtue of its contribution to practical life; and it suggested the need for "constants" in the curriculum, but did not name them. Precisely because it captured the consensus elements of the curriculum "struggles" so faithfully, *Cardinal Principles* provoked little controversy (Krug, 1964).

Cardinal Principles was clearly as much of a watershed document as the report of the Committee of Ten. If the report of the Committee of Ten was the first nationally recognized call for the professionalization of curriculum planning, *Cardinal Principles* was an assertion that educational professionals, now largely composed of faculty in schools and colleges of education, their graduates, and allies in school administration, should play the leading role in such planning, rather than either faculty representing other parts of universities or lay boards of education. Moreover, by moving away from sharply dichotomizing the high school student body into those destined for college and those destined for "life" (a distinction that still allowed considerable influence for experts in both academic and vocational subject areas) and toward the concept of "general education" for all (which reduced the importance of academic *and* vocational subjects in secondary schools), the report advanced the ideas and ultimately the interests of professional educators even further. More important, it guided the future development of high schools.

SUMMARY

The relationship between history and policy often is more assumed than demonstrated. However, with regard to the nineteenth-century high school, the distortion of history and the creation of specific curriculum policies seem closely related indeed. In their quest for power and legitimacy, leaders of the emerging profession of education revised the history of the nineteenth-century high school as part of their effort to implement a new order in American education, one in which experts rather than lay school boards determined policy and practice in schools. By describing the nineteenth-century high school curriculum as aristocratic and irrelevant, by depicting these schools as pawns of university presidents, professional educators laid the intellectual foundation for a dramatically new institution, the comprehensive high school. Moreover, by casting the nineteenth-century high school in so negative a light, they were better able to convince politicians and the public that the new programs and curricula of the comprehensive high school would lead to greater educational democracy.

How well did the professional educators succeed in that process? To what extent did the ideas of *Cardinal Principles* take hold in American high schools? To what extent did those ideas shape policy and practice? How did high school students respond to these changes? In the next chapter, we look at the political and educational changes that transformed American education in the first part of the twentieth century. In doing so, we shift our focus from developments in the nation generally to events in one city, Grand Rapids, Michigan. A national leader in Progressive educational politics and curriculum reform, Grand Rapids provides an excellent site in which we can examine how leaders of the education profession joined with local politicians to introduce new ideas about secondary education in an urban school system and how students responded to these changes.

NOTES

1. The University of Michigan arranged with individual high schools to admit, without examination, any of their graduates who had taken a suitable course of study preparatory to college and who came with the recommendation of the principal of the school. To participate in the system, each high school had to agree to inspection by representatives of the university every 3 years and to maintain at least one course of study that would qualify students to enter some degree program at the university.

2. This list of ideas and our portrayal of the consensual aspects of Progressive high school curriculum reform is based on the following sources: Bobbitt (1915, 1918, 1924); Briggs (1926, 1931); Brown (1909); Charters (1923); Counts (1926); C. Davis (1914, 1927); Hanus (1904, 1908, 1913); Inglis (1918, 1924); Johnston (1912); Judd (1918a, 1918b); Kandel (1930); Lewis (1914); Rugg (1926/1969, 1931); Russell (1922); Russell and Bonser (1914); Smith (1916); and Snedden (1917, 1922, 1927).

2

Vocationalizing the High School?
Curriculum Expansion During
the Progressive Era

THE PROFESSIONAL EDUCATORS who took control of curriculum planning in the early twentieth century had high ambitions. In working toward a greatly expanded and highly differentiated high school curriculum, they expected that high schools would become more closely aligned with "real" life. As a result, enrollments would increase, the interests of both boys and girls would be better served, children from all social classes would find something useful there, and the high school would become the truly democratic institution that the public demanded. In this chapter we explore which, if any, of the reformers' goals were realized and to what degree. In the process, we analyze how and to what extent these reforms expanded vocational programs in the high schools and how students responded to them in terms of their actual coursetaking. We also consider many of the claims made by reformers about the relationships between a differentiated curriculum and high school enrollment increases, the diversity of the student body, the reactions of the "public" to the reforms, and the ways in which these changes affected students differently depending on their social class and their gender.

To understand educational change in the first 3 decades of the twentieth century we must examine how all the various factors contributing to building a new modern high school played out at the local level. While there may have been many forces pushing toward greater uniformity after the turn of the century, there still was no "typical" American high school in this era. Students did not attend "the American high school"; they attended high schools in Gary or Poughkeepsie, Selma or Helena, Phoenix or Philadelphia, and they were only abstractly members of national cohorts in 1900 or 1910. In actuality, they were eager, apprehensive, or indifferent members of the entering ninth grade of local high schools. Despite the efforts of the Committee of Ten and the Commission on the Reorganization of Secondary Education, they didn't choose courses of study laid out on some national grand plan. Rather they enrolled in whatever courses their local high school offered, paying close attention to district or state requirements for graduation. The experiences of these high school students were shaped more by local than national events.

This chapter, then, begins with a detailed analysis of the high schools of a single city, Grand Rapids, Michigan, between 1900 and 1930. First, we discuss the politics of curriculum reform, examining how the reform of the governance system was achieved and how this reform process relates to the question of transforming the high school. Then we look at the building and reorganizing of the system of high schools, the growth in the size and diversity of the student population, and the expansion of curricular offerings. Based on an analysis of the transcripts of four cohorts of students who attended high schools in those years, we look at the distribution of the students by class and gender across the curriculum options that were offered. From this analysis, we try to understand how different groups of students were reacting to the changing high school environment. Finally, we compare the curriculum choices made by students in Grand Rapids with the available evidence on high school coursetaking patterns in other cities, the state of Michigan, and the nation to determine whether what happened in Grand Rapids fell within the range of what seems to have happened elsewhere. Through this "nested" analysis we particularly explore the extent to which vocational education transformed the Progressive Era high school. In the process we hope to illuminate the general pattern of high school development in these years while also capturing the richness of what students experienced.

POLITICS AND CURRICULUM IN GRAND RAPIDS, 1890–1920

Grand Rapids is a particularly good site in which to explore the impact of Progressive Era curricular change on public high schools. A representative, moderate-sized manufacturing city, it was known for much of the twentieth century as the "furniture making capital of the nation." With a population of 87,600, Grand Rapids ranked as the forty-second largest city in the nation in 1900, forty-seventh in 1920, and fifty-second in 1940. It had a large immigrant population, many of whom hailed from Holland, but it also included sizable numbers of Italians, Germans, Greeks, Poles, and other Slavs. By the early 1940s, there was a small but growing Black population as well (U.S. Bureau of the Census, 1943b).

During the Progressive Era, Grand Rapids boasted of a nationally renowned, innovative school system particularly in the areas of vocational education and vocational guidance (Spring, 1972; Violas, 1978).[1] Consequently, Grand Rapids provides an excellent opportunity to explore curricular and programmatic change systematically and on the school level as well as offering glimpses into the coursetaking patterns of six cohorts of students.

The city followed a pattern of Progressive political and educational reform that was nearly identical to that of other major cities in this period. In the late nineteenth century a group of elite reformers with strong ties to the business community (and strong support from some education professionals) began a vigorous campaign against alleged corruption on the large, ward-based school board. These reformers sought to transform both educational governance in the city and the curriculum of the city's high schools. In 1906, they triumphed. They took control of the new, much smaller school board, hired a group of educational experts to "modernize" the system, and greatly expanded the range of vocational courses and programs offered in the high schools.

Not only did events in Grand Rapids follow the traditional historiographic model of Progressive reform, but several unique aspects of these developments strengthen the case for focusing on this city to see the impact of Progressivism on secondary education. First, the campaigns to reform the system of school governance and to greatly expand the high school curriculum were explicitly linked in Grand Rapids. As a consequence, the debate about high school curriculum change was subject to more public involvement and more direct political action than were similar debates in other cities. Second, voters in Grand Rapids had three separate opportunities to vote on bonding proposals specifically related to high school curriculum reform. These elections provide us with an exceptionally good record of the views of various community groups on this issue, and the voting records enable us to glimpse how people from different social strata responded to the push for curricular reform. Third, following the success of the Progressive reformers, Grand Rapids became a national model for vocational guidance, a program designed to help young people match their interests to future jobs. This national recognition gives greater significance to our exploration of the degree to which vocational education had an impact on the coursetaking experiences of high school students in this city. Finally, Grand Rapids was one of the earliest cities to adopt both the junior high school and the junior college.

Prior to the 1890s, educational leaders in the city showed little if any enthusiasm for either reforming the board or expanding high school enrollments or course offerings. As the president of the school board argued in 1884, "We are essentially a manufacturing community. A large percentage of those who attend our schools leave them either before, or at the close of the grammar grades. . . . It should be, then, the object and aim of this board to educate those who are pupils of the lower departments thoroughly" (Grand Rapids Board of Education [hereafter GRAR], 1884–85, p. 9).

In the 1890s, however, a group of socially elite reformers initiated a three-pronged reform effort that sought to (1) end corruption on the school board, (2) reduce the size of the board, and (3) enlarge the high school and broaden its curriculum. At the time, the board was composed of 24 members, two members elected from each of the city's 12 wards. The high school program focused largely on academic subjects, although a few commercial and pedagogical courses provided "vocational education" for some students. By the end of the decade, the reformers had achieved none of their goals. Indeed, in 1900, voters soundly rejected a ballot proposal that called for the size of the board to be cut by half, with only one member elected from each ward (Angus, 1982; Lydens, 1966).

Despite this setback, elite reformers received new hope early in the century because of a major scandal over the city water supply. Amid the water scandal, school board member Edwin F. Sweet, a socially prominent lawyer, began railing against the supposedly corrupt practices of the school board and the American Book Company, which he claimed was reaping great profits by secretly controlling the board and its textbook purchases. Sweet argued that the actions of corrupt board members in league with the textbook company gave ample evidence of the need to reduce the size of the school board and change the form of school board elections. In addition, Sweet and his allies vigorously supported changing the high school curriculum by adding modern, vocationally oriented courses and programs. Using the issue of corruption to whip up public support for reform, Sweet captured the mayor's office and from that bully pulpit (and as an ex-officio member of the school board) he continued his denunciations of the American Book Company, board members, and the quality of education offered in the city's high schools. In these efforts, he was strongly supported by the Grand Rapids Civic Club, an organization of business and professional leaders formed in the wake of the water scandal; the Ladies Literary Club, an organization of socially prominent women; and the Grand Rapids Board of Trade, the local Chamber of Commerce (Angus, 1982; Goss, 1906).

The first part of this reform campaign to come before the public was the effort to change the high school curriculum. In 1900, the reformers gained a new ally in school superintendent W. H. Elson. In his report to the board in 1903, Elson heartily endorsed their call for high school curriculum reform:

> Grand Rapids is a manufacturing city and 95 percent of its high school students who do not go on to college must make these occupations their life work. Our high schools should offer elective courses in manual training in wood and iron, mechanical and architectural drawing, domestic science, domestic art, and sanitation; in addition they should offer something more than the mere technique of bookkeeping, stenography and typewriting; they should include elective courses in English, also German and Spanish, the physical sciences including physics, chemistry, physical and commercial geography, an elementary course in industrial history, bookkeeping, commercial arithmetic, commercial law, penmanship, stenography and typewriting. . . . Offer these opportunities to the boys and girls and our high school enrollment will at once show distinct gains, and thus will the school serve a larger constituency and be worth more to the community.[2] (GRAR, 1902–03, pp. 70, 72)

In February 1904, the school board committee responded to these suggestions by placing a "manual training" bonding proposal on the spring ballot. Specifically, the proposal called for a bond of $200,000 to build a new manual training high school on the south side of the city and add manual training facilities in the two existing high schools, Central and Union. During this period, supporters and detractors of the proposal alike used the term "manual training" to refer to much more than shop and drawing classes for boys. Rather, the term referred to a large curriculum reform package that included art and drawing, home economics, music, physical education, and industrial arts. Few of these courses were designed specifically to prepare students for jobs, but many supporters thought that the courses undoubtedly would make going to high school more attractive to young people, and high school graduates more valuable to employers, especially in the offices, furniture factories, and design and printing shops that dominated the local economy. The bonding proposal was strongly supported by the Civic Club, the Board of Trade, and the Democratic candidate for mayor, Edwin Sweet, as well as his Republican opponent. The most notable opposition came from the city's labor unions, specifically the Trades and Labor Council, which took a stand reminiscent of nineteenth-century battles over educational priorities by urging the school board to build more regular schools instead of investing in manual training.[3]

Despite strong support from civic leaders, the proposal was soundly defeated at the polls. Advocates of the proposal, however, maintained that the vote did not reflect the real attitudes of the people. Two weeks before the election, the predominantly working-class west side of the city, which would vote heavily against the proposition, was extensively damaged by a flood. Supporters of manual training believed that the voters rejected the proposal because they were unwilling to increase their taxes in the wake of the disaster rather than because they disapproved of the proposal itself (Grand Rapids Civic Club, 8/17/04). Consequently, the reformers convinced the school board to place the proposal on the September ballot. The same interest groups lined up on the issue as had in the spring election, although newly installed Mayor Sweet refused to take a stand on the referendum and one of the major newspapers, the *Post*, sharply criticized the plan, arguing that once committed to this course of action the board would seek ever-increasing amounts of money for extending manual training. By contrast, the other major papers in the city, the *Evening Press* (hereafter *Press*) and the *Herald*, supported the proposal. However, the extensive debate about manual training in the local press did not improve the idea in the eyes of the voters. In a much larger turnout, the proposal again was defeated, this time by a three to one margin, as one commentator put it, by a "flood of votes rather than a flood of water" (Angus, 1982).

Dismayed but not deterred by this setback, the reformers made one last attempt to convince the voting public to approve funds for major curricular changes in the high schools. In January 1905 a school board committee headed by George A. Davis, one of the wealthiest furniture manufacturers in the city, presented a report urging the board to issue $104,000 in bonds to build manual training annexes at the two existing high schools. Davis attempted to get the board to issue the bonds without public approval, but he was outvoted in this effort, and the proposal was placed on the Spring 1905 ballot (Grand Rapids Board of Education *Proceedings* [hereafter GRP], 1904–05; Lydens, 1966). The alignment of interest groups and newspapers was similar to the previous two elections, with especially strong support for the proposal coming from the Civic Club, the Board of Trade, the *Press*, and the *Herald*. In addition, this time Mayor Sweet gave his backing to the effort. At first, the *Post* opposed the proposal, chastising Davis and the "manual training boomers" for their initial attempt to circumvent the public and approve the bonds without a vote. Nevertheless, on the eve of the election the *Post* gave the plan a mild endorsement, as did the *Chronicle*, nominally the labor paper. Despite all these endorsements, the proposal once again went down to defeat, albeit by a narrower margin (Angus, 1982).

When we analyzed the precinct-level election data (see Table 2.1),* we found that two variables, social class and "distance-from-school," showed the strongest relationship to the outcome of the elections. All three of the elections divided along class lines—the wealthier wards and precincts strongly supporting the proposals, while the poorer wards, especially the middle- and working-class wards on the west side of the city, generally opposed them. But in the Spring 1904 election, with a new South High School still on the ballot, "distance-from-school" appears to have played a role as well, as voters in one middle- and working-class ward located on the south side of the city strongly supported the proposition, possibly because they believed that their students would have relatively easy access to the proposed high school.[4]

These findings are consistent with all the other information we have about public attitudes on this issue. Individuals with greater wealth and status were the strongest supporters of the manual training proposals, while individuals of more modest means generally cast their votes against them. Board members who differed from the vote of their wards on this issue were turned out of office. However, the negative votes cast in some middle- and working-class precincts appear to have been based less on opposition to the curricular reforms in principle and more on doubts that their children actually could take advantage of the proposed programs.

In late 1904 and early 1905, reform leaders in Grand Rapids found themselves repeatedly thwarted by the popular will. Therefore, Mayor Sweet and his allies decided to circumvent the public altogether. Under the guise of making modest revisions to the city charter, they skillfully engineered an elite takeover

---

*In addition to the tables found in the text and the appendices, supplementary tables are available from the authors on request or may be found on deposit in the Bentley Historical Library, University of Michigan, Ann Arbor. These supplementary tables include a more detailed presentation of student enrollment rates in specific courses at the national aggregate level for some years and a complete list of courses offered in the Grand Rapids public high schools from 1900 to 1990. Requests to the authors may be made by email, dangus@umich.edu or jmirel@learnlink.emory.edu.

Table 2.1. Analysis of Precinct-Level Vote Returns on Two Referendums on High School Manual Training, Grand Rapids, 1904 and 1905

Variable	Marginal Contribution to Regression Equation	
	1904	1905
Mean age of household heads	.011	.008
Mean nuclear family size	.026	.046
Percent white collar	.104	.265
Percent U.S. born	.016	.001
Distance from school	.039	.043
	$R^2 = .753$	$R^2 = .723$

of the board of education. The campaign began with the mayor announcing new allegations of corruption on the part of several school board members and the American Book Company. Amid the furor raised by these new allegations, the mayor appointed a charter revision committee that drafted a proposal to abolish the ward-based school board and replace it with a seven-member body elected from the city at large. Supporters of the change argued that the new governance structure would eliminate corruption and run the schools in an efficient, business-like manner. Rather than submitting this proposal to the voters, however, as did the reformers in 1900, Sweet and his allies went directly to the Michigan legislature for approval of the change (Angus, 1982).

Not surprisingly, these efforts sharply divided the city along class lines. The Civic Club and the Board of Trade strongly endorsed the changes, while the Grand Rapids Socialists, the unions, and west side politicians opposed them. By far the strongest argument put forth by the opponents was that city-wide elections would virtually disenfranchise the western, mostly working-class section of the city since the costs of at-large campaigning and the lack of name recognition by less prosperous city residents would handicap westsiders in any at-large election. The consequences of an at-large election, opponents argued, would be to leave the west side of the city unrepresented on the new school board.

These interest groups eventually met and clashed at a stormy public meeting in late April 1905. The Board of Trade had called the meeting to lobby the Kent County delegation to the Michigan legislature on the issue, and practically all the major political and civic leaders in Grand Rapids attended. When the dust settled after at least 8 hours of debate, the charter revisions were only slightly altered—the new board would have nine rather than seven members elected at large. Despite a last, futile effort by one city council member to get a popular referendum on the proposed changes, the legislature passed the bill authorizing a nine-member, at-large board, and the governor quickly signed it (Angus, 1982).

The election for the new board took place in early April 1906 and produced almost a clean sweep for the elite, Progressive reformers. Although 45 people from diverse backgrounds entered the race (including a large number of incumbent board members), eight of the nine winners were listed in the Grand Rapids social register, seven were either professionals (lawyers or doctors) or corporate officials, seven lived on the wealthy east side of the city, six belonged to both the Board of Trade and Civic Club, and eight were endorsed by the Civic Club. The "odd man out" in this assemblage was an ethnic Dutch hardware dealer from the west side of the city (Angus, 1982).

Manual training was not a dominant issue in the campaign, but it was present nonetheless. As early as September 1904, an editorial in the Grand Rapids *Post* denounced the efforts to reduce the size of the school board, noting that the people who were trying "to place that body beyond the reach of the people . . . [were also] the chief promoters of the $200,000 bonding high school manual training scheme" (p. 1). The results of the 1906 election confirmed that assessment, with three of the strongest manual training advocates, George A. Davis, Josephine A. Goss, and W. C. Sheppard, leading all candidates in the vote totals (Angus, 1982; Lydens, 1966; see also Goss, 1906).

With the elite takeover of the board, a new group of leaders came to dominate educational policy making in the city. Foremost among them was George Davis, who served on the board for 25 years, half of them as president. His vision of vocationalized secondary schools became the standard for curricular changes. In addition, the reform board quickly promoted or hired a group of educational administrators who were deeply committed to progressive curricular reforms. The first of these was W. A. Greeson, who had once served as the principal of Central High School and who at the time was dean of Lewis Institute in Chicago, the nation's first junior college. In 1906, the board appointed him superintendent, a position that he retained until 1924. The second, but clearly the more important, was Jesse B. Davis, who became principal of Central High School in 1907. Davis had been a successful high school teacher and assistant principal in Detroit and was a strong supporter of vocational education. Davis would serve Grand Rapids for 14 years, bringing the city's schools to national prominence, then moving on to serve as assistant superintendent for secondary schools of Connecticut and later as professor of education at Harvard. These three men became known as the Greeson triumvirate, and they worked closely with one another to reshape secondary education in the city (Davis, 1956; Lydens, 1966).

Commenting on these developments, the editor of the *Post* declared, "The high-school-manual-training faddists have captured the new Board of Education. Now look for propositions to build a high school with manual training attachments in every corner of the city" (p. 1). In that prediction, the editor was only partly correct. The board never again went to the people to vote on reforming the high school curriculum. Rather, because of an unexpected U.S. Supreme Court decision in 1906 concerning taxes owed to the Michigan primary school fund by various railroads, the school board received a one-time windfall of several hundred thousand dollars. The board immediately allocated the money for restructuring the high schools of the city along "modern" lines. Educational progressivism in all its varied aspects finally had triumphed in Grand Rapids, despite the repeated objections of the majority of voters in the city (Grand Rapids *Post*, 4/4/06, p. 1; Lydens, 1966; Starring & Knauss, 1968).

The reformers sought to align the program of studies in these schools with the ideas articulated in *Cardinal Principles of Secondary Education* and other expert opinion. One of the main reasons why Grand Rapids provides such a good site to examine the impact of Progressive curricular reform on high schools is the degree of success the reformers achieved in realizing that goal. By the mid-1920s, Grand Rapids was recognized nationally as a model of secondary curricular reform. Indeed, the "Greeson triumvirate" implemented virtually all of the key elements of *Cardinal Principles* and they justified these policies in similar terms (and with an equally flawed sense of history) to those used by the curricular reformers who dominated the national scene.

One of the first challenges facing the educational reformers in Grand Rapids was convincing an obviously skeptical public that the new, practical programs were the best examples of modern, democratic education and that these programs advanced the cause of educational equality. In January 1911, the Grand Rapids *Press* ran a 12-part series on secondary education in the city in which prominent local and state educators lauded the curricular and programmatic changes at the city's two high schools (Grand Rapids *Press*, 11/4/11, 1/5/11, 1/6/11, 1/18/11, 1/19/11, 1/23/11, 1/26/11). The most important article in the series included a lengthy interview with Central High School Principal Jesse B. Davis. Like the curriculum theorists discussed in Chapter 1, Davis believed that high schools in the past had been committed to elite, academic education that was largely irrelevant to most students entering the institution. Yet he saw promise in recent changes in secondary education, declaring, "High school education is just now in a state of transition. It is growing more practical and far more useful to the masses than it was just a few years ago. It now aims to serve the wants of all classes of pupils not the wants of a few who desire to go to college." The key to this transition, Davis maintained, was vocational education that would enable a boy entering high school to "select any one of the hundreds of vocations of life and under the elective system we will shape his course to fit him as far as possible for the career he has chosen. It is the same way with the girl" (Grand Rapids *Press*, 1/11/11).

Eight years later, in the wake of World War I, Superintendent William A. Greeson echoed and embellished these sentiments by comparing the traditional, academic high schools of the United States with the aristocratic high schools of Germany under the Kaiser. In essence, Greeson argued that high schools designed "to prepare the chosen few for college" were un-American because they threatened to divide the country into classes (based on those who attended high school and those who did not) that ultimately would become fixed "through custom and inheritance." True educational democracy, he believed, was possible only in the new "cosmopolitan" high schools where students could choose courses from a wide array of options. Vocational classes were central to these schools. Indeed, Greeson advocated prevocational classes in the new junior high schools to prepare students for making the correct vocational choices for their futures (Greeson, 1914).

Perhaps no statement more succinctly captured their belief in the democratizing power of vocational education than the motto "Equal Educational Opportunities for All" that was emblazoned on the cover of the handbook for students at the new Davis Technical School, established by the reformers in 1920 (Davis Vocational and Technical High School, 1933). Greeson, Davis, and other educational leaders in Grand Rapids paid more than lip service to these ideas. Between 1905 and 1930, they introduced curriculum reforms that embodied many of the ideas discussed in Chapter 1, including substantially increasing the number of subject areas and courses in the comprehensive or, as Greeson called them, "cosmopolitan" high schools. The new courses were clearly in line with the main ideas articulated in *Cardinal Principles*; indeed nearly all were practical and relevant courses designed to fit students for "life" rather than college.

HIGH SCHOOL GROWTH AND CURRICULUM CHANGE IN GRAND RAPIDS

The process of building a new curriculum was thoroughly entwined with the process of building new, modern high schools to house that curriculum. At the turn of the century, Grand Rapids had two high schools: Central High School, located on the bluffs east of the Grand River in a neighborhood of large homes owned by the city's elite families, and Union High School, located on the "flats" a few blocks west of the river in a working-class neighborhood. The combined enrollment of the two schools in grades 9 through 12 was 1,141, 9% of the total public school enrollment in Grand Rapids (see Appendix B, Table B.1). These high schools focused squarely on academic education organized into "courses of study" in which much of the coursework was specified. In 1900, these courses of study were commercial, engineering, scientific, normal, and 2-year, 4-year, and 6-year foreign language. To graduate, students were required to take 3.5 or 4 years of English, 2 years of history, and 2.5 years each of math and science (including algebra, plane geometry, and physics). The schools offered 28 different courses in seven subject areas—English, foreign language, mathematics, science, social studies, commercial, and art. The three commercial classes and a single art class in drawing were the only nonacademic courses offered at the time.

By 1910, the number of different courses had jumped to 46 and the number of subject areas increased to 11. The period from 1906 to 1910 marked the single largest expansion of the curriculum (both in terms of the number of courses and the addition of new subject areas) during the entire period preceding World War II. Joining the seven subject areas from 1900 were industrial arts, home economics, health and physical education, and music. Most of the new courses were nonacademic courses: four new courses each in art and music, three new courses each in industrial arts and home economics, and two additions each in commercial and health and physical education. Enrollment in grades 9 through 12 had reached 1,451.

The 1910–11 school year marked the true beginning of "modern" education in the Grand Rapids high schools. A new Central High School building opened in midyear and by the end of the year, a large shop addition had been completed at Union. Over the next 5 years, enrollment in grades 9 through 12 grew steadily, reaching 1,892 by 1915. Under Greeson's leadership, the city adopted a 6-3-3 plan of organization that necessitated building a series of new junior high schools across the city. The old Central High School building was remodeled for this purpose and in 1913 began offering classes for grades 6 through 9. The reformers had predicted that such a reorganization would retain more students beyond eighth grade, and Central Junior High seems to have done exactly that (see Appendix B, Table B.1).[5]

In Fall 1915, the long-proposed South High School was ready for occupancy, phasing in the grades over 3 years. Realizing that any attempt to impose a vocational high school on the city's south side would be politically unwise, the board established South High School as a comprehensive school with facilities for a modern curriculum but not emphasizing industrial subjects over academics. By the end of the decade it had the largest enrollment in the city.

But perhaps the most important development of the decade was the opening of a vocational continuation school in 1919. In that year, the Michigan legislature passed a new state continuation school law, the James Act, requiring large cities to provide one-day-per-week continuation schools for young people between the ages of 14 and 18 who previously had dropped out. The law penalized school districts that did not provide continuation schools and also mandated penalties for parents and employers who failed to enroll eligible young people in such schools. Consequently, Grand Rapids established a Vocational and Part-Time Continuation School in rented buildings in January 1920. The school opened with an enrollment of 617 part-time and 158 full-time students. Before the year was out, these numbers had doubled, and they continued to rise even though the legislature reduced the upper age to 17 in 1921.

Initially, the curriculum of this school was tied directly to the needs of the local economy and was narrowly focused on four trades for boys—furniture crafts, machine shop, automotive, and drafting—and two for girls—cooking and sewing. A commercial course also was offered, along with academic work in English, civics, mathematics, and science. All programs in this school were 2-year courses, open to eighth-grade "graduates" and older students. In 1922, the board broke ground for a new building for this school and the following year started holding classes for 185 full-time and 1,238 part-time students in the still incomplete structure. While this was clearly the vocational high school for Grand Rapids, offering a large number of courses that were not offered in the industrial arts departments of the other high schools, it quickly began to take on curricular characteristics similar to the comprehensive high schools in the city. According to the official history of the school, in 1923,

> [M]any students began to clamor for high school credits at this school; some for positions that they wished to fill and some for college entrance. It was because of this demand that in February, 1925, the curriculum was extended to a four year technical course and the school name changed to The Vocational and Technical High School. . . . Bowing to these demands, school officials increased the number of academic courses available to the students. In 1926, the State High School Inspectors approved the academic curriculum of the school and the school gained accreditation from the University of Michigan. (Davis Vocational and Technical High School, 1933, pp. 9–10)

In addition to "Davis Tech," two other high schools came on line during the 1920s. In 1924, Creston High School opened as a 6-year school with 203 students in ninth grade. In 1926, a second 6-year school, Ottawa Hills High School, opened. Throughout the 1920s, enrollments grew steadily. By mid-decade, total high school enrollment stood at 5,032, a figure that did not include the 270 full-time and 1,365 part-time students in the vocational and technical school, who were always listed separately in the annual reports. High school enrollment stood at just under 20% of total system enrollment, a figure that Superintendent Greeson believed was the point that marked universal high school attendance at least as far as ninth and tenth graders were concerned.[6]

Indeed, between 1900 and 1925, high school entrance came close to being a norm for most eighth-grade "graduates" in Grand Rapids. Over this quarter-century, larger and larger percentages of eighth graders and later ninth graders enrolled at least for a time in high schools. Before 1910, no more than two-thirds of all the eighth graders who left school in June returned as first-year high school students the following September; by 1920 almost 100% did so.[7] Like school officials across the country, educational leaders in Grand Rapids attributed this increase to the establishment of the junior high school. Yet, the "holding power" of the high school also increased. By 1930, enrollment in ninth and tenth grades was about equal. Still, only about half of high school entrants graduated, and the large enrollments in the continuation school attested to a persistent dropout rate.

At least with respect to graduation requirements and course offerings, school leaders tried to make high school graduation as common as high school entry. By 1920, graduation requirements had been reduced to 3 years of English, 1 year of history, and 1 year each of mathematics and science (see Appendix B, Table B.3). In addition, to support the commitment to vocational education, 1 year of vocational subjects was required of all graduates. These reduced academic requirements could be met by taking courses that curriculum planners saw as more practical and relevant—Bible narrative, contemporary literature, journalism, debate, drama, practical math, general math, general science, girls' physiography, civics, government—all of which were added between 1920 and 1930. World history and European history replaced such traditional and formidable courses as Greek and Roman history, ancient history, and medieval and modern history.

The expansion and modification of nonacademic course offerings also continued in the 1920s, but at a slower pace. In addition to the skilled trades courses associated with the establishment of Davis Tech, such as cabinet making, a number of industrial arts courses, including machine shop and printing, were added to the new or remodeled comprehensive high schools. The home economics departments added a course in clothing, another called "personal regimen," and, in a few schools, interior decorating. In the commercial area, stenography and typewriting were split into separate courses, and typing became a popular elective for those intending to go to college.

Most of these changes can be understood as a working out in practice of Jesse Davis's belief that "[a]ll education is vocational, or should be. All education is preparation for some life work" (Davis, 1914, p. 138). With that in mind, Davis and other school leaders not only greatly expanded the curricular offerings, but they also revised the course of study within various subject areas in order to make the traditional classes more relevant and practical for students. In describing these changes, Davis noted, "The 'career motive' was used by all teachers to inspire a new interest in their fields of study. The teachers of Latin had their pupils preparing lists of words derived from Latin that were of special value to the lawyer, the doctor, the scientist, the writer. History teachers had pupils looking up the origins or historical backgrounds of the vocations in which they were interested. The applications of science, mathematics, and the practical arts to engineering, manufacturing and to business made most interesting reports" (Davis, 1956, pp. 179–180; see also Grand Rapids *Press*, 1/18/11, 1/23/11).

The most extensive revisions appeared in English classes. At Central High School, for example, English teachers assigned a series of essays with vocational themes, such as "Vocations: The Employment of Boys and Girls" and "The Trained Worker and the Professions," designed to help students choose and prepare for "their life's work" (Davis, 1912, p. 714; see also Grand Rapids *Press*, 1/19/11). Even the school library was reconceptualized to aid students in their vocational inquiries. In phrases that echoed his larger view of the high school itself, Jesse

Davis (1916) dismissed traditional school libraries as mere repositories of the "classic literatures of antiquity" and argued instead for new library services that would provide students with "information with regard to the great call of the world to service, and for the best ways to prepare oneself for his chosen field of endeavor" (pp. 553–554). These changes to high school organization and curriculum were so significant that historian Paul Violas (1978) claims the Grand Rapids reforms were the "most often cited experiment modifying traditional school subjects" (p. 213) for vocational purposes.

The national attention that these curricular changes received was only part of the reason that school reformers across the country regarded Grand Rapids as a model of progressive innovation. Even more important to that reputation was the school system's leadership in the area of vocational guidance. Jesse Davis was at the center of this effort, introducing vocational guidance at Grand Rapids Central in 1908. In developing the program, Davis acted on a number of assumptions about education, work, and counseling that paralleled the ideas of such better-known proponents of vocational guidance as Frank Parsons and Helen Woolley. All of these individuals sought to improve the "match" between youth and jobs and to bring some "rational planning" into the process through which young men and women entered the work world. All of them shared the conviction that much of the world's misery was due to mismatches between people and jobs. As Davis (1914) put it, "All about us we find men struggling along in occupations for which they have no liking or fitness" (p. 6). The stepson of a Baptist minister, Davis saw the need less in terms of social engineering than of helping young people to find their "calling."

In 1911, Davis moved to give the program more structure. He obtained released time for six teachers who supervised large homeroom classes, called session-rooms, to provide vocational counseling for about 250 students each. Session-room teachers continued to play that role until the 1930s, when they were finally replaced by full-time counselors. Also in 1911, Davis established a Vocational Placement Bureau to serve dropouts as well as high school students. A strong supporter of continuation schools, Davis envisioned the bureau as an agency that would encourage dropouts to seek additional education. He also created a Junior Board of Trade that arranged Saturday field trips to offices, factories, and shops throughout the city to acquaint high school students with available occupations (Davis, 1912, 1914, 1956).

The Grand Rapids system of vocational guidance attracted national attention and became a national model, albeit without the uniquely spiritual aspect that Davis espoused. In 1913, the National Society for the Promotion of Industrial Education met in Grand Rapids in order to see it in operation. Over the next few years, Davis traveled across the country lecturing about vocational guidance and describing the success of the Grand Rapids program. The reputation of the program was so great that during several summers, Davis taught the first courses in guidance offered at the Universities of Michigan and Minnesota and at Teachers College, Columbia University. In addition, Davis played an instrumental role in founding the National Vocational Guidance Association, becoming its second president in 1914. That same year he published *Vocational and Moral Guidance*, an influential text that went through several editions and remained on the market for more than 2 decades (Krug, 1964; Spring, 1972; Violas, 1978).

Without doubt, Davis and the Grand Rapids schools played a pivotal role in the development of progressive secondary education. The important question, however, is what was the actual impact of these curricular and programmatic changes on the educational experiences of the young people in the schools? Progressive curriculum reformers assumed that their reforms would change high schools into institutions that appealed more strongly both to students from varied social class backgrounds and to boys, who were substantially underrepresented in secondary education. Did these reforms have the predicted effect of "democratizing" high school enrollments? Did the new curricula attract larger numbers of boys into secondary education? Did students from working-class backgrounds follow substantially different courses of study than other students? Were the high schools actually transformed by the expansion of vocational education? We now turn to these questions.

CURRICULUM DIFFERENTIATION IN THE PROGRESSIVE ERA

During the 1920s, Grand Rapids appeared to perfectly embody the hopes and dreams of the curriculum reformers, as well as to serve as a harbinger of national trends. The city's social and economic elite were firmly in control; they had appointed a group of energetic and committed educational experts to transform curricula and programs in the high schools, greatly expanding the curricular offerings and adding dozens of nonacademic courses; they built new, architecturally advanced high schools as rapidly as resources permitted; they helped pioneer the reorganization of secondary education by building junior high schools and opening a junior college; and they instituted the nation's first school-based system of vocational guidance. Coinciding with these changes, high school enrollment had risen well above the national average, reaching over two-thirds of the 14–17 age group by 1930.[8] On the eve of the Great Depression, Grand Rapids' five comprehensive high schools enrolled 370% more students than in 1900.[9]

To understand how all these Progressive Era changes in secondary education affected the high school experience of students, we collected and analyzed the high school transcripts of six cohorts of students, those entering the ninth grade in the years 1900, 1910, 1920, 1930, 1935, and 1940. While these transcripts differ in format over time and in detail from school to school, they provide at least a record of the courses taken by each student, the grade or mark received in each course, a modest amount of information about the parents, and in some cases such additional information as the class rank of graduates, a listing of extracurricular activities, or perhaps an IQ score. These records are in one sense cross-sectional snapshots of high school students, but in another sense they are longitudinal, since they record the whole period of time each student attended secondary school. We supplemented this transcript information with information from a variety of other sources, tracing individuals in street directories, yearbooks, and end-of-semester class reports, and tracing the high schools over time in their frequent accreditation reports submitted to the University of Michigan accrediting bureau.

Transcript data allow us to go well beyond conventional interpretations to consider in what ways, if any, the student body became more diverse, how going to high school and graduating from high school were distributed with respect to gender and social class, what courses students took as they faced an expanding range of curricular options, and what the timing of these developments may tell us about the interpretive paradigms that have dominated educational history. We present the results of our analysis in narrative form. The data that support our interpretation are found in Appendix B, Tables B.4–B.9.

In 1900, the high schools of Grand Rapids placed major emphasis on academic subjects. Students chose or were assigned to a "course of study" in which much of the coursework was specified, and few electives were offered. The typical high school student took 3 years of English, 2.5 years of math and science, 2 years each of history and foreign language, and 1 year each of commercial subjects and art (drawing). About a third of the students took no foreign language courses, and 69% took no commercial courses. Those who took several semesters of commercial courses were less likely to graduate than those who did not, probably because these courses made the students more readily employable.

At this time, girls outnumbered boys among high school students by a factor of three to two. While the grading standards were extremely tough, with the average mark in most subjects between a D+ and a C, girls consistently received higher marks than boys in all subjects. Even at this early time, girls were less likely than boys to take more than the required amounts of mathematics and science, but their enrollments in all other subjects were comparable.

With respect to social class background among the 1900 freshman cohort, for every 3 ninth-grade students from white collar families there were two students from blue collar families. Students from white collar homes were substantially overrepresented in the high schools, since the white to blue collar ratio in the male, over age 45 work force in Grand Rapids at the time was three to seven. However, differences between students from white collar and blue collar backgrounds in terms of what they studied, how long they went to school, and what marks they received were small and largely insignificant. Even school completion rates were similar for those reaching high school, with white collar students completing only one semester more, on average, than blue collar students. While the high schools enrolled only a small share of those who had started school 8 years earlier, those who did manage to attend, even for a short period, were treated quite evenhandedly and the experience enhanced their future job prospects.[10]

The 1910 cohort attended high schools that were in rapid transition. While the school reformers had expanded the high school curriculum greatly by the time this cohort entered, not all their ideas were fully realized until this class graduated. Most of the curricular changes that were introduced took place outside the academic departments. In this transition period, students took more English courses, perhaps because the guidance program based on English composition was in place, and fewer science and foreign language courses. The new domestic arts and industrial arts departments opened with a whimper rather than a bang, with two-thirds of girls and a third of boys taking no courses at all in these areas.

With high school enrollment increasing by about 20% between 1900 and 1910, boys claimed a slightly higher share of high school places, and the occupational class distribution was virtually unchanged. Girls continued to get better marks than boys, particularly in the study of languages. Boys continued to take more math and science, while girls took more foreign language and surpassed the boys in enrollments in commercial courses. There were still very few differences related to class background, but students from blue collar homes took commercial courses, and also music courses, at significantly higher rates than students from white collar homes. Graduation rates were highest among students who took a good deal of math, science, and foreign language, although they differed very little by gender or social class.

By the time the next cohort of ninth graders entered the Grand Rapids high schools in 1920, the schools had changed in many ways, including a reduction in the number of academic courses and an increase in the number of nonacademic courses required for graduation. In 1913, school leaders abandoned the "course-of-study" system in favor of a list of graduation requirements with specific required courses and electives. The new requirements clearly downgraded the importance of the academic subjects, English from 4 years to 3, history from 2 years to 1, mathematics from 2.5 years to 2, and science from 2.5 years to 1. In addition, school leaders required 1 year of vocational subjects. These changes made it considerably easier to graduate, since students generally received higher marks in nonacademic areas such as vocational courses than they did in academic subjects. As a result, graduation rates rose to 60%. Also, partly as a result of the changes in requirements, enrollments in English classes declined quite sharply and enrollments continued to slide downward in mathematics, foreign language, and art. Enrollments rose in commercial courses, stayed even in industrial arts, and nearly tripled in domestic arts.

In the years just prior to America's entry into World War I, boys attained enrollment parity with girls but fell back to about 1910 levels by the end of the war. Girls got increasingly better grades, even in mathematics and science. All grades on average were getting higher, particularly in commercial, vocational, and art courses. By today's standards, however, grading was still rigorous, with girls' average marks in history and science only reaching a C by 1920.

Total enrollment in the high schools increased by 160% between 1910 and 1920, but it is virtually impossible to sort out the relative strength of such factors as curriculum change, school construction and expansion, higher rates of completion of the lower grades, the establishment of the junior high school, and general improvements in transportation and the standard of living of workers, all of which may have contributed. Even in the face of this massive increase, the occupational background ratio actually shifted back in favor of white collar students, 60 to 40. Since the white to blue collar ratio in the work force remained the same in 1920 as it was in 1900, the degree of white collar overrepresentation in the high school also remained the same.[11] Only one notable change occurred over these 20 years—the percentage of students from professional homes fell by 7 percentage points, from 13 to 6, while the percentage from the homes of clerical and sales workers rose by the same amount. This shift occurred because the "pool" of potential high school students from professional homes was nearly exhausted and could not continue to rise at the same rate as overall enrollments.

In Grand Rapids, at least, the dramatic curriculum changes introduced in the comprehensive high schools after Progressive reformers took control did not result in immediate increases in the proportion of working-class students (see Appendix B, Table B.4). But if we factor in the 775 mostly part-time students enrolled in the continuation school in 1920, among whom the ratio of white collar to blue collar students was, by contrast, two to eight, a somewhat different picture emerges. The overall city-wide ratio becomes 52 to 48, still in favor of white collar students, but by a smaller margin. What the reformers had not achieved through curriculum reform, they were achieving through legal compulsion.

Differences in coursetaking related to gender and class background were both more numerous and wider in 1920 than in former years. Girls took significantly less mathematics and significantly more commercial courses than boys.[12] Students from blue collar homes also took more commercial courses, but far fewer foreign language courses. With a declining emphasis on the academic subjects, students were beginning to be sorted along the dimension of whether they viewed their high school experience as preparatory for college or for the work world. They also appear to have been choosing courses with regard to the kinds of future jobs that might be open to them.

It is important to note, however, that the "showcase" vocational courses, domestic arts and industrial arts, played practically no role in this trend. The vocational orientation of blue collar students, if that is what it was, was expressed by taking commercial courses preparatory for white collar jobs, not for blue collar jobs in industrial or domestic arts. As other historians have noted, commercial courses were the vocational subject of choice for girls (Kantor, 1988; Powers, 1992;

Rury, 1991; Tyack & Hansot, 1990). If we distinguish between taking a few semesters of such commercial classes as typing or bookkeeping for personal development purposes and taking commercial classes in greater numbers for vocational training purposes, then girls clearly dominated the latter category. Their higher average resulted from many more of them taking five semesters or more in the commercial field.

Over the decade of the 1920s, the emphasis in curriculum development was placed on (1) expanding offerings in industrial arts and home economics, and (2) developing academic courses of a more general, more practical, and less rigorous sort. Total enrollments in grades 9 through 12 expanded by a factor of 85% to over 6,800 students (7,360 students if the full-timers at Davis Tech are included). Boys made up between 46 and 49% of each entering cohort over the decade. But by far the most interesting development of this period was the sharp shift in the occupational makeup of the 1930 class, in which blue collar students gained a majority of high school places, 55 to 45.

School officials in Grand Rapids undoubtedly believed that these enrollment shifts were due mainly to the curriculum reforms they had instituted, but clearly other factors were operating. One was the still mandatory continuation school. Although its numbers were declining, it enrolled over 1,100 students, 612 of whom were part-timers. For another, the percentage of students from three of the four white collar categories fell by 5%, and the estimated enrollment of students from two of these actually declined, suggesting an exhausting of these potential "pools." But this maximizing of white collar attendance did not halt the rise of high school enrollments, for two reasons. Enrollments continued to rise because increasing educational requirements for work made staying in school more attractive to working-class youngsters, and because the prospect of mandatory continuation school made that decision easier to reach. In the late 1920s, however, a new and even more powerful factor came into play, namely, youth unemployment.

In the 1920s, the attendance department of the Grand Rapids schools issued permits to students to leave school for full- or part-time work or to work after school. By mid-decade, over 2,500 permits were being issued annually for various purposes. As Appendix B, Table B.2, shows, these numbers declined drastically over the remainder of the decade and into the 1930s. This decline signaled a worsening employment picture for young people well before the Great Depression hit the nation. During the same period high school enrollments grew steadily and students remained in school longer. In his report for 1926–27, explaining the continued growth in high school enrollment, Superintendent Butler took note of the "increase in holding power" of the schools and its links to the weakening youth labor market. He wrote that high school growth "may reflect the economic conditions of the city since it has become more difficult year by year since 1920 for boys and girls of employment ages to secure positions" (GRAR, 1926–27, p. 12). Enrollments in the continuation school showed a similar relationship to the shrinking job market for young people. The number of part-time students, those 14 to 17 who had jobs but by law had to be enrolled in the continuation school, peaked in 1924 at 811 and declined thereafter. Equally telling was the fact that the number of persons aged 19 or older enrolled in the schools rose from about 200 at mid-decade to 640 in 1932.

It seems clear that the decline of the teenage job market beginning in the mid-1920s severely restricted the choices facing young people in Grand Rapids. Indeed it appears that this decline largely accounts for the increased attendance of working-class youngsters that occurred between the 1920 and the 1930 cohorts, but that we believe to have occurred mainly after 1925. We discuss the importance of these enrollment shifts due to the growing economic crisis in greater detail in Chapter 3,[13] but here we can ask whether the loss of employment prospects influenced the coursetaking patterns of Grand Rapids young people.

Overall, between 1920 and 1930, English, math, social studies, and industrial arts saw modest increases in the average number of semesters taken, and foreign language study continued its decline. The state of Michigan required that all students take physical education for at least one period per week and the 1930 cohort took six semesters on average. An increase of one semester in the number of elective credits required for graduation led to an increase in music enrollments.

More important, the separations along gender and class lines, which had begun to show themselves in the 1920 cohort, became deeper and wider in the 1930 cohort. Girls came to dominate the commercial courses. More than four times as many girls as boys took over four semesters of commercial courses. Girls still lagged behind in mathematics enrollments but also, surprisingly, in music. The other vocational subjects also were strongly gendered.

What increasingly divided students by social class background up to 1930 was just two areas of the curriculum, foreign languages and commercial subjects. The pattern suggests that students from white collar backgrounds were using the high school mainly to prepare for college and for occupations that required further education, while blue collar students were taking the commercial courses to prepare for entry into lower white collar occupations. As the proportion of working-class students rose from about 40% in 1920 to 55% in 1930, the number of boys taking industrial arts at a vocational concentration (more than 1 year) nearly doubled, and the average number of semesters taken by blue collar boys was double that of students from white collar backgrounds, who continued to prepare for college.

With the economic downturn reducing the likelihood of college attendance, white collar girls took nearly the same amount of work in the commercial field and domestic arts as girls from blue collar families. Thus, among the girls, class differences carried little weight; among the boys, they were critical. Moreover, within social classes gender differences were significant. White collar boys took more math and fewer commercial courses than white collar girls. Blue collar girls took more English, more foreign language, more commercial, and less math or music than blue collar boys.

While we explore the impact of the Great Depression on the American high school more closely in Chapter 3, suffice it to say that by 1930 the high schools in Grand Rapids were far more democratic in terms of the class background of the students than they had been in 1900, but they were far less egalitarian in terms of the types of programs that these students followed.

In all, the educational reformers of Grand Rapids saw only some of their objectives for the high school come to fruition in the first 3 decades of the twentieth century. Their vision of a "democratic" high school composed of diverse groups of students eagerly taking relevant, practical courses materialized more slowly than these educational leaders had wished. True, by 1930 the student body of the Grand Rapids high schools was more diverse than in earlier years, but more disappointing to the reformers was the fact that large numbers of students did not seek their vocational callings in the domestic and industrial arts classes. Rather they followed fairly traditional academic programs. Indeed, despite the enormous amount of time, energy, and money these school leaders directed toward "vocationalizing" the high schools, and despite changes in course requirements that mandated vocational courses for graduation, as late as 1930 most students still followed a course of study not greatly different from the course of study students followed at the turn of the century.

What was truly different about the high schools in 1930 was that for some students, mainly boys from blue collar homes, the range of educational options was considerably narrower than it had been 30 years before as these students took increasingly more vocational courses. Similarly, some girls, again mainly from blue collar homes, increasingly opted for commercial courses as vocational preparation rather than for personal development. Both these trends indicate that on the eve of the Great Depression the high schools were more sharply divided along class and gender lines than in 1900. These trends also indicate the problematic nature of the definition of equal educational opportunity that guided the reforms in Grand Rapids. More students from diverse backgrounds were attending high school than ever before, but the educational experiences of these students were diverging along class and gender lines more clearly than ever before. This pattern is the essence of what reformers called democracy's high school, which equalized the opportunity to *attend* high school by providing curricular programs that were profoundly *unequal* in the adult roles for which students prepared.

ENROLLMENT AND HIGH SCHOOL COURSETAKING CHANGES ACROSS THE COUNTRY

We began this chapter arguing that the best way to understand the nature of high school development in the Progressive Era was to study events in great detail at a local level. A potential problem with that approach is that events in any one locale might be so anomalous as to make them irrelevant to the larger questions being posed. Certainly, many aspects of Progressive reform in Grand Rapids were distinctive, including the degree of success elite reformers had in capturing the school board, the commitment of these reformers to vocationalizing the high schools, and the early introduction of vocational guidance into the system. As we noted earlier, we chose Grand Rapids in part because of these developments, but we also recognize that they might call into question the generalizability of the findings we have presented. In this section, we use a varied group of studies of high school students and curriculum reform to see whether the gender or social class composition of high school enrollments changed in other parts of the country in ways that were similar to those in Grand Rapids. We also briefly look at Black secondary school enrollments. Finally, we investigate similarities in the impact of curriculum reforms on student coursetaking, particularly in vocational education.

There are limits to this broader analysis. Few endeavors in educational history have yielded more disparate findings than inquiries into who went to high school at particular times in American history. Affecting high school enrollments in different sections of the country were such idiosyncratic factors as the size of communities in which high schools were located, the ebb and flow of the local economy, the availability of jobs for adolescents, the proximity of high schools to prospective students, the seating capacity of those schools, as well as the cultural norms of families and groups with high school-age children (Katz, 1968; Labaree, 1988; Perlmann, 1988; Ueda, 1987; Vinovskis, 1995). Studies that examine the social class backgrounds of high school students—and they are numerous—yield contradictory findings. Few of these studies are comparable to one another, and fewer still try to assess change over time. Finally, because the various studies often focus on questions different from ours, findings from these studies are more suggestive than conclusive.

Nevertheless, data from these studies do suggest that the pattern of developments in Grand Rapids regarding gender, social class, and coursetaking fit neatly into the larger patterns in this era. These data also confirm that as in Grand Rapids, vocational education, particularly courses in industrial arts and home economics, accounted for only a modest share of student coursetaking.

Gender and Racial Diversity Nationwide

The one factor of high school attendance on which there are fairly reliable and consistent data over a long period of time is gender. Annual or biennial reports of the U.S. Commissioner of Education reported national aggregate high school enrollment by gender at least from the 1890s. These show a pattern similar to that for Grand Rapids, including a decline in the boys' share of places during World War I. At the start of the twentieth century, girls held 58% of public high school places. This share declined to 55% by 1916, rose to 57% in 1918, then began to decline again after the war, to 56% in 1920, 52% by 1928, and 51% by 1930. Girls also represented a consistently higher share of high school graduates, about 60% in 1900, 1910, and 1920, and 55% in 1930. In all, these female/male ratios are quite similar to what we found in Grand Rapids.

Too few Black students were present in Grand Rapids at this time to give us any insight into their high school experiences. This is not surprising because as late as 1930 over 80% of Black Americans lived in the southern states (Wilkerson, 1939). A number of studies do provide data on Black high school enrollments in the South and they present a consistent picture of limited opportunities for Black young people due to virulent racism and the de jure segregation of schools. In 1899, the U.S. Supreme Court dashed any hope of Blacks having equal access to high schools by ruling in *Cummings v. School Board of Richmond County, Georgia* that the doctrine of "separate but equal" *did not* mean that Blacks automatically had the right to a high school even if Whites had one. This ruling led to pervasive discrimination against Black young people who sought secondary education (Anderson, 1988). In 1910, for example, 10.1% of White young people aged 15–19 were in high school compared with only 2.8% of Blacks. By 1933–34, the percentages had gone up for both races but the ratio remained largely unchanged, with 55% of Whites aged 14–17 in high school but only 19% of Blacks. Most of the Black students who were in high school lived in urban areas (Anderson, 1988; Margo, 1990; Wilkerson, 1939). As we shall see in Chapter 3, despite their small numbers, African American high school students also faced intense pressure from curriculum reformers to shun academic courses and follow vocationally oriented programs.

Cross-Sectional Studies of Social Class and High School Enrollment

Assessing the ratio of white to blue collar students in high schools across the country is considerably more vexing than considering gender ratios. To do so, we examine three different kinds of studies: cross-sectional snapshots that provide data on specific states and cities, a few longitudinal analyses of enrollments in several cities, and, most rare of all, cohort studies in a small number of cities.

The most influential cross-sectional data on social class and high school enrollments in the early twentieth century were reported in George Counts's *The Selective Character of American Secondary Education* (1922). Counts studied four cities, St. Louis, Seattle, Bridgeport, and Mt. Vernon, New York, with a combined high school enrollment of over 17,000 students. He asked students to complete questionnaires in their classrooms while supervised by their teachers, thus guaranteeing nearly complete responses and almost a 100% response rate. He analyzed the data intelligently and carefully and developed a new system of categorizing occupations that became the standard for other researchers for many years.

Counts's findings on these four cities suggest that Grand Rapids was fairly typical in its proportion of white collar to blue collar students in 1920. His aggregate findings show that white collar students made up 62% of the total population surveyed, blue collar students 35% (including 2% agricultural), with another 3% that could not be categorized. The distributions differed among the individual cities, however. In St. Louis about two-thirds of the students were from white collar homes. In Seattle, the white to blue collar ratio was 57 to 39%, in Bridgeport, 54 to 43%, and in Mt. Vernon, 74 to 23%. Grand Rapids, with its 59% white collar and 38% blue collar enrollment, closely parallels the proportions in the two medium-sized cities, Seattle and Bridgeport.

Counts's study inspired a number of similar investigations and even the recoding of data for comparison purposes that had been collected much earlier using different occupational classifications (see Appendix E, Table E.1). Taken as a whole, these data present no unequivocal patterns. There is, however, a tendency for the proportion of white to blue collar students to vary according to the size of the community, suggesting that one ought to compare Grand Rapids only with cities of similar size (Dear, 1933; Gaiser, 1923; Lide, 1931; Uhl, 1925).[14] For example, a 1923 study of the high schools of Wilmington, Delaware, and a 1922 study of Spokane, Washington, cities about the size of Grand Rapids and Bridgeport, found similar white to blue collar ratios of 52 to 47%, and 48 to 41%, respectively (Gaiser, 1923; U.S. Bureau of Education [hereafter USBE], 1918b).

As we noted, the vast majority of these studies capture just a single moment in time. Even when earlier similar data were available for a particular city, researchers seemed unaware of that fact and did not utilize them. Moreover, these studies underscore the care that researchers must take in claiming that cross-sectional local findings indicate long-term national trends. Counts, following the instincts of a sociologist rather than a historian, argued that while the high schools remained quite "selective" in 1920, they were surely less "selective" than in the past. Few of the scholars who followed him challenged his unsubstantiated claim about the weakening "selectivity" of high schools, whatever their own data might have suggested (but see Dear, 1933). Thus, Counts reinforced rather than challenged the dominant view of curriculum reformers that a larger student body meant a more diverse student body and that the reforms they advocated were actually making the high schools more democratic.

Studies of Social Class and High School Enrollment Changes over Time

One of Counts's cities, St. Louis, provides perhaps the longest-running data collection on the social class background of high school students of any place in the country (see Appendix E, Table E.2). Beginning in 1860 and continuing annually until 1897, school administrators collected and displayed information about the social class background of students in each of the city's schools. These data show surprisingly consistent patterns of class distribution, with the percentage of white collar high school students ranging from two-thirds to three-quarters over the period, even while enrollments rose from 387 to 2,000. Counts's 1920 data showed that although high school enrollments had soared by another 280% during the intervening quarter-century, the proportion of white to blue collar students was still about what it had been 50 years before (Counts, 1922).[15]

Another cross-time comparison can be made from data collected from the public high schools in Wisconsin in 1891 and 1923 (Uhl, 1925; Wisconsin, 1892). In 1891, among just under 5,500 high school students, the percent from white collar backgrounds was 27.1, from blue collar backgrounds, 33.8, from agricultural backgrounds, 29.7, and unclassified by occupation, 9.5. In 1923, on a student base of just under 40,000 students, the respective percentages were 31.1, 33.9, 28.9, and 6.1, a very similar distribution. The relatively stable composition of the student body indicated by the two Wisconsin surveys lends no support whatever to the curriculum reformers' claims that the high school population was becoming more diverse with respect to social class.

We found only two other studies providing data representing the same places at two or more points in time. One is a replication of Counts's study of Seattle and Bridgeport carried out by U.S. Office of Education researchers in 1932 as part of the National Survey of Secondary Education (Kefauver, Noll, & Drake, 1933). The authors reported that, while high school attendance had increased substantially over the 11 years between Counts's study and the replication, these two cities experienced insignificant changes in the white to blue collar ratios in opposite directions, with the blue collar share decreasing slightly in Seattle and increasing slightly in Bridgeport. However, since the data did not include enrollments in the state trade school in Bridgeport or in Seattle's Edison Vocational School, which had opened in 1930, the replication probably understated the blue collar proportion in both cities.[16] Even given this understatement, in Bridgeport our calculations show a shift in white collar to blue collar ratio from 68/32 to 54/46, a shift comparable to what happened in Grand Rapids.

The most interesting and detailed study that we found of social class and high school curriculum was conducted in 1937 by researchers from the Rochester Civic Committee on Unemployment aided by funds from the Works Project Administration. Designed and directed by Harold S. Rand, a researcher for the Rochester Municipal Research Bureau, this study (hereafter the Rand study) examined the employment status of former Rochester high school students. The study was unique among the dozens of youth and youth employment investigations done in this period because it focused on cohorts of entering ninth graders, much as we have done in Grand Rapids. The researchers identified three cohorts of Rochester students, those entering high schools in 1924–25, 1927–28, and 1930–31 (a total of 8,470 students), analyzed their high school transcripts in considerable detail, and carried out lengthy interviews with a subset of 5,266 of these students to determine their subsequent job histories and their attitudes toward their schooling and their lives in general.[17] In all, the Rand study offers a superb picture of a broad cross-section of young people in this era.

Rochester is a particularly fruitful city to compare with Grand Rapids because George Counts chose it as one of the 15 cities he examined in a study of high school course enrollments in 1926, a study that was later replicated as part of the National Survey of Secondary Education (Loomis, Lide, & Johnson, 1932). Using Rand's occupational data and Counts's course enrollment data we can compare coursetaking trends between Rochester and Grand Rapids in some detail and see how developments in both cities fit into the larger, national context (see Appendix E, Tables E.3–E.6).

In 1923, Rochester had four high schools and two brand-new junior high schools (Rochester Board of Education, 1923). The system was organized on the 6–3–3 plan. Responding to sharply increasing enrollments in the high school grades, by 1930 the city had replaced one high school with a new building and had built a large new high school in an area not previously served, converted the two junior high schools into 8–12 schools, converted two elementary schools into junior highs, and enlarged the Rochester Shop School and changed its name to Edison Technical High School (Rochester Board of Education, 1928). Total high school enrollment had risen from just over 6,000 in 1923 to over 10,500 in 1930.

Despite that dramatic increase, the gender ratio of the students remained virtually unchanged, with girls holding slightly more than half of the high school places. The same was not true of the social class background of the students. Using a category system similar but not identical to the one we used in Grand Rapids, the Rand study showed that the percentage of high school places held by students from working-class backgrounds increased from 55% among the 1924 cohort to 71% among the cohort entering in 1930, a huge shift given the relative stability of the occupational structure over time (see Appendix E, Table E.3). While the size of the entering ninth-grade class rose by one-and-a-half times, the number of students from the homes of unskilled workers rose by a factor of five, and their relative share of total high school places rose from 4% to 11%.[18]

These enrollment changes appear to us, as they appeared to Harold Rand, to be the direct result of a worsening economic situation in Rochester. In 1926, beginning with a building construction decline, the economy in Rochester deteriorated rapidly. By 1928 the city was in recession and in 1929 joined the rest of the nation in a full-blown industrial collapse (McKelvey, 1961). These developments forced young people out of the labor market and into school, a trend that we explore more fully in Chapter 3.

Changes in Curriculum and Coursetaking

We have argued that in Grand Rapids, an extraordinarily Progressive-minded city, the high school was not radically transformed into a vocational training institution during the early years of the twentieth century. What evidence is there to determine whether this pattern coincides with general trends? The studies of high school coursetaking we have found are remarkably consistent and uniformly point toward one conclusion—while the number and variety of vocational courses were greatly increased, enrollment data suggest they played a fairly minor role in the educational experiences of high school students prior to 1930.

Not surprisingly, the Progressive curriculum reformers were interested in documenting "scientifically" what effects their efforts were having on public high schools. Consequently, a number of studies focusing on changes in the structure of curricula, course offerings, and graduation requirements were carried out during the period, including some attempts to replicate earlier studies (Bradley, 1929; Counts, 1926; Lawson, 1940; Loomis, Lide, & Johnson, 1932; Stout, 1921; Van Dyke, 1931). Generally, these studies did not look at what students were actually taking. From this vantage point, the results must have been heartening to education professionals. In the 35 high schools studied by Loomis, Lide, and Johnson, the number of different course offerings increased by 475% between 1906 and 1930. Most of the increase was in the nonacademic subjects, with emphasis on the practical. Graduation requirements were reduced, particularly in mathematics. The researchers found that by 1930 algebra was a requirement in only 46% of the high schools and geometry was required in only about a third.

The best sources of usable data on course enrollments bracketing the years from 1900 to 1930 are the Reports of the U.S. Commissioner of Education, published annually until 1916 and then biennially (Latimer, 1958). In the 1870s and 1880s, the U.S. Bureau of Education reported the numbers of students enrolled in various courses of study—classical, English, modern language—for private and public high schools. In 1886, it also began to report enrollments in specific subjects—Latin, Greek, French, German, and English—in the form of percentages for states, regions, and the nation. Mathematics and science were added to the list in 1887. Over time, increasing numbers of schools reported and more subjects were listed. Enrollments in nonacademic subjects were not reported in either the detailed tables or the summary tables until 1910, with one exception, 1900–1901.

The 1900–1901 report provides a starting point for assessing changes in course enrollments. The report contains a table of subject percentage enrollments in 146 high schools in the 50 largest cities, with a combined enrollment of 109,029, representing about 20% of total aggregate public high school enrollment in the nation (USBE, 1902, 1908).[19] The table includes enrollments in drawing, manual training, and four commercial subjects, commercial law, commercial geography, bookkeeping, and stenography. Just under half of the students were enrolled in a drawing course in that year, one-fifth were enrolled in a commercial course, and less than 10% were taking a course in manual training. Further, these combined nonacademic enrollments represented less than 15% of total course registrations.

The report on city school systems (those over 8,000 population) for 1900 indicated that only 92 out of 568 cities (16%) even offered manual training in the high school grades (USBE, 1902). Thus, Grand Rapids was by no means unique in offering drawing and commercial subjects to many of its students and in not offering manual training in 1900. These figures also provide a baseline from which we can gauge the growth of vocational enrollments over the succeeding decades.

In 1910, the Bureau reported on 10,213 public high schools with an aggregate enrollment of 915,061 students, 56% of whom were girls (U.S. Bureau of Education, 1911, Ch. 25). Unfortunately, the tables that reported enrollments in specific courses did not include either manual training or commercial courses, but did include agriculture and domestic economy. These latter two subjects enrolled 4.7% and 3.8% of students, respectively. Between 1900 and 1914, the Bureau also maintained a special report on manual training and industrial schools. This series makes clear that there was an increase in the number of cities offering manual training in this period, but it provides no clue as to the numbers of students enrolled in manual training courses.

Another set of tables helps to quantify the number of students in public high schools in manual or technical training courses. For 1910, these figures were 16,834 boys and 9,803 girls in 257 schools, or about 3% of the total enrollment recorded for that year (Ch. 26). This could well be a serious undercount, however, since the term "courses" could mean either courses of study or individual course offerings; moreover, students enrolled specifically in manual training high schools were not included in these figures. The figures provided for 265 public manual training and industrial schools of secondary grade were 75,880 boys and 45,516 girls. When these various categories are totaled and divided by the combined enrollments in manual training and comprehensive high schools, we arrive at the estimate that about 20% of high school students were enrolled in at least one class in manual arts, domestic arts, or agriculture in 1910. Even this readjusted count, however, is not an impressive showing for the movement to vocationalize American education.

The most useful series of tables to illuminate what happened after 1910 was one started in 1910–11 in which the numbers of high school students enrolled in seven leading courses of study were reported for the country, for each of five regions and for each state (see Table 2.2). It reported that more than 76% of the students were enrolled in academic courses of study, about 11% in commercial, just over 6% in technical/manual training, and slightly over 3% in home economics.

Two important trends are evident in these data. First, following a sharp swing from academic toward vocational courses of study between 1910 and 1914, the proportion of vocational courses of study steadily declined until the end of this

Table 2.2. Percentage Distribution of Public High School Students by Course of Study and Percentage of Boys in Each, United States, 1910–11 Through 1923–24

	1910–11		1914–15		1915–16		1917–18		1923–24	
	All Students	Boys	All Students	Boys	All Students	Boys	All Students	Boys	All Students	Boys
Academic	76.3	43.0	62.5	45.1	65.3	45.2	69.0	41.6	72.5	48.0
Commercial	10.7	46.5	12.5	44.2	14.1	43.2	15.4	37.5	13.5	33.4
Technical or manual training	6.4	78.2	8.4	94.7	7.3	96.0	5.4	90.0	4.9	95.9
Trade training							0.9	66.5	1.3	77.9
Agriculture	1.9	57.0	5.4	57.0	3.5	64.5	2.1	69.5	1.8	85.2
Domestic economy	3.2	0.9	9.6	0.5	7.9	0.2	5.6	1.3	5.0	0.2
Teacher training	1.4	14.3	1.5	13.6	1.9	12.9	1.5	11.5	1.1	13.4

Sources: U.S. Bureau of Education, 1912, 1915, 1917a, 1918c, 1926.

data series, 1923. The second trend is the increased differentiation of curriculum choices by gender. While girls represented about 54% of commercial students in 1910, this had risen to two-thirds by 1923. Agriculture shifted in the opposite direction, with the percent of girls falling from 43 to 15 over the 23 years. The other courses of study reported—manual training, trade training, teacher training, and home economics—were sharply differentiated by gender throughout the period. It should be noted that these course of study distributions do not correspond directly to the types of classes students were taking in high school, since, as we saw in Grand Rapids, academic track students may well have taken vocational classes and, most assuredly, vocational track students took many courses in English, math, science, and social studies.

The course enrollment study of 1914–15 begins to provide a better picture of coursetaking trends, since the vast majority of the nation's public high schools, and certainly all the larger urban ones, were reporting. However, except for bookkeeping, the tables for that year omitted enrollments in commercial subjects, placing these in a separate report on business courses in public high schools. By the 1921–22 data collection, the course list included all the commercial subjects, as well as the other vocational courses. A significant addition for the 1927–28 data collection was the inclusion of enrollments in physical education and a separate field in which schools could list all the enrollments in all the courses not specifically named in the survey. The data from these surveys are displayed in Appendix A, Tables A.2–A.4.

This data array underscores in several ways that Grand Rapids was not anomalous. First, commercial enrollments significantly led other vocational enrollments. Second, the share of students taking a commercial course rose from one in five to one in two, a trend similar to but even wider than in Grand Rapids. Third, by the end of the 1920s, the largest commercial enrollments were in typing, a class taken by many students for personal development rather than vocational training. Fourth, enrollments in the showcase fields of industrial arts and domestic arts increased substantially, but they still remained an extremely small part of the high school coursetaking experience. Fifth, proportionate enrollments in art actually fell, probably as a result of mechanical drawing classes being shifted from art to the industrial arts department. These tables suggest that the 1917 Smith–Hughes Act, seen by some historians as a watershed event in the vocationalizing of the high school, had no perceptible effect on enrollments in the vocational fields. By the late 1920s, industrial arts, home economics, agriculture, trade training, and teacher training combined accounted for less than 10% of all course enrollments in American public high schools.[20]

Is it possible that shifts in subject field enrollments between the 1914–15 and 1921–22 data collections were the direct result of World War I rather than of efforts by curriculum reformers? The most obvious effect of the war was on foreign language enrollments. The proportion of American high school students taking a

German class was about 25% in 1915 but was less than 1% by 1922. While German clearly led the way in the decline of foreign language enrollments, Latin, which had nothing to do with the war, was close behind. Just under half of all high schoolers took Latin in 1910, while by 1922, Latin enrollments fell slightly below one-quarter. Increases in the proportions taking French or Spanish failed to make up these losses. Total foreign language enrollments dropped from 73% of students to 55% between 1915 and 1922. The slide continued well after the war hysteria was over, however, with total enrollments falling to 36% by 1934.

The U.S. Office of Education was not the only agency to trace course enrollment changes in the high school during these decades. Two other studies, a 1925 survey of schools accredited by the North Central Association of Colleges and Secondary Schools (NCA) and a 1926 investigation of high school curricula conducted by George Counts, provide useful comparisons to Grand Rapids, focusing as they do on both educationally "progressive" schools and larger urban schools. The NCA high schools tended to be large schools, usually in urban areas, including, for instance, the large technical and commercial high schools in cities such as Chicago, Cleveland, and Detroit. In 1914, the North Central Association began to produce from its individual school reports a series of detailed studies on the public and private high schools within its purview. Its 1925 study was the only one to include data on course enrollments (Davis, 1925). Enrollment figures were displayed for the 1924–25 school year in 72 course offerings and 11 subject families, by each of the 19 states and by gender (see Table 2.3).

Our analysis of these enrollments shows that only 20% of total course enrollments were in the vocational subjects, and more than half of these were in the commercial field. Just under half of all students were taking a commercial class, and one in three was taking a class in industrial arts, domestic arts, or agriculture. In eleventh and twelfth grades, the time when one might expect students who intended to use such classes for vocational preparation to be enrolled in them, only one in five was taking a class in one of these last three fields of study. As in Grand Rapids, boys were more heavily enrolled in math and science classes than were girls, while girls dominated commercial enrollments by a two-to-one margin. The nonacademic share of coursetaking varied from a high of 31% in Illinois and Missouri to a low of 17% in Arkansas. Overall, when compared with the national data for 1927–28, the NCA distribution by subject field was within one or two percentage points in each field.

The NCA data tell us nothing about changes over time, but they do support the conclusion that as late as the mid-1920s high schools of similar quality across the country were still not the strongly vocationally oriented institutions that Progressive reformers had intended them to be. George Counts's (1926) study of student coursetaking in 15 cities also illustrated that situation. Given three key factors in these cities—the success of Progressive Era governance reforms, the commitment of the reformers to vocational education, and the industrial charac-

Table 2.3. Subject Field Enrollment, Percent of Students Enrolled and Percentage Distribution by Gender, North Central Association Accredited High Schools, 1924–25

Subject Field	Girls Enrolled			Boys Enrolled			Total Enrolled		
	n	%	Distribution (%)	n	%	Distribution (%)	n	%	Distribution (%)
Total enrollment	356,209	52.5		322,726	47.5		678,935	100.0	
English	305,338	85.7	20.7	280,630	86.6	21.7	585,968	86.3	21.2
Foreign languages	169,593	47.6	11.5	129,300	40.1	10.0	298,893	44.0	10.8
Mathematics	175,581	49.4	11.9	201,361	62.5	15.6	376,942	55.5	13.6
Science	134,731	37.8	9.2	160,313	49.7	12.4	295,044	43.5	10.7
Social studies	218,891	61.5	14.9	203,546	63.0	15.7	422,437	62.2	15.3
Commercial	213,614	59.9	14.5	95,781	29.6	7.4	309,395	45.6	11.2
Household arts	99,727	27.9	6.8	429	0.1	0.0	100,156	14.8	3.6
Industrial arts	1,122	0.3	0.1	93,510	28.9	7.2	94,632	13.9	3.4
Agriculture	6,020	1.7	0.4	15,792	4.9	1.2	21,812	3.2	0.8
Music	119,953	33.6	8.1	96,440	29.8	7.4	216,393	31.9	7.8
Art	27,397	7.7	1.9	17,633	5.5	1.4	45,030	6.6	1.6
Total academic	1,004,134		68.2	975,150		75.3	1,979,284		71.5
Total nonacademic	467,833		31.8	319,585		24.7	787,418		28.5

Source: Davis, 1925, pp. 24, 72–79. See also Davis, 1920.

Notes: The high schools surveyed were in 19 states: Arizona, Arkansas, Colorado, Illinois, Indiana, Iowa, Kansas, Michigan, Minnesota, Missouri, Montana, Nebraska, New Mexico, North Dakota, Ohio, Oklahoma, South Dakota, Wisconsin, and Wyoming. This survey excluded enrollments in health and physical education, enrollments that were highly significant in those states that had adopted physical education requirements for secondary schools.

ter of many of the cities—Counts expected vocational education to play a prominent role in these high schools. To assess student coursetaking patterns, Counts
computed "the percentage of the total number of pupil recitation hours" in 11
subject areas for the second semester of the 1923–24 school year. While the ratio
of academic to nonacademic courses in these schools was lower than that in the
other studies, 62.5 to 37.5%, the relative importance of the vocational subjects
was about the same.[21] Only 12.4% of the students' recitation time was in commercial subjects, 7.5% was in industrial arts, and 4.7% was in home economics.
Students spent a larger percentage of time in physical education courses, 7.7%,
than in industrial arts.

Counts, who, like the reform leaders in Grand Rapids, believed that vocational subjects would help change the selective character of the high schools and
bring about greater educational equality, expressed his disappointment with these
findings:

> As the movement toward vocational education got under way, it manifested such
> strength that many expected the industrial arts rapidly to assume a position of dominance
> in the high-school curriculum. This expectation has not been fulfilled. . . . The industrial
> arts were shown . . . to play a relatively humble role in the curriculum. . . . The fortunes
> of home economics in the secondary school have been much the same as those of
> industrial arts. . . . The girls who were supposed to rejoice at the opportunity of being
> better equipped for the responsibilities of the home and motherhood have been in-
> terested in other things. They have chosen the college-preparatory courses because they
> desired to continue their education, or the commercial courses because they wished to
> earn money. (pp. 98, 103)

Although the data from these studies represent different areas, collection
methods, and approaches to characterizing student coursetaking, they tell a remarkably consistent story. Yet none of them are based on student transcripts, as
was our analysis of coursetaking in Grand Rapids. We found only two studies that
were structured in this way, the study of youth problems in Rochester, New York,
discussed earlier, and a portion of the 1932 National Survey of Secondary Education entitled *The Program of Studies* (Loomis, Lide, & Johnson, 1932).

In the years examined by Rand and his colleagues, 1924–1934, the Rochester secondary schools offered five courses of study: college preparatory, commercial, vocational, technical, and home economics (Rochester Board of Education,
1928). In each of the three cohorts, the largest percentage of students were in the
college preparatory course of study, but this declined over time from 40% to 29%,
while those following a commercial course rose from 15 to 24% (see Appendix E,
Tables E.5 and E.6). The combined share of those taking industrial arts and home
economics rose from 4 to 13% between the 1924 and 1930 cohorts. Those taking
the college-oriented technical course remained flat at about 5%. From 30 to 36%

of the students were listed as in "no course" but these seem to have been mostly ninth graders who left school before making a course decision.

Slightly less than half of all the Rochester students stayed to graduate, and about a third left after 1 year or less. The number of years of high school completed did not change much between cohorts. The graduation rate among students from homes where the parents were American, English, or Russian was 60%, compared with 38% among Italians, 41% among Poles, and 52% among Germans. Furthermore, about 30% of the students in these latter groups cited "financial reasons" for dropping out of school, twice as many as in the former groups. The graduation rate also differed by occupational class background, with about two-thirds of white collar background students graduating compared with about one-third of those from the homes of unskilled laborers.

Several of the trends evident in Rochester between 1924 and 1930 are similar to developments we found in Grand Rapids between 1920 and 1930. For example, the commercial course of study became more gendered over time, as the share of girls choosing this course rose from 25 to 39% while the share of boys rose from only 6 to 9%. Girls received higher marks than boys, and average marks were mostly below a C average, but were rising. Not surprisingly, marks were lowest in foreign language courses and highest in practical courses. The number of students taking at least one course in foreign language declined from 59 to 47%, while those taking a practical course increased from 30 to 35%.

As we noted, Counts (1926) chose Rochester as one of his 15 cities, and Loomis, Lide, and Johnson (1932) later replicated his study, offering us a way to put Rand's findings in a broader context. These scholars found that between 1924 and 1931 the enrollment share of English, mathematics, and foreign language decreased, science increased a bit, and social studies remained the same. Among the nonacademic subjects, the shares of industrial arts, home economics, commercial, art, and physical education increased, while music declined. The big gainer was industrial arts, moving from a 1% share to over 9%, while foreign language lost about the same amount, from 20% to just over 11%. The academic share of coursetaking fell sharply from 73% to 60% in just 7 years. As the number of students from lower blue collar and Italian families increased, so did enrollments in industrial arts classes. We believe that this is not a coincidental relationship, but we are unable to establish a direct causal link because we do not have the individual-level transcript data.

In all, the Rochester study provides additional support for our contention that the experience of high school students in Grand Rapids was well within the "mainstream" of secondary coursetaking during the 1920s. While the share of vocational courses did rise for students in the 1930 cohort (who graduated in 1934 or 1935), it seems clear that this development was largely due to the Great Depression rather than to the curriculum changes introduced by professional educators.

The portion of the 1932 National Survey of Secondary Education that addressed questions about coursetaking analyzed the transcripts of the 1926 entering cohort of students in 13 high schools in five cities, and added the data on four additional cities from another study (Gamble, 1931; Loomis, Lide, & Johnson, 1933). Also included was a comparison of the transcripts of *graduating* cohorts of six of these high schools in 1890, 1900, 1910, 1920, and 1930.[22] These data provide a good opportunity for additional comparison, offering a look at changes in vocational education over time in large cities where special-purpose high schools were available.

Among the 1926 cohort, the nonacademic share of coursetaking in the nine cities ranged from a low of 17% among the Washington, DC, graduates, who were all college preparatory students, to a high of one-third in Long Beach, California, and Springfield, Massachusetts. The median share was 27.6%. The data for Providence, Springfield, and Denver are particularly important because they include graduates from vocational high schools. The nonacademic share for Providence was 28.0%, for Denver, 19.2%, and for Springfield, 32.6%. These three cities with vocational high schools had almost exactly the same median share of nonacademic subjects as all nine cities, 27.7%.

The study by Loomis et al. (1933) also provided a more detailed breakdown of nonacademic coursetaking for five cities. The commercial share of coursetaking varied from 9.4% in Denver to 16.9% in Providence, with a mean of 13.1. The authors commented:

> Commerce was the most popular nonacademic field. In fact in three of the five cities, a larger percentage of work was completed in commercial subjects than in all other nonacademic subjects combined. . . . The old standard subjects of stenography, typewriting, and bookkeeping accounted for more than half of the time devoted to commerce. (p. 224)

The combined totals of industrial and domestic arts ranged from 3.4% in Washington to 8.8% in Joliet, with a mean of 6.4%. For two cities, Providence and Springfield, the study provided separate distributions for the technical and commercial high schools. Even in these schools, with one exception, the majority of courses taken were academic classes. For each of the two technical high schools, the nonacademic shares were 35%, and for the two commercial high schools, they were 41 and 52%. This last figure is the only instance we have found of a high school prior to 1930 in which the nonacademic share was roughly equal to the academic share of courses taken by graduates.

Finally, the cross-time comparison of the graduates in three of these cities did not show a steady increase in the nonacademic share. In fact, the pattern of change was surprisingly uneven. Between 1890 and 1900, the nonacademic percentage increased by a factor of four, from 3.6 to 16.0. Over the next decade, it increased to only 16.7%. Then, during the teens, it rose to 21.2% and remained at exactly that level for the 1930 graduates. This pattern is likely the result of the way high schools were built in these three cities. In 1890, the group included a comprehensive high school, a classical high school, and a commercial high school. Over the next decade, a comprehensive, a manual training, and a technical high school were added. Between 1900 and 1910, only another comprehensive school was added. If more high schools in other states and regions were included in this calculation, the progress of the nonacademic subjects might indeed appear to follow a smoother course, but not necessarily a greater one. Like the students in Grand Rapids, the students in these three cities could only respond to the opportunities actually available in their time and place.

SUMMARY

Vocational education clearly made important inroads into American high schools in the first 3 decades of the twentieth century. As the century opened, the courses with immediate vocational relevance in most urban high schools were limited to commercial courses such as bookkeeping and commercial law and some courses in mechanical and architectural drawing. Only a few cities offered opportunities to take subjects such as woodworking, sewing, cooking, and metalworking in the high school grades. By contrast, in 1930, many American high schools provided an amazing array of vocational courses. For example, in that year, the high schools of Los Angeles offered 129 different courses in industrial arts, 47 courses in home economics, 16 courses in agriculture, and 42 commercial courses (Loomis, Lide, & Johnson, 1933). Courses in the traditional academic subject fields—English, mathematics, science, foreign language, and social studies—also had multiplied but not to the same extent. At the same time, aggregate secondary school enrollments in the nation had soared from just under 700,000 in 1900 to over 4.8 million in 1930, and the ratio of these enrollments to the size of the 14–17-year-old population rose from 11.4 to 51.4% (see Appendix A, Table A.1). No wonder so many historians have argued that during this period the high school was transformed into an entirely new kind of educational institution, a mass terminal institution in which the vast majority of American youth could be shaped for the vocational futures that awaited them. This is certainly what the professionals who had taken command of school governance in the period had planned for them.

But the students and their parents seem not to have heard the message. Of the students who managed to stay out of the job market long enough to attend high school, and this was a steadily increasing number, the great majority did not flock to the vocational training "opportunities" that were being opened to them. The plain fact is that the overwhelming proportion of high school courses taken by most students were in the traditional academic fields of English, mathematics, science, and social studies. Only the study of foreign language fully succumbed to the attacks that Progressive reformers mounted against it, and its losses were largely absorbed by two other academic fields, English and social studies. Many students took no vocational classes at all, and many who did took so few that we must think of these as personal development classes rather than as vocational preparation.

This is not to say that the efforts of the Progressive reformers had no effect at all. They projected a model of secondary education in which the curriculum would be tailored to the "needs" of the individual, or at least to the interests, talents, and "probable destiny" of various groups of students. In the early part of this period, it seems that high school students who did not aspire to continue their education into college, whether they were working class or middle class, saw their own "probable destiny" in white collar work, a rapidly expanding portion of the work force, and they used the high school commercial offerings to get them there. After 1920, however, the coursetaking patterns show that students tended to be more sharply distinguished by gender and social class background, a result that we can only assume satisfied the Progressives' educational agenda. However, we doubt that even this outcome can be "credited" to their efforts.

Sometime after the mid-1920s, a new factor, the weakening of the teenage job market, began to strongly influence the high school attendance and curriculum decisions of American young people. Progressive reformers had largely ignored such economic variables in thinking and writing about high school attendance and nonattendance. When their own dropout studies consistently reported that economic hardship was the primary cause of early withdrawal, they contemptuously dismissed this as an excuse to cover school failure or boredom with the curriculum (Angus, 1965). We argue in the next chapter that as the national economy began its slide toward the Great Depression in the late 1920s, high school-age youth were the first affected, and what they chose or were forced to do had a greater impact on the long-term shaping of the American high school than all the curricular innovations, textbooks, accreditation standards, and school surveys put together.

NOTES

1. On Davis's leadership of the vocational guidance movement, see Spring (1972).

2. Board member Josephine Goss, who had attended the NEA meeting of that year, reported that "[m]anual training received more attention and occupied more time of the members than any other department of the NEA. It was stated without contradiction that wherever manual training high schools are established they draw almost an entirely different set of pupils. In many cities they have doubled high school attendance" (GRAR, 1902–03, p. 29).

3. When Mrs. Goss and Superintendent Elson appeared before the monthly meeting of the Trades and Labor Council, they were told specifically that the Council supported the issue of bonds for the purpose of building more schoolhouses, but opposed the extension of manual training (Angus, 1982).

4. For this analysis, we created a social profile of each precinct using the Michigan State Census of 1904. The distance variable was created by measuring the distance from the center of each precinct to the nearest existing or proposed high school over existing transportation lines.

5. This junior high school became a model for other cities when Thomas Briggs of Teachers College featured it in the first textbook on the subject (Briggs, 1920).

6. In 1923, Superintendent Greeson calculated that high school enrollment should be optimized at about 20% of system enrollment. This figure had been exceeded by 1925 (GRAR. 1923).

7. Often the ninth-grade enrollment exceeded the previous year's eighth-grade enrollment since a few students were admitted as tuition students from the nearby country schools.

8. This ratio is, at best, a rough way to gauge the expansion of high school enrollments, since it tends to give the impression that if 14–17-year-olds were in school, they were in high school. The U.S. Census reported that 84.8% of those ages 14 to 17 in Grand Rapids had attended school in 1930, as contrasted to the 67.8% that the ratio suggests.

9. There were also a number of small Protestant (mainly Dutch Reformed) and Roman Catholic high schools in the city enrolling a total of about 1,100 students by 1930.

10. An analysis of the first jobs obtained by the males of the 1900 cohort showed that 80% of those who attended high school for any length of time entered a white collar job, compared with just 50% of those who did not continue past the eighth grade. By the 1920 cohort, with two-and-a-half times as many students attending high school, the percent of boys entering white collar first jobs had fallen to 70, but for those who dropped out it also had fallen, to 40.

11. These percentages for blue collar students are larger than other historians have suggested. For more on the percentage of working-class students in nineteenth- and early-twentieth-century high schools, see Vinovskis (1995); Perlmann (1988); Ueda (1987); and Angus (1981).

12. By 1914, business arithmetic was counted toward the 2 years of mathematics required for graduation. See the discussion of business arithmetic in Chapter 5.

13. While the relationship between rising youth unemployment and high school attendance in the 1920s has often been noted, a relationship which was particularly apparent in industrial cities, no one has pinpointed the precise timing of these developments (see Fuller, 1983; Grubb & Lazerson, 1982; Osterman, 1979; U.S. Department of Labor, Children's Bureau, 1933; Walters, 1984).

14. For a more detailed discussion of these studies, see Angus (1981). On similar findings involving nineteenth-century high schools, see Vinovskis (1995). Comparison between places is made difficult by the facts that different data collection methods produced widely differing amounts in the "unclassified" category, and there seems to be no sound way to categorize agricultural workers within a scheme designed to imply a social class hierarchy.

15. Counts made no reference to these earlier data and, in fact, claimed that despite the degree of "selection" he found, the situation had been much worse in the past, a claim based on no data whatever.

16. When Counts collected data for Seattle, the situation there was in flux. Following a 1919 general strike led by the Wobblies, the work force in manufacturing jobs fell from about 40,000 in 1919 to 13,000 in 1921. This must have affected the youth labor market and forced many working-class youth into the high schools a full decade before the Great Depression. The period of most rapid high school enrollment increase in Seattle was 1917 to 1921, following which Seattle led the nation in high school attendance rates.

17. The report of the Rochester study is an unpublished typescript, which we located in the Northwestern University Library with the call number L371.8 C582a. All references in this section are to this report, and no page numbers are provided because the report is not effectively paginated. Efforts to locate the original code sheets, notes from interviews, transcripts, and so on, were unsuccessful. Our account of the findings is derived solely from the tables provided in the study report and some retabulations of data available in those tables. While many of the tables displayed data separately for those who entered high school in September and those who entered in January, we have combined these groups in our summary of the study's findings.

18. There was also a major shift in the ethnic diversity of the student body, led by an increase in the number of students from Italian homes from 8% to 22% over the same half-decade. Benjamin Franklin High School served an area of the city in which up to 70% of the population was foreign born or of mixed or foreign parentage; by 1930, it had the largest enrollment in the city, with Italian, German, and Polish students making up about 36% of the student body.

19. Girls made up 60% of these enrollments, exactly the same relative share as in Grand Rapids.

20. We have followed a long-standing convention in listing subject fields as academic or nonacademic. In the most recent study by Westat, courses in the arts have been shifted to the academic category (NCES, 1997, Table 8).

21. The difference in academic/nonacademic ratio is due entirely to Counts's inclusion and the other studies' exclusion of physical education enrollments.

22. For a list of these high schools, see Loomis, Lide, and Johnson (1933).

3

The Transformation of the High School
During the Depression and War

AMONG POLITICAL AND ECONOMIC historians, the eras of the Great Depression and World War II stand as periods of enormous change in American life (Schwarz, 1993). Educational historians, however, generally dismiss the crises and controversies surrounding public schools in these eras as sound and fury signifying little (Cremin, 1961; Tyack, Lowe, & Hansot, 1984). This chapter challenges these assessments, arguing that during the depression and war American secondary education underwent a profound transformation in which the nature and function of high schools changed dramatically and in which curricular differentiation took on an entirely new dimension. During this period, high schools shifted from institutions concerned primarily with academic and vocational preparation to institutions largely responsible for custodial care. In curricular terms this shift meant that high schools decreased their emphasis on preparing young people for future adult roles and responsibilities and instead increasingly directed their attention to immediate and clearly relevant problems of youth. Four interrelated developments led to that transformation.

First, the Great Depression shattered the youth labor market and forced huge numbers of young people to return to or reluctantly remain in school. Second, the emergence of the youth problem and the enormous increase in high school enrollments unleashed a series of political struggles and policy debates the outcome of which influences secondary education to this day. In the 1930s, school leaders scrambled to accommodate rising enrollments amid sharp budgetary retrenchment (Mirel, 1993; Tyack, Lowe, & Hansot, 1984). Consequently, this period witnessed the first major effort by school leaders to secure federal aid to education (Smith, 1982). However, in their struggle for funding, school leaders became embroiled in hostile battles with social scientists and New Deal leaders about whether schools were the best place to serve young people in this crisis. Educators won those battles in the early 1940s with the destruction of the New Deal youth programs, a development that gave the comprehensive high school a monopoly position on "meeting the needs of youth" and ensured that federal aid to education would flow in only one direction, to public schools.

Third, in order to convince politicians and policy makers that high schools deserved this monopoly position, educational leaders had to demonstrate that their curricula were indeed relevant and useful to the new waves of students who were swelling secondary enrollments. Toward this end, curriculum specialists, particularly in "lighthouse" urban school districts, implemented courses and programs that initially took their cue from *Cardinal Principles of Secondary Education*. However, these reforms eventually went well beyond the recommendations contained in that manifesto, by rejecting both traditional academic courses and more modern vocational ones and instead focusing on courses and programs to meet the immediate "needs of youth."

Fourth, the decline in high school enrollments and the rapid expansion of vocational programs during World War II did *not* halt the curricular trends begun in the 1930s. Indeed, in the 1940s as the high school solidified its monopoly, the "needs" curriculum became even more vital to its success. From that perspective, the life adjustment movement of the late 1940s must be reconceptualized as *following* rather than initiating curricular trends. Driving these curricular developments was the increasingly important role that secondary schools were playing in the postwar economy, namely, keeping young people out of the labor market (Grubb & Lazerson, 1982). By 1950, American high schools had become in large measure custodial institutions.

This chapter details the profound and enduring shift in the basic relationships among youth, high schools, and employment that took place in the 1930s and 1940s. In the first half of the chapter, we examine the crisis of youth caused by the Great Depression and the war, the political and policy struggles engendered by that crisis, and the responses of educational professionals to these challenges, particularly those responses that focused on curricular reform. In the second part, we resume our analysis of the high school experiences of youth, focusing on precisely how these national debates and curricular changes influenced the educational experiences of young people in these two critical decades. Continuing our cohort analysis of high school students in Grand Rapids, we closely examine young people who entered high school in 1935 and 1940. In addition, we consider school-level data from Detroit, a school system serving a diverse student population that was also on the cutting edge of curriculum reform in this era. We demonstrate the significance of our findings from the local level by linking them to data in Michigan and the nation.

POLITICS AND THE YOUTH PROBLEM

Since at least the 1890s, a variety of social reformers have tried to arouse the nation to action against the problem of child labor. That "crusade for the children" pitted union leaders, child welfare advocates, and Protestant clergy against employers, parents, and, sometimes, leaders of the Roman Catholic Church. Educators also played an important role in the struggle against child labor in part because opponents of the practice saw universal schooling as the solution to the child labor problem (Trattner, 1970). Among the most important developments arising out of the Great Depression was the triumph of child labor opponents on both aspects of their crusade. The depression drastically curtailed and in some areas virtually destroyed the youth labor market. At the same time, high school enrollments soared and the prospect of universal school enrollment for 5–17-year-olds appeared to be within sight.[1]

Yet even before anti–child labor advocates recognized, let alone savored, these triumphs, a new crisis, "the youth problem," emerged. The youth problem was ironically the reverse of the child labor problem—rather than too many young people working, huge numbers of young people could find no work at all. With joblessness came a series of related crises, including increased delinquency, crime, sexual promiscuity, alienation, and manifestations of political radicalism. As these crises gained national attention, the youth problem engendered a political and jurisdictional battle over which institutions could best deal with this new and troubling situation. While this political and jurisdictional battle was in some ways similar to the earlier one fought over child labor, those who thought that schooling was the best solution to the youth problem faced a new set of opponents. Rather than struggling with employers and more conservative elements of American society, educators in the 1930s and 1940s squared off against New Deal politicians and leading social scientists who saw such institutions as the Civilian Conservation Corps (CCC) and National Youth Administration (NYA) as the best agencies to prepare young people for their transition into adulthood.

The Youth Crisis and the New Deal

The depression had a particularly devastating impact on the lives and aspirations of young people. Unemployment hit them harder than any other segment of the population. Every national survey conducted in the 1930s and early 1940s found youth unemployment substantially higher than that of all other groups. In 1930, for example, youth between the ages of 15 and 24 made up over 23% of the labor force but almost 28% of the unemployed. By 1933, young people accounted for over a third of the unemployed and in 1937, when economic conditions throughout the country were somewhat improved, the young still accounted for almost 36% of the unemployed. In raw numbers that meant that in 1937 nearly 4,000,000 young people who were willing and able to work could not find jobs. Even in 1940, as industry began to gear up for war, almost 35% of the total number of unemployed were between the ages of 14 and 24, a group that made up only 22% of the total labor force (NYA, 1944; see also Henry, 1947).

These aggregate numbers mask the even bleaker employment situation facing the very youngest group of job seekers, Blacks, and young women. When
broken down by age, researchers found that the younger the job seeker, the higher
the rate of unemployment. One study done in 1935 found that 16–19-year-olds
had four times higher rates of unemployment than 20–24-year-olds (Karpinos,
1941). Also, throughout this period, Black youth and young women had consistently higher rates of unemployment than young White males. In 1937, 35% of
Blacks aged 15 to 24 were unemployed compared with 29% of Whites, and 43%
of young women were unemployed compared with 32% of young men (NYA,
1944; Rainey, 1938; Rawick, 1957). Furthermore, as we saw in Chapter 2, there
is evidence that the employment situation for young people had begun to worsen
in the mid-1920s in some cities, earlier than for other workers.

This rapid deterioration of the youth labor market had a number of serious
consequences that contributed to the emerging youth problem. As early as 1932,
the nation discovered between 200,000 and 300,000 teenage tramps (of whom an
estimated 10% were young women) criss-crossing the country seeking work
(Minehan, 1934; Rawick, 1957). The large numbers of out-of-work and vagrant
youth also heightened fears of increased crime, violence, and sexual promiscuity.
In addition, a small but highly vocal group of young people were gravitating to
radical left- and right-wing organizations, and in marches, demonstrations, and
meetings encouraged open rebellion against the government and the economic
system (Chamberlain, 1939; Lowitt & Beasley, 1981). Equally troubling were fears
about juvenile delinquency, a concern that increasingly became part of national
debates about the youth problem (Mirel, 1984).

As dramatic as these developments were, by far the most significant consequence of the collapse of the youth labor market was the explosion of high school
enrollments. In 1930, slightly less than half of all 14- to 17-year-olds had dropped
out of school, usually to seek employment. But in the face of the collapsing labor
market, many of the nation's teenagers remained in or returned to school, pushing high school enrollments up by nearly 30% between 1930 and 1934 alone. Not
surprisingly, the greatest increases were among older students who would have
left school had jobs been available. Between 1930 and 1934, the number of students in eleventh and twelfth grades rose 38% and 43% respectively (Angus, 1965).
In many cities, high school enrollments rose spectacularly. For example, between
1930 and 1940, high school enrollments in Milwaukee climbed from 14,290 to
24,780 (Kritek & Clear, 1993). In San Francisco only 29% of the students who
had entered the school system as first graders graduated high school in 1930. A
decade later, the proportion had jumped to 86% (Zilversmit, 1993).

These increases in high school enrollment could not have come at a worse
time for most school systems. During the depression, tax delinquencies rose hand-
in-hand with unemployment, and by 1932 most public schools experienced severe revenue reductions that usually meant the termination of building programs,

mass firings of teachers, or sharp salary reductions for school employees (Mirel, 1993; Tyack, Lowe, & Hansot, 1984). Each of these responses to retrenchment made accommodating the flood of high school students far more difficult. In Detroit, for example, enrollments in the city's comprehensive high schools jumped over 43% between 1929 and 1934, a period in which the school board slashed its budget by over one-third, implemented a temporary hiring freeze that led to a sharp decline in the number of teachers, and placed a moratorium on all school construction and renovation. In the 1938–39 school year, Detroit's high schools were serving almost 20,000 more students than a decade earlier, yet only 366 more teachers had been hired in the entire system and only one new high school had been brought on line by converting a junior high building (Mirel, 1984).

Across the nation similar experiences with retrenchment, combined with studies showing the large-scale inequities in school funding between the various regions and states, galvanized efforts by the National Education Association to win federal aid for education. While New Deal rhetoric initially led educators to believe that such aid would be forthcoming, by the mid-1930s, educators, particularly NEA leaders, were thoroughly disenchanted with the Roosevelt administration. Two major developments led to that disenchantment. First, leading New Dealers in both the White House and Congress refused to support federal aid to education as long as educators maintained the position described by Tyack, Lowe, and Hansot (1984) as federal assistance without control. Second, neither President Roosevelt nor any of his top aides had much confidence in the ability or willingness of school leaders to deal with the youth problem in all its varied manifestations (Fass, 1989; Rawick, 1957; Tyack, Lowe, & Hansot, 1984; Zeitlan, 1958).

In the eyes of the New Deal leaders, the schools were too inflexible to deal with large numbers of unemployed out-of-school youth—youth whom many federal officials believed the schools had rejected and who, in turn, had rejected the schools (Rainey, 1938). Consequently, the New Dealers deliberately created two new agencies, the Civilian Conservation Corps (CCC) and the National Youth Administration (NYA), to address the most serious problem young people faced, getting a job. These programs became the main point of contention between the NEA and the New Deal, not merely because professional educators believed the politicians were threatening their "turf" but also because the CCC and NYA siphoned away federal funds that the educators believed should be going to the beleaguered public schools (Fass, 1989; Rawick, 1957; Smith, 1982; Tyack, Lowe, & Hansot, 1984; Zeitlan, 1958).

Roosevelt established the CCC in 1933 in part to deal with the problem of teenage vagrants. It quickly expanded into the larger of the two New Deal youth programs, eventually sending some 2.5 million young people into national parks and forests where they engaged in a variety of socially and ecologically useful projects. Working full-time at modest wages, CCC members were able to send some money back to their families to supplement their relief payments. Throughout its history, the CCC was one of the most popular programs of the New Deal. Nevertheless, as the 1930s wore on, educators denounced both the CCC and the NYA as unwarranted and dangerous federal encroachments into the field of tax-supported education (Fass, 1989; Mirel & Angus, 1985; Rugg, 1947; Salmond, 1967).

The reaction by educators to the creation of the NYA in 1935 was typical of these attacks. Speaking at the National Education Association convention in July of that year, George Strayer of Teachers College declared, "The President has not only deliberately ignored the Office of Education . . . but he has gone against the best interests of the young people involved, he has denied the competence of the school people with their years of experience and has set up a dual administration dealing with youth guidance" (Rawick, 1957, p. 192). Most galling to the professional educators, as Strayer intimated, was Roosevelt's rejection of a proposal by U.S. Commissioner of Education John Studebaker to make the new youth agency an adjunct of the public schools. The Studebaker plan would have given federal aid to local school districts, which, in turn, would have provided vocational guidance, training, and placement services to young people. Instead, Roosevelt opted for a program of direct relief for youth under the auspices of Harry Hopkins and the Works Project Administration.

Unlike the agency envisioned by Studebaker, the primary function of the NYA was to supply funds for youth relief and employment rather than for youth training. Ultimately, about 1.75 million young people between the ages of 16 and 24 served in the NYA. NYA employment fell into two broad categories. The first was "work–study" positions within high schools, colleges, and universities, paying only $6.00 a month but enabling many poor families to keep their teens in school (Fass, 1989; NYA, 1944; Rugg, 1947). The second category consisted of jobs for youth who had already left school and were unable to find work in the private sector. These jobs generally were cosponsored by state governments, local municipalities, or public service institutions such as hospitals and paid $15 to $22 a month (Zeitlan, 1958).

School leaders at first supported the job-creation aspect of the program, but they became increasingly worried when the NYA began adding such services as vocational training, guidance, and placement, activities that, as in Grand Rapids, had been the stock in trade of progressive high school curriculum reform. That encroachment into the high schools' domain further aggravated the jurisdictional dispute between school leaders and the NYA (Mirel & Angus, 1985). Even more troubling for the educators was the support the New Deal agencies received from leading social scientists who also saw nonschool agencies as the best approach to dealing with the problem of youth unemployment and transition into adult life. The most important social scientists involved in this controversy were those from the American Youth Commission (AYC).

The American Youth Commission

The creation and operation of the CCC and NYA were based not solely on New Dealers' distrust and disdain for professional educators. These agencies were, in fact, strongly supported by research conducted by a new, influential reform agency, the American Youth Commission. In 1935, the prestigious American Council on Education created the AYC to study and focus attention on the "thousands of youth [who] were roaming the country as destitute young tramps" and on the thousands more flooding into the high schools "at a time when school taxes remained unpaid and school budgets were being drastically cut" (AYC, 1942, p. ix; see also Flack, 1969). The Commission produced a series of studies that quickly set the standard for all youth-serving agencies, including a number of classic studies on the problems of Negro youth, which were among the first sophisticated works of social science to call attention to the dire impact of segregation on the lives of young African Americans (Davis & Dollard, 1940; Frazier, 1940).[2]

The most important of these studies in shaping the outlook and agenda of the AYC was the Maryland Youth Study by Howard M. Bell (1938). Based on a carefully constructed sample of over 14,000 Maryland youth, Bell's study was the first to suggest that the number of unemployed youth might be as high as 4,000,000 nationwide, a figure confirmed by the 1937 federal census of unemployment. The study argued that the central feature of the youth problem was the prolonged period of enforced idleness between the time teens left school and the time they were able to find work.

The AYC commissioners were "startled and shocked" by what this study and similar surveys revealed. They wrote:

> [A]s we shifted our attention from one aspect of youth to another, taking up questions in the fields of secondary education, use of leisure time, marriage and the home, health and fitness, juvenile delinquency, citizenship, and the special problems of rural youth and of minority groups, we found ourselves meeting the economic situation at every turn. . . . Through this process it became apparent that major attention must be given to the problem of employment opportunity for youth in all of its manifold ramifications. (AYC, 1942, p. xii)

Here, then, was a new perspective on America's youth problem. Unlike educators and anti-child labor activists who saw increased schooling and curriculum reform to attract and keep new students as the solution to youth unemployment and related youth problems, the AYC focused on the period between school leaving and work entry that the depression had either caused or revealed. The AYC was convinced that work experience was a vital part of the education of young people (at least from about 16 years of age), that all aspects of a healthy transition from youth to adult life depended on it, and that institutions such as the CCC and

NYA were better able to provide this experience than were the nation's second-ary schools. Indeed, as the AYC saw it, instead of meeting all the needs of all the youth, the schools had met almost none of the needs of youth from poor families and few of the vocational training needs of any youth. Moreover, the AYC argued that most of the reduction in child labor in America had resulted from changes in the economy rather than from curriculum reform in schools. It maintained that these very changes called for a new national policy, one of publicly provided jobs for youth during periods when the private sector of the economy could not put youth to work (AYC, 1942).

Throughout its short history, the Commission was committed to the idea that the major problem of youth was the problem of employment; and this conviction set the tone for its final report in 1942, which argued that "[t]he most fundamental problem of youth is precisely the problem of full employment under peacetime conditions" (p. 89). In the report, which contained a detailed analysis of the causes of the depression and the failure of the economy to rebound from the economic disaster of the 1930s, the Commission concluded that without considerable government intervention in business and industry, the high unemployment conditions of the depression era would return after the war. Consequently, the AYC maintained that the government would have to continue providing programs such as the CCC and NYA to facilitate young people's transition from school to the labor force (AYC, 1942).

Despite the fact that the AYC strongly supported federal aid to education and proposed policies in which schools would work collaboratively with such youth employment agencies as the CCC, the general thrust of AYC positions clearly challenged the hegemony of public schools. First, the AYC rejected the fundamental proposition of public school leaders that high schools, particularly comprehensive high schools, were the best institution to deal with youth problems. By repeatedly arguing that new, nonschool agencies were necessary to solve the youth problem, the AYC and its allies directly challenged the "imperial" ambitions of school leaders who saw the expansion of high schools as the only effective way to deal with youth problems.

Second, by calling for actual job experience rather than more vocational education, the AYC questioned the ability of curriculum reform to deal effectively with the youth problem. As we have seen in the previous chapter, school leaders had touted vocational programs as the centerpiece of high school expansion. The AYC, however, did not believe that school systems could provide the broad range of vocational preparation that was necessary, and that therefore educators would have to work in partnership with other agencies in the future. In proposing this policy, the AYC attacked the utility of current vocational programs and questioned a key article of educational faith, that curricular change had led to enrollment increases. As the AYC studies showed, enrollment increases were due more to economic developments—either the increasing ability of parents to forego children's wages in the 1920s or the collapse of the youth labor market in the, 1930s—than to curricular reform (Bell, 1938). In short, the AYC saw the schools as incapable of meeting all the needs of youth. The Commission contended that work experience, coupled with continuing part-time training, was an essential, not incidental, part of the youth-to-adult transition. Moreover, it argued that society had the responsibility to provide a paying job to youth whenever and wherever one could not be provided by private business.

Third, by arguing that school leaders had shown virtually no interest in the problems of out-of-school youth, the AYC and its allies unmasked the claims of school leaders who argued that they had fashioned high schools so that they could serve all American youth. In 1942, Charles H. Judd, who had left the University of Chicago to serve as associate director of education for the NYA, asked rhetorically, "Did the schools show in 1933 and 1935 the slightest insight into the youth problem or any disposition to take care of young people who were out of school and out of work?" (p. 31). In fact, the AYC and its allies claimed that school leaders were concerned only about American youth who were *in school*. From that perspective, the need for new, nonschool agencies to deal with out-of-school youth was imperative.

Obviously, each of these challenges had to be met by educators seeking both to protect the gains they had made toward universal high school enrollment and to get a larger share of federal funds. The organization that spearheaded these efforts was the Educational Policies Commission (EPC).

The Educational Policies Commission

The National Education Association and the American Association for School Administrators initially created the EPC in response to the severe educational budget cutting that took place in the worst years of the depression. Consequently, from its inception in 1935 to at least the early 1950s, the EPC viewed almost every issue through a single lens: How can spending for public education be increased without relinquishing any professional control over educational affairs (Hampel, 1986; Krug, 1972; Tyack, Lowe, & Hansot, 1984)?

The earliest policy statements of the EPC dealt with the aims and purposes of education in a democratic society, a theme strongly reminiscent of the use of the term "democracy's high school" in the Progressive reform literature. Yet during the depression this theme gained added force as radical youth movements gained attention. The EPC statements are also notable for their implicit assumption that, in a democracy, the aims and purposes of the schools are what the professionals say they are, not what the electorate decides they should be. In this regard, the EPC statements were simply reassertions of the ideas about who should determine educational policy, as described earlier. Here, however, professional educators were asserting their right to set policy on the national rather than local level (EPC, 1937, 1938a, 1938b).

During the mid-1930s, educational leaders and school officials had accepted and even supported the CCC and NYA as long as they believed it was politically and financially expedient to do so. However, as Congress granted these New Deal programs larger budgets (which educators felt should be going to public schools) and as the programs' successes began calling into question whether schools were the best agencies to serve American youth, educators asserted their political will. In the early 1940s, the EPC began a concerted attack on the two federal youth agencies that were becoming increasingly vulnerable due to the economic and political changes brought about by the war (Fass, 1989; Rawick, 1957; Zeitlan, 1958).

The first volley in this attack was a pamphlet, *The Relationship of the Federal Government to the Education of Youth of Secondary-School Age*, issued early in 1941 by the National Association of Secondary-School Principals of the NEA. Written by EPC member G. L. Maxwell and Francis Spaulding, dean of the Harvard Graduate School of Education, the pamphlet acknowledged the "great services rendered to youth by the federal emergency agencies" during the depression and admitted that the public schools exhibited many "shortcomings" in dealing with the youth crisis of those years. "Nevertheless," the authors firmly declared, "in long-term planning for the years ahead, the responsibilities for all public educational services to youth of secondary-school age should rest with the public schools" (Maxwell & Spaulding, 1941, p. 24).

A far more strident volley appeared soon after, as the EPC manifesto, *The Civilian Conservation Corps, the National Youth Administration and the Public Schools* (EPC, 1941). Unlike the Maxwell and Spaulding pamphlet, this document studiously ignored all the substantive criticism of secondary education that had been raised during the depression and focused instead on the single issue of federal funding of the two youth agencies. The EPC argued that the CCC and NYA had diverted vitally needed funds from public schools and set the dangerous precedent of a wasteful "parallel" educational system run by the federal government. The EPC maintained that everything these agencies were doing could be done more effectively by local public schools, an idea specifically denied by the NYA, the AYC, and even some professional educators such as Charles H. Judd (EPC, 1941; Judd, 1941).

This manifesto summarized all the arguments that NEA leaders used on members of Congress as the politicians deliberated the fate of the New Deal youth agencies in the 1942 and 1943 sessions. These arguments helped seal the fate of the programs, which were already under severe budgetary pressure as Congress sought to drastically cut domestic spending in order to pay for the war and as Republicans attempted to dismantle key New Deal initiatives. Regardless of which of these factors played the largest role, the outcome was almost inevitable and in

June 1942 and July 1943 first the CCC and then the NYA were eliminated (Rawick, 1957; Salmond, 1967; Schwarz, 1981; Zeitlan, 1958).

Despite their victory over the New Deal youth agencies, educational leaders greatly feared the revival of these programs at the end of the war. Along with many economists and political leaders, educational leaders worried that once the war ended the depression would return, with massive unemployment and restless youth again becoming major issues (AYC, 1942; Schwarz, 1981). In such a situation, they believed that the CCC and NYA would garner renewed support in Washington and across the country. With those fears in mind, in 1944 the Educational Policies Commission published *Education for All American Youth*, which presented in the clearest possible terms the attitude of school administrators toward postwar educational problems. The document consisted of two fictitious "histories" of the postwar period showing what might happen if America made the wrong decision and what a wonderful world it could be if the suggestions of the EPC were adopted. The villains of this story were the federal youth programs.

This volume rested on the firm conviction that the extension, adaptation, and improvement of secondary education were essential both to the security of American institutions and to the economic well-being of the nation. Moreover, the EPC members believed this had to be carried out within the framework of existing local and state educational systems. The only legitimate role the EPC saw for the federal government was encouraging and financing the expansion of high schools. If the local and state leadership did their parts, the EPC argued, it would be neither necessary nor desirable for the federal government to operate such "educational" services as the CCC and NYA (EPC, 1944).

This policy statement did indeed represent an awareness of the problems of youth, but in an incredibly superficial form. The report totally ignored the deeper problems facing young people that had been identified by the AYC and others, and it showed a complete unwillingness to be critical of the prevailing educational and economic situation. In essence, school leaders responded to years of criticism about their failure to meet the needs of American youth with a bland assurance that with bigger budgets and greater institutional control over young people's lives all would be well. However, if these school leaders were to make a plausible case for the restoration of their monopoly position, they had to show that high schools could indeed, through curriculum reform, meet the needs of "all American youth."

CURRICULUM REFORM IN THE DEPRESSION AND WAR

The intensity of the debate over which institutions could best serve American youth was heightened in large part by the fact that most of the participants shared several ideas about the future of American society and particularly about the American economy. Perhaps the most important of these ideas, as Arthur Schlesinger,

Jr. (1958) has noted, was the "sobering sense" that with the Great Depression "the age of economic expansion had come to an end" (p. 180). Consequently, leading economists and social policy makers worried about how to more equitably distribute jobs, goods, and services in a "mature economy." Strongly linked to this idea was the belief, expressed succinctly by members of the American Historical Association's Commission on the Social Studies, that "the age of individualism and *laissez faire* in economics and government is closing and that a new age of collectivism is emerging" (American Historical Association, Committee on the Social Studies, 1934, pp. 16–17). As the American Youth Commission (1942) saw it, "since most adults are no longer in a position to provide self-employment, much less provide employment for their children, the age-old responsibility for assuring youth a start in life has largely become a social responsibility" (p. 23).

These ideas had powerful repercussions on educational policy making and curriculum development. Educational leaders quickly grasped that if individual initiative was not enough for improving the quality of one's life, hope for a decent future increasingly would be linked to mass, public institutions. Indeed, educators had seen clear evidence of these trends as the collapse of the youth labor market forced even the most ambitious young people back to school or into the federal youth employment programs. In 1934, the NEA, for example, believing that its earlier manifesto, *Cardinal Principles*, reflected the discredited philosophy of individualism, issued a new report, *Issues of Secondary Education*, authored by Thomas Briggs. Arguing that the age of entrepreneurship and a growing economy was over, the report assumed that unemployment would continue to be a permanent feature of young people's lives and called for the acceptance by educators of the responsibility of planning for youth (Committee on the Orientation of Secondary Education, 1934). From that perspective, it is easy to see why participants on both sides of the jurisdictional battle for control of youth policy saw the outcome of that struggle as so profoundly important. But how did this battle help determine the direction of high school curriculum?

As we noted, one key to the triumph of public schools in that struggle was convincing politicians and to a lesser extent the public that high schools actually could meet the diverse needs of young people in this new era. In a 1940 article in the *Atlantic Monthly*, Harvard President James B. Conant provided a clear picture of how this might be done. Conant, who served on the EPC when it prepared *Education for All American Youth*, argued that if America was to survive the immediate challenges of communism and fascism and solve the more fundamental problem of restoring young people's hope for the future, it had to revive "equality of opportunity" in a society where the prospects for lone individuals looked bleak. Public secondary schools were central to this mission since, Conant (1940) wrote, they can "aid us in recapturing social flexibility, in regaining that great gift to each succeeding generation—opportunity, a gift that once was the promise of the frontier." In order to carry this out, he maintained, high schools had to continue their increasingly successful drive for universal enrollment, strengthen their ability to assess talent and guide ambitions, and equip students "to step on the first rung of whatever ladder of opportunity seems most appropriate. And an appropriate rung must be found for each one of a diverse group of students" (p. 600).

In many ways, Conant's vision fit squarely into the institutional structure that Progressive educational leaders had devised in the 1910s and 1920s, especially in terms of "individualizing" the curriculum and relying on an expanding guidance program to steer young people to "appropriate" career choices. But the enormous changes in American society and the economy that had been brought on by the depression, particularly the massive increase in high school enrollments, pushed educational policy and high school curriculum reform well past all earlier efforts. Indeed, Conant saw the need for a "reconstruction of our schools" in order to deal more effectively with the "horde of heterogeneous students [that] has descended on our secondary schools" (Conant, 1940, p. 602). Specifically, he called for a thorough revision of curricula to "include programs for developing the capacities of many who possess intuitive judgment on practical affairs but have little or no aptitude for learning through the printed page." Essential to this process, Conant believed, was "[e]xtreme differentiation of school programs" (p. 602). And, as important as altering high school curricula, Conant declared that educators must convince parents to accept the intellectual "limitations imposed by nature" (p. 601) on their children and then accept the guidance of professional educators in determining their children's future.

Here then was the apotheosis of the Progressive Era vision of equal educational opportunity. Upon gaining a monopoly position over the lives of young people in the early 1940s, high schools became the site of a vast educational and social experiment in which the Progressive vision of equality, curriculum, and guidance came to fruition. In the process, the function of the high school changed dramatically, shifting from an institution that prepared young people academically and vocationally for the adult world to an institution whose primary purpose was to meet the immediate needs of youth while keeping young people separate from the adult world. This new custodial orientation would dominate high school curriculum making and student coursetaking for nearly half a century.

In fashioning this new role for American high schools and in dramatically altering the nature of the curriculum, educational leaders took a number of interrelated precepts for granted. These precepts included: (1) most of the new students pouring into high schools were less academically and vocationally talented than previous generations of students; (2) since most of these students were incapable of following either the college preparatory or vocational tracks in comprehensive high schools, it was crucial for educators to undertake new curriculum initiatives that would meet all the needs of youth, including their need for developing practical "life-skills"; (3) the new curricula increased equal educational opportunity for these students especially when compared with traditional programs;

and (4) such curricula were vital to keeping students in high school for as long as possible. We will examine each of these precepts in turn.

The Declining Level of Talent of High School Students

As Edward Krug noted, for much of this century secondary educators claimed that each successive wave of high school students was less capable of mastering the curriculum than previous waves of students (Krug, 1972). As early as 1904, for example, G. Stanley Hall decried the increasing high school enrollment, claiming that these new students constituted a "great army of incapables . . . who should be in schools for dullards or subnormal children" (quoted in Kliebard, 1986, pp. 14–15). During the 1920s, amid continued high school growth, educators reiterated these views. In 1925, Detroit's assistant superintendent for secondary education argued that a third of all high school students were "congenitally incapable of doing high school work as it is now constituted" (quoted in Krug, 1972, p. 111; see also Powell, Farrar, & Cohen, 1985).

The explosion of enrollments between 1930 and 1939, from almost 4.8 million to over 7.1 million (from just over half of all 14–17-year-olds to nearly three-quarters), raised these concerns about declining student ability to a new level. School leaders from New Jersey to California bemoaned the arrival of high school students whom they categorized as "dull" or "dull normal" or as having "poor mental equipment" (Greet, 1972, p. 74; see also Zilversmit, 1993). A widely cited 1934 article by E. W. Butterfield described the situation somewhat more diplomatically but the essence of his argument was the same: The new group of students flooding "into the secondary schools varies greatly in scholarly ability but, as a whole, is not characterized by high psychological intelligence." Butterfield estimated that these students now made up "the new fifty per cent" (pp. 267–268) of high school enrollments. By 1939, such organizations as the National Association of Secondary-School Principals were citing the 50% figure as the basis for demanding major changes in high school curricula that would address the needs of these students of low intelligence (Powell, Farrar, & Cohen, 1985; Ravitch, 1983).

Other factors also contributed to the belief that the depression era students were less capable than previous generations of students, notably class bias and racism. When the depression shattered the youth labor market, children from working-class and poor families could no longer find jobs and crowded into schools in record numbers. Only children from the very poorest families continued to shun the classroom and seek employment (Karpinos, 1941). Once in school, poor and working-class students encountered deeply held prejudices about their intellectual abilities (Krug, 1972). In addition, during World War II many northern urban school systems experienced a huge influx of Black students whom educators also believed were incapable of handling either the traditional academic or vocational programs (Homel, 1984; Mirel, 1993).

Were these assumptions justified? Given the widespread use of IQ tests, especially in urban school districts, one might assume that these beliefs about the lack of talent of this new wave of students had at least some "scientific" basis. Some evidence, however, calls even that assumption into question. One study, for example, comparing IQ scores of high school students in 1920 and 1934 in three towns near Minneapolis, found that despite dramatic increases in enrollments average IQ scores of the 1934 students were *higher* than those 14 years earlier (Roessel, 1941). Similarly, A. B. Hollingshead's classic study *Elmstown's Youth* (1949) found that students in high school in 1941 had "intelligence quotients [that] averaged considerably higher than the general population of the United States" and, even among students from the lowest socioeconomic backgrounds, the average IQs were overwhelmingly in the average or above average range (pp. 174–175; see also Johns, 1938).[3] Such studies, however, were inconclusive and most received little publicity. Most important, given the depth of conviction professional educators had on this subject, it is doubtful that any research would have shaken the belief that the majority of high school students could not handle academic work and therefore needed less challenging curricula.

The Necessity for Curricular Reform

The explosion of high school enrollments coupled with the belief in the declining ability levels of students brought about renewed efforts to transform the high school curriculum.[4] Given the more than 3 decades of attacks on the traditional high school program, it is hardly surprising that during the 1930s and 1940s denunciations of the "academic high school," with its college preparatory emphasis, became one of the most prominent features in debates about curriculum. The 1938 report to the president by the federal Advisory Committee on Education (1938) provides a typical denunciation of the traditional, academic high school program. After noting the huge upsurge of new high school students, the committee, whose membership included leaders of the AYC and such prominent educationists as Charles Judd, Arthur Moehlman, and George Zook, declared:

> It would at once appear that the traditional linguistic-mathematical curriculum of the college preparatory school is no proper training for young persons who will leave the full-time school at age 17, 18, or even 20. Universal secondary education affords little justification for desperate attempts to retain subjects as general requirements that have little other than their antiquity to commend them for purposes of general education. (pp. 98–99; see also Kliebard, 1986)

These ideas had three main consequences for educational policy. First, they reinforced the need to provide different educational programs for students of varying ability. A typical example of this stance appears in the report on methods of instruction prepared for the AHA's Commission on the Social Studies. After presenting a thoughtful and cautious review of the research on ability grouping, the author declared, "[I]t is obvious that pupils whose abilities vary widely cannot be expected to master the same course of study" (Horn, 1937, p. 64).[5]

Given that assumption, professional educators turned to a second problem directly related to the first. The flood of new students and the continuing youth problem reinforced the beliefs of many educational professionals that high schools had not changed enough to adapt their programs to less able students. Commenting on the general irrelevance of the curriculum in most high schools, the 1934 NEA report, *Issues of Secondary Education*, noted that "a very considerable proportion of the new enrollment is comprised of pupils of a different sort—boys and girls who are almost mature physically, who are normal mentally, *but who are unable or unwilling to deal successfully with continued study under the type of program which the secondary school is accustomed to provide*" (Commission on the Orientation of Secondary Education, 1934, p. 64, emphasis added; see also Thayer, Zachry, & Kotinsky, 1939).

By the end of the decade, these views could be found in the policy statements of such prominent organizations as the American Association of School Administrators (1938) and the federal Advisory Committee on Education (1938), both of which denounced traditional high school programs and trumpeted calls for major curricular reform.

The third and perhaps the most fascinating aspect of these calls for transforming high school programs was that, unlike previous efforts, *they did not assume that expanding vocational education was the answer*. Indeed, depression era educators believed that neither the academic nor vocational tracks could successfully accommodate the new wave of students. As the chair of the committee to revise the high school curricula in Detroit put it, "One of the important problems of the secondary school in the next decade will be to formulate curricula and reorganize subject matter for those pupils who have not the ability to master subjects in the college preparatory and commercial curricula" (Rivet, 1934, p. 502). At the 1936 NEA conference a teacher from Brighton, Massachusetts, summarized these beliefs succinctly: "Due to the economic depression which has increased the number of pupils of low IQ's who have been forced to remain in school because there is no employment for them, schools have emphasized social trends and personal use because these pupils are incapable of reaching vocational standards" (Stuart, 1936, p. 349).

What led to this loss of faith in vocational education as the cure to what ailed traditional high schools? As the above quotes indicate, much of the reason lies in the educators' assumptions about the low levels of intelligence and skill of the new wave of students. But other factors also played an important role. Unquestionably the high rates of teenage unemployment in the 1930s badly demoralized educational policy makers generally and vocational educators specifically. More troubling were the findings of youth surveys that routinely showed that young people with high school vocational training were no better off in finding jobs than those without it (Bell, 1938; Rand, 1937; Stutsman, 1935). In addition, during the period of the worst budgetary retrenchment, 1931–1935, some high schools cut or dropped vocational programs, yet students still poured into high schools, belying the educators' belief that vocational programs encouraged students to return to or remain in school (Angus, 1965).

Above all, vocational educators began to recognize the great changes that were sweeping through the American economy, particularly the rapid growth in semiskilled jobs with extremely low training requirements. In his second major study for the American Youth Commission, *Matching Youth and Jobs* (1940), Howard Bell argued that most high school students needed only general vocational training and "occupational adjustment." This argument was based on his study of a sample of jobs that covered roughly 70% of the American work force. The study found that "approximately 47 per cent of these jobs demand nothing in the way of education beyond an ability to read, speak, and write," only 24% required either high school attendance or graduation, and just 9% required college attendance or graduation (Bell, 1940, p. 56; see also Reeves, 1942).

All these factors contributed to the loss of faith in vocational education as the centerpiece of high school curriculum reform. Few individuals exemplified this shift in attitudes more clearly than Charles M. Prosser. Prosser had served as executive secretary of the National Society for the Promotion of Industrial Education and was an early and effective advocate of vocational preparation at the secondary level. He was credited as being the man who almost single-handedly brought about the compromise between the American Federation of Labor and the National Association of Manufacturers that resulted in the passage of the Smith–Hughes Act. Yet, during the depression, Prosser lost much of his enthusiasm for vocational education and began urging schools to adopt what he termed "life-education subjects." Although he never directly attacked vocational programs, he argued for a strictly utilitarian standard of value that did not look much beyond the immediate present.

In his 1939 Inglis lecture at Harvard, Prosser warned the nation's educators that if they did not make substantial changes to the high school curriculum, "some new agency similar to the Boy Scouts, CCC, or NYA . . . may be created to which would be assigned the duty and responsibility for giving neglected youth the sort of life education which high school refused to provide" (pp. 86–87). He then sketched an outline for a life-education curriculum in which vocational education played a diminished role in favor of such courses as civic problems of youth and social amenities and manners (Prosser, 1939).

Prosser's ideas, however, were not radically different from those that leading educators and even their critics in such organizations as the AYC and NYA had been advocating for some time. As early as 1933, for example, the North

Central Association issued a revised set of objectives for secondary education that reduced the seven cardinal principles to four. These four objectives were entirely practical in their orientation, including maintaining "health and physical fitness"; exploring "vocations and vocational efficiency"; developing "successful social relationships" (in the civic, domestic, and community areas); and learning the "right use of leisure" (cited in Douglass, 1947, p. 31). In 1936, the Department of Super-intendence of the NEA issued a call to revise the social studies curriculum, declaring:

> Whether in the fourth grade or in the twelfth grade, the instruction of superior pupils needs to differ from that of inferior pupils. In general, dull pupils should develop the true essentials of social living—the ability to get along agreeably and effectively with the people with whom they associate daily; some power as consumers to evaluate the merits of various solutions to vexing social, economic, and governmental problems; some ability to choose among candidates for leadership; some appreciation of the cultural heritage represented by the conventional course in social studies; and so on. Bright pupils need all this and more. (p. 99)

The following year, the American Youth Commission issued a similar set of objectives that stressed citizenship, home membership, enjoyment of life, physical and mental health, vocational effectiveness, and continued learning. Like the NCA, the AYC called for a "practical curriculum" that identified the present needs of youth and responded to them. The approach AYC members favored was a general program of studies for all youth that was relatively undemanding and focused on such areas as tools of learning, health, and family living (Douglass, 1947; Reeves, 1942). The 1938 report of the federal Advisory Committee on Education recommended that high schools "reorganize their curriculums, even for the young people expecting to enter college, in such a way that the required core curriculum does not contain any subjects unjustified on the basis of their general social utility" (p. 99). That same year, the American Association of School Administrators' *Youth Education Today* repeated all these ideas and urged high schools to adopt curricula "centered in the actual problems and opportunities of modern life. The dynamic and life-centered curriculum should help to harmonize youth's educational development with his fundamental needs and interests, with his social environment, and with his whole life career" (p. 14).

Such efforts encouraged the further evisceration of academic programs (no-tice that the NCA proposals went even farther than *Cardinal Principles* in drop-ping from their objectives any mention of academic skills or knowledge) *and* the weakening of vocational education. Curriculum reformers in the 1930s and 1940s were steadily moving high schools away from their traditional preparation of young people for adult roles and responsibilities and toward a concentration on the im-mediate lives and needs of youth.

Examples of the adoption of these ideas and their translation into curricular form in schools across the country are legion (see, for example, Calguire, 1975; Greet, 1972; Hofstadter, 1963; Krug, 1972; Ravitch, 1983; Zilversmit, 1993). In Minneapolis, as high school enrollments soared from 12,167 in 1930 to 16,075 in 1934, Assistant Superintendent Prudence Cutright claimed that many in this flood of new students had "limited academic abilities," and initiated revisions of the high school curriculum to steer them away from academic and vocational courses (Franklin, 1982). The main vehicles were to be such social studies courses as Community Life Problems, a ninth-grade class that featured field trips to government agencies and local businesses, and Modern Problems, a required 2-semester course for seniors that replaced sociology, economics, and American government and focused on such topics as "population, labor, housing, family life, and consumer needs" (pp. 19–20). In 1946, however, Superintendent Willard Goslin declared that the school program was still removed from the realities of life. Inspired by the work of the Educational Policies Commission (of which Prudence Cutright was a member), Minneapolis introduced a new 2-year course, Common Learning, in which juniors and seniors got practical, life education in a combined English and social studies program organized around "the personal and social problems common to young people of the school" (Franklin, 1982, pp. 21–22).[6] The Minneapolis English teachers who were involved in the Common Learning course sounded an old but revitalized theme: "There must be a relaxing of standards. We must learn to distinguish between everyday, utilitarian English and professional, scholarly English. Most high school students will only use the first, and the whole school program cannot be geared to meet the needs of the few who expect to enter college" (pp. 21–22).

Detroit became a national trend setter in curricular innovation during the 1930s and 1940s when such local educational leaders as Associate Superintendent Paul T. Rankin (who served on the Educational Policies Commission and wrote an important section of *Education for All American Youth*) played prominent, national roles in shaping and implementing curriculum for the new wave of high school students (Hampel, 1986; NEA, 1944). The city experienced massive secondary enrollment increases of almost 11,000 students (43%) from 1929 to 1934. By 1940 enrollments were nearly double what they had been at the start of the depression (Mirel, 1993). As in other cities, educational leaders in Detroit looked at many if not most of these students as less capable of mastering either the academic or vocational programs (Rivet, 1934, 1937). As the depression began, Detroit high school students followed one of four curricular tracks, college preparatory, technical, commercial, or general, placed there on the basis of standardized test scores, grades, teacher recommendations, and family consultations with counselors or administrators (Moehlman, 1922; Detroit Public School Staff, 1943; Mirel, 1984). The major changes were concentrated in the general track, rather than the college preparatory or the vocational tracks, and were aimed largely at students "of low ability" (Rivet, 1937, p. 453; see also Rivet, 1934).

To make it easier for students to graduate, school officials allowed the substitution of descriptive biology, chemistry, or physics, large lecture classes with demonstrations, in place of the laboratory versions of these courses, which had been required in 1930. In social studies, required courses in civics and economics were replaced with Problems in American Life, a less rigorous course that included such life-education materials as units on juvenile delinquency, finding a job, traffic safety, and how to rent an apartment (Mirel, 1984).

In English courses, school leaders urged teachers to emphasize useful knowledge and to downplay reading classic literature and writing compositions. The most important language skills for the modern English classroom, these leaders declared, are "conversation, discussion, story-telling, explaining, arguing, speech-making, letter-writing, and the making of reports both oral and written" (Shattuck & Barnes, 1936, pp. 5–6). But the course most powerfully symbolic of the new life-education principles was the Personal Service or Standards class. Appearing in some high schools as early as 1935, these classes were designed as electives for juniors and seniors in the general curriculum. In the young men's section of the Personal Service course at one high school, the students studied the "problems of diet, dress, etiquette, jobs, relations with girls, [and] personal hygiene" (Rivet, 1937, p. 455). The courses for young women contained units on "appearing to advantage," homemaking, the use of leisure time, family finance, interior decorating, bride and trousseau, and "the American woman as citizen" (Cameron, 1940, p. 206).

Even during World War II, when the Detroit schools became a center for vocational training for the war industries, these life-education trends continued with only a small shift toward vocational coursetaking among high school students. By the late 1940s, the general track was serving the largest percentage of Detroit students of any of the four tracks, and the decline in academic and vocational coursetaking was continuing apace (Angus & Mirel, 1993).

The New Curricula and the Rhetoric of Equal Educational Opportunity

The movement toward custodialism in high school education did not go without challenge. During the 1930s and 1940s, such prominent scholars as Mortimer Adler of the University of Chicago, a few professors of education such as William Bagley and Isaac Kandel of Teachers College, as well as parents, business leaders, and newspapers across the country denounced the degradation of academic education and its replacement by life-education courses (Adler, 1939; Franklin, 1982; Kliebard, 1986; Krug, 1972; Mirel, 1993; Ravitch, 1983).

These criticisms fell into two broad categories. One essentially followed the line of argument laid down in the Committee of Ten report that all students were capable of taking rigorous academic courses and that the dilution of the curriculum was undercutting the basis of democratic education. In 1934, for example, a Hartford high school principal, Gustave Feingold, gave an impassioned speech decrying the belief that

> the bulk of our high school population is moronic and unfit for the profitable pursuit of high school studies, as we know them. We have been hearing of late, for instance, that 50 percent of high school enrollment is made up of the sons and daughters of conductors, factory workers and scrubwomen, and since they will themselves become motormen, truck drivers, and charwomen, the education of the high school ought to be of a type which will prepare them for that sort of life . . . the spreading of the idea that 50 percent of high school enrollment is unqualified for the traditional high school studies is nothing less than a libel against the youth of the nation. (Feingold, 1934, pp. 828–829)

The second school of criticism also decried current curricular trends but took a very different approach to solving the problem of the modern high school, arguing that most of the new wave of students should not be in high schools at all. The 1936 Inglis Lecture by an assistant superintendent of the New York City schools, John L. Tildsley, provides a powerful example of these ideas. Tildsley declared that "the public secondary school may be moving toward bankruptcy . . . because it is failing to educate in any true sense the great mass of the boys and girls who throng its doors" (pp. 2–3). Tildsley, however, was even more disparaging of the new students than were the progressives, stating that more than half were "misfits" who were "unqualified to do the work of the high school" and who should be attending continuation schools instead (pp. 7–8). He claimed the curriculum reforms were designed for "misfits," and would eventually debase the courses for the better students (pp. 16–17).

Leading educationists rarely differentiated between these two types of criticism and instead argued that both were efforts to return to the antidemocratic and inegalitarian past history of the high school. Speeches such as Tildsley's (especially in prestigious forums like the Inglis Lecture) provided evidence for the progressives that their great nemesis, the traditional academic high school, still had strong supporters; that these supporters still held the undemocratic belief that only a small number of talented students should attend high schools; that these "conservatives" maintained that the high school curriculum should still be focused on the academic preparation of that elite group; and that these "conservatives" were at best either seeking a European-style, two-tiered education for American students or at worst giving up on the majority of these students entirely. In all, this caricature was enormously useful to the curriculum reformers. In comparison to

Tildsley's vision, the changes the progressives offered appeared democratic, compassionate, and fair. To the extent that the reformers could keep this straw figure in the public eye, and, as we will see, over the next few decades they were enormously successful in that regard, they could continue to claim that the utilitarian courses they were introducing advanced equality of educational opportunity.

In addition to these arguments, the reformers had one other powerful claim working in their favor. Due to the great changes occurring in the American economy, particularly the declining number of jobs for young people, high schools had to substantially increase their holding power as part of the effort to maintain full employment for adults. The educational leaders of this era firmly believed that if they did not speed up the adoption of more relevant new courses, students would drop out of school and create serious problems for themselves and the economy.

The Changing Economy and the Need for a Custodial High School

By the mid-1930s, it was quite clear to educators across the country that the high school had become a refuge for unemployed youth. The Detroit principal who chaired that city's high school curriculum reform committee noted that "the economic situation . . . has forced into the secondary schools thousands of young people who formerly left school at the age of sixteen or seventeen to go to work. There are no jobs for them now and there will not be for some time to come" (Rivet, 1934, p. 502). As the Educational Policies Commission (1938a) put it, "The choice offered to many individuals is not between work and school, but between school and deteriorating idleness" (p. 3).

Yet more was occurring in this period than high schools simply becoming way stations for youth during an economic downturn. Behind this trend was a fundamental shift in the relation between secondary education and the American economy. In the 1910s and 1920s, the primary mission of high schools was the preparation of young people for adult roles and responsibilities in the economy either through academic or vocational education. While that mission did not disappear during the 1930s and the 1940s, it was rapidly relegated to a secondary position as the need to keep young people out of the labor market became a crucial social and economic necessity. Indeed, all the participants in the jurisdictional dispute over youth policy shared this belief. The EPC (1938b), for example, declared, "Nor must it be forgotten that every youth and adult added to the school enrollment tends to reduce the competition for jobs" (p. 3). Howard Bell (1940) of the AYC concurred: "It appears that whether young people who leave school at the lower grade levels succeed or fail in their efforts to secure employment, the result is what might be reasonably interpreted as an ultimate social and economic loss. If they get jobs, they displace adults and thus aggravate the national problem of unemployment" (p. 97).

This sense that high schools must increase their holding power was therefore part of a much broader social and economic transformation taking place in America. During the depression, keeping young people from competing with adults for jobs became an important aspect of educational as well as economic policy. Similarly, after World War II amid fears of renewed depression and concern about whether those returning from military service would find jobs, the national interest once again led economists, political leaders, and educators to redouble their efforts to keep young people in school and out of competition with adults. Thus, the custodial function of the high school, the idea that it is far better for every teenager to be in high school than anywhere else, regardless of what they might be learning there, was strongly reaffirmed during the war and postwar years.

Educators took for granted the idea that students dropped out of school mainly because of their lack of interest in the traditional curriculum. As early as 1908, for example, E. L. Thorndike made that point, arguing that the primary reason for dropping out of school was students' "incapacity for and lack of interest in the sort of intellectual work demanded by the present course of study" (p. 10). By the 1930s, such ideas were part of the conventional wisdom of educational professionals. Writing in 1940, John Dale Russell and Charles H. Judd declared:

> The fact remains that most young people today are not able to enter industry or other types of gainful employment before age eighteen and in many cases not before age twenty. The best method of occupying the time of such young people is an important problem, and the solution to this problem by requiring an extended educational period, regardless of the immediate value of the education as such, may be socially wise. (p. 303)

They noted that both the traditional academic and vocational programs were inadequate for that task and urged a re-emphasis on such aspects of *Cardinal Principles* as education "for citizenship, for worthy home membership, and for effective use of leisure time" (p. 303).[7]

But before these ideas could be fully implemented, school leaders had to surmount one last great hurdle that seemed to confirm their worst fears about the inadequacy of high school programs (despite over 3 decades of reform!)—the sudden decline in high school enrollments during World War II. As the United States began to mobilize, first for defense and then for war, most of the trends and conditions of the depression era began to reverse. Chief among these developments was the decline of youth unemployment and the trend toward "overemployment." In 1940, there were still more than 8 million unemployed persons. By 1943, the rapidly expanding economy had reduced this to virtually nothing, and by 1945, "[t]he labor force exceeded by 7,300,000 the normal labor force that would have been expected in peacetime conditions" (Seidman, 1953, pp. 152–153). This expanded labor force included 1.9 million women over age 35, 600,000 young married women who had never been employed before, and 2.8 million teenagers, many of whom were high school dropouts. The U.S. Children's Bureau estimated that the number of workers 14 through 17 years of age increased from 1 million in 1940 to nearly 3 million in April 1944 and approached 5 million in the summer months of 1943 and 1944 (Merritt & Hendricks, 1945).

Correspondingly, secondary school enrollments plunged. Aggregate high school enrollments in the nation as a whole had reached over 7.1 million in 1939–40, but in 1941 they actually declined for the first time in history and they continued to decline throughout the war, falling to just over 6 million in 1943–44. Entry into the armed forces and a decrease in the high school-aged population accounted for only a fraction of this decline. Mainly, it was due to "the great increase in the number who left school for work, many cutting short their courses in mid-term" (Merritt & Hendricks, 1945, p. 759; also see U.S. Office of Education, 1956).

Beginning in the summer of 1943, a host of organizations attempted to reverse this tide of dropouts. Between 1943 and 1946, for example, the Children's Bureau and the U.S. Office of Education jointly sponsored a National Go-to-School Drive. In terms of numbers of students returned to school, however, the drive and others like it were dismal failures. The goal for Fall 1945, for example, was to induce a quarter-million young people to return to school, yet public high school enrollment increased by only 68,677 between 1944 and 1946, and even this modest increase was due largely to such factors as returning military personnel and a declining demand for teenage workers (Angus, 1965).

The drop in high school enrollments during the war was a serious challenge to the vision of the comprehensive high school put forth by educational leaders. Having convinced Congress to abolish the federal youth programs in the early 1940s and having deflected the criticism of the American Youth Commission by claiming that high schools alone could bring about a successful transition from youth to adulthood, secondary educators now had to live up to the overheated promises that the Educational Policies Commission had made in *Education for All American Youth*. The essence of these promises was simple: With professional educators free to fully plan and control the high school curriculum and with adequate resources to greatly expand curriculum to meet the varied needs of the increasing numbers of students, the comprehensive high schools could prepare all youth for successful citizenship, family life, and employability. Despite the frequent criticism directed at the high schools in the 1930s and early 1940s—that educators never cared about working-class students or the dropouts, that vocational education demanded both classroom training and real work experience—the EPC asserted that with only some modification of the ideas contained in *Cardinal Principles*, the comprehensive high school could meet all the needs of youth.

The curricular initiative put forth after the war to deliver this promise, recover the losses in enrollments due to the war, and re-establish the trend toward universal attendance that had been interrupted by the war was called the "life-adjustment movement." In 1947, the Division of Vocational Education of the U.S. Office of Education invited a group of educators to Washington to help formulate a vision of secondary education, and particularly vocational education, that could meet the challenges of the postwar world. This conference provided educators with one of their first real opportunities to demonstrate how they would reshape secondary education now that the threat of federal agencies and the demands of war were gone. The fact that these educators came to Washington at the behest of the U.S. Office of Education was a strong indication of how the political climate had changed since the termination of the CCC and NYA. Educators clearly no longer feared the prospect of federal involvement in education because the U.S. Office of Education (which educators had always felt comfortable with) was now the primary federal agency dealing with schools. Equally important was the emphasis of the conference on secondary students now that the high school had a virtual monopoly over their educational lives.

After several days of inconclusive debates and nearing adjournment, the conference leaders turned to Charles M. Prosser to give some shape to the discussions. Prosser tried to do this by shifting the focus away from either the traditional college-bound student or the "terminal" student for whom vocational education originally had been developed. Prosser argued that only about 40% of high school-aged youth could be well served by these two curricular regimens, and that postwar efforts should be directed toward developing a curriculum for the other 60% who were not being served by either program. This idea took the form of the famous "Prosser Resolution," which called on all high schools to develop "life-adjustment training" for this 60% (Cremin, 1961; Hampel, 1986; Ravitch, 1983).

While the idea of life-education or life-adjustment education was certainly not new, the Prosser Resolution had the effect of mobilizing the U.S. Office of Education and vocational educators, who created a National Commission on Life Adjustment Education to lead curriculum reform. One result was that, for at least the next 30 years, virtually all "youth problems"—unemployment, teenage pregnancy, drug use—and even some major national problems—the Cold War, international economic competition—would be debated on a national level as if they were *curriculum* problems. Another result was that, over the same 30 years, national educational leadership would remain committed to a depression era vision of a highly differentiated, custodial high school that had little belief in the capacities of its students to master challenging subject matter.

Despite its supporters' claims that life-adjustment was a new and exciting initiative, knowledgeable observers realized that most of it was nothing more than a warming over of predepression educational philosophy mixed with some depression era curricular practices. Prosser's unserved 60% was none other than the "new 50%" that Butterfield had acknowledged in urging schools in the 1930s to take a more custodial role. The life-education program espoused by leaders of the movement did not go much beyond the ideas presented by Prosser in his 1939

Inglis Lecture or the curricular reforms put into place in such urban districts as Minneapolis and Detroit. Life-adjusters wanted to provide course offerings for the unserved 60% that would have immediate relevance to their lives, promote self-esteem, build character, acquaint students with their communities, and gradually engage them with the wider world. As Diane Ravitch (1983) has argued, life-adjustment education "consisted of guidance and education in citizenship, home and family life, use of leisure, health, tools of learning, work experience and occupational adjustment," all tailored to some educational professionals' ideas of the tastes, inclinations, and, above all, abilities of "non-academic and non-vocational" adolescents (p. 65).

The one area where the life-adjustment movement *did* break new ground was in its attempt to realize James Conant's 1940 vision in which both curriculum and guidance would operate to *lower* the career aspirations of the majority of students. Here was a dramatic shift in the perceived function of the high school, from an institution commonly associated with increasing social mobility to one deliberately trying to get young people to limit their aspirations and accept menial roles in society. This undertaking was based on the assumptions we noted earlier: that the period of economic expansion was over (i.e., the economic frontier had closed) and that most students (especially the poor and minorities) had limited academic and vocational abilities.

The life-adjusters believed such students needed an education that would train them for the limited economic and social roles they would fill in American life and provide them with a more "realistic" sense of their futures. As one of their pamphlets (Rummel, 1950) put it, "Most boys and girls are headed for jobs that require little training. These youth need and want an invigorated *general* education that relates to their everyday lives" (p. 5). In a figure showing "actual [career] opportunity in 1940," the pamphlet encouraged students to stop hoping to become doctors, architects, and lawyers, for which few opportunities were available, and instead shift their attention to positions such as taxi drivers, clerks, salespeople, and mechanics, for which opportunities were great. In many ways, this attempt to lower aspirations was the ironic culmination of the progressive quest for equal educational opportunity through curricular differentiation.

Finally, Prosser's estimate that 20% of American students would be going on to college, made on the eve of the most rapid expansion in college attendance in history, induced many high schools to place far fewer students in the college preparatory curriculum than the colleges were prepared to admit. The increasing competition for the best-prepared students forced many colleges and universities to admit students who had followed the weakened general track, thus lowering academic standards still further.

The question remains, Did this profound ideological shift in the way secondary educators viewed the purpose of the high school have a powerful impact on enrollments, curriculum choices, and student coursetaking? Was this new vision widely translated into practice and did the students cooperate? In order to get a better sense of the impact of these proposed changes, in the next section we turn again to coursetaking and transcript data from Grand Rapids, Detroit, Michigan, and the nation as a whole. We pose three broad questions: (1) what were the patterns of high school enrollment increase during these eras? (2) In what ways did high school curriculum change over time? and (3) to what extent and in what ways did the high school coursetaking experience vary with gender and between different class, ethnic, and racial groups?

GRAND RAPIDS, 1930–1944

When Leslie Butler succeeded William Greeson as Superintendent of the Grand Rapids Public Schools in 1924, he took over a "model" progressive school system. The system consisted of 34 elementary schools, five junior high schools, three senior high schools and two more soon to open, a vocational and technical school, and a 2-year junior college. When the state raised its compulsory attendance age from 14 to 16 years, Butler argued for two "prevocational" junior high schools, one of which was built. In curriculum development, Butler seemed more interested in the upper elementary and junior high school levels, and there was only modest change in high school offerings during his administration.

On the eve of the Great Depression the Grand Rapids schools appeared to be in excellent condition. The buildings were adequate to house the students and nearly all were in good physical condition; the district's bonds were nearly retired and it had built all new buildings and additions since 1925 on a pay-as-you-go plan. It had begun to reduce staff by eliminating many special teachers and some administrative positions and by increasing class sizes.

As the youth labor market in the city weakened in the late 1920s and collapsed in the 1930s, its relation to high school attendance was quite clear. Part-time enrollments in the city's continuation school, which peaked in 1926 at 811, plunged to 227 by the mid-1930s. Conversely, until 1930, the number of full-time students in the vocational and technical school lagged well behind the part-time enrollment. But with the opening of a large addition and the expansion of the academic curriculum, the school's full-time enrollment rose sharply from 500 to over 1,300 students in 3 years (see Appendix B, Table B.2). Enrollment in the comprehensive high schools increased by 500 students between 1924 and 1929, then increased by another 500 in just one year, between 1929 and 1930. Enrollments soared early in the 1930s, tailed off when the economic situation seemed to improve, eventually peaked at over 5,300 by the end of the decade, and dropped sharply with the onset of the war. By the end of the 1940s, enrollments had not returned to their 1930 levels.

The boys' share of high school enrollments reached and slightly exceeded half when they were forced to stay in school during the worst years of the depression. With the possibility of military service and/or war employment, their share fell sharply back to pre-World War I levels. Continuing the trend toward a higher blue collar share of high school places that we saw in comparing the 1920 and 1930 cohorts, the blue collar proportion of Grand Rapids high school students passed 60% with the 1940 cohort. All the Grand Rapids high schools enrolled increasing numbers of the sons and daughters of semiskilled and unskilled workers, but Union High School and Davis Tech were most strongly affected. By 1940, over 80% of Union's students were from blue collar homes, and at Davis it was about 90%.

Grand Rapids school leaders introduced only a few curricular changes during the 1930s to accommodate these young people. We noted that in Detroit educational leaders encouraged the development of general track courses, aimed particularly at students of low ability, and essentially ignored college preparatory or vocational courses. While we did not find the same rhetoric, we see the same trends in Grand Rapids. Examples are the introduction of ungraded sections of English for low achievers; the expansion of such noncollege preparatory mathematics offerings as general math, practical math, shop math, and business math (which met the graduation requirement in math); the movement toward more general and "relevant" history courses, such as world history and Latin American history, and even more, the development of courses in modern problems, occupations, and problems in democracy; and the offering of such science classes as hygiene and sanitation and girls' physiology. Even in the vocational areas, most of the new courses were aimed not so much at improving vocational training as at being useful to adolescents in their daily lives. Some of these courses were similar to "personal standards" classes in Detroit such as boys' foods, personal regimen, art in the home, safety, interior decorating, and costume design. School officials also separated typing from stenography and shorthand to aid those students who took typing as a personal development course, rather than as a vocational subject. The only new offerings with a clear vocational orientation were bookbinding, nursing and home care (in Davis Tech), office practice, and office machines.

Our transcript data on Grand Rapids students provide a unique opportunity to explore more deeply the curricular experiences of these depression era students. If boys seem to have been somewhat more affected by shifts in the job market, were there significant differences between the courses taken by boys and by girls? If during this period for the first time, large numbers of the sons and daughters of semiskilled and unskilled workers attended high school, were there major differences between the courses they took and those taken by white collar students? Bear in mind that our 1930 cohort attended high school during the worst years of the depression, the 1935 cohort were in high school during a slightly improving but mixed economic picture, while those entering in 1940 faced the prospects both of an improving labor market and of military service.[8]

Many of the trends that we identified in comparing the 1920 cohort with the 1930 one continued to be evident in the next two cohorts we studied, those entering in 1935 and those entering in 1940 (see Appendix B, Tables B.6–B.10). Foreign language and mathematics enrollments continued to decline, enrollments in science rose slightly, and then fell back, and English and social studies enrollments were relatively stable. In the vocational areas, industrial arts, trade and industry, and domestic arts all rose a bit between the 1930 and 1935 cohorts, but among the wartime cohort, only trade and industry continued to gain.

More interesting were the enrollments in commercial courses, which rose for the 1935 cohort, then fell back to 1930 levels. The pattern was not the same for all students, however. The easiest way to see the point is to focus on those students taking more than 4 semesters of commercial subjects, that is, those we see as taking commercial courses as a vocational field (see Appendix B, Table B.6). Among girls, this percentage increased sharply between 1935 and 1940 from 43 to 48%, as many of the young men went off to war and as young women were expected to defer marriage and go to work. Among the males, there was a very large increase between 1930 and 1935, from 12 to 25%, as the economy seemed to present some glimmers of hope; the percentage then fell back sharply to about 1930 levels, perhaps as white collar clerical jobs seemed irrelevant to the war effort. This shift was most dramatic among blue collar boys, from 9 to 28 and back to 8%. We think a plausible explanation may be that while blue collar boys felt forced into high school by high unemployment, once unemployment eased a bit, they may have seen a high school education as the chance to move into white collar jobs, following the lead of previous generations. America's entry into World War II capped these aspirations and pushed these boys into more "blue collar" forms of vocational training. The share of blue collar boys taking vocational-level amounts of industrial arts and trade training rose from 24% in the 1935 cohort to 45% in the 1940 cohort.

What about the development of the "softer" electives in English, mathematics, and social studies? How popular were these courses and who took them? In English, we coded speech, dramatics, journalism, and debate separately from the regular English offerings. Averaged across all the students, the mean amounts taken of such courses increased over time but not much, a half semester in 1930, six-tenths of a semester in 1935, and seven-tenths in 1940. Three-quarters of the 1930 cohort took none of these English alternatives, and this fell to two-thirds among the 1935 cohort, and then rose to 70% among the 1940 group. There were no statistically significant differences between subgroups in the taking of these electives, but females and white collar students had slightly higher averages. The alternatives to college preparatory math were the "practical" math courses mentioned above. Related to the pattern we saw in commercial enrollments, the numbers in practical math courses increased from 1930 to 1935, then fell back, but not to their 1930 level. In this case, the increase of shop math as an adjunct to trade and industry courses may have counterbalanced a decline in commercial math enrollments. Girls took significantly more of these practical math alternatives in all three cohorts, 1.5 semesters to 1 in 1930, about 2 to 1 in 1935, and 2 to 1.2 in 1940. Blue collar students also took more practical math, no doubt reflecting their greater vocational orientation throughout this whole period, but only a half semester more on average in each cohort. The share of students taking none of these practical math classes fell from two-thirds in 1930 to one-half in 1935 and 1940.

As for social studies, in 1929 school leaders shifted the one-semester required course in civics to the seventh and eighth grades and, to make room for advanced civics, changed the graduation requirements from 4 semesters of history to 2 semesters of American history and 2 semesters of social studies electives. With this change, the number of students taking at least one of the nonhistory social studies electives rose from 30% in 1930 to 48% in 1940, but almost no students took more than a year of such courses. The average amount taken was almost identical to the amounts taken of alternative English courses in all three cohorts. When these courses were first offered for the 1930 cohort, blue collar students took them only half as often as white collar students, but in the later cohorts the differences were slight. There were no significant gender differences in any cohort, but by the 1940 cohort, the trend was for girls to take more of them.

We noted in Chapter 2 that curriculum differentiation along both gender and class lines seemed to deepen significantly between the 1920 and the 1930 cohorts. What happened to such differences during the depression and war? In 1930, girls got better grades, significantly better in some fields, and took less mathematics and music, but more commercial and art. Among the 1935 group this pattern continued, except that declines in music enrollments for all students eliminated any gender difference in that area. In the war cohort, girls still took less math but significantly more of all other academic subjects except English, and continued to lead by a wide margin in commercial enrollments. Nearly half of the girls took more than 4 semesters of commercial courses, while less than 10% of the boys did so. Except for a brief recovery toward predepression levels of male enrollments in commercial courses, gender differences during this period were much as they had been at its beginning (see Appendix B, Table B.8).

The simplest way to see what happened with respect to class differences is to refer again to Appendix B, Table B.10, where we have divided the students into curricular "tracks" based on a series of inferences.[9] First, based on our analysis of the curriculum trends of the period and of shifts in curriculum ideology, we would expect the percentage of general track students to rise; and indeed it did, but not greatly, from about 28% of students to one-third. Since both foreign language and mathematics enrollments were falling, it is no surprise that the share of academic track students, by our definition, was going down, from 1 in 3 to 1 in 5.

Students taking either a commercial or vocational course rose during the period, from just under 40 to just over 45%, with commercial gaining more between 1930 and 1935 and vocational gaining more in the war cohort.

We take these figures to mean that, while educational leaders may have been placing much less emphasis on the vocational preparation function of the high school, the students were not, particularly those students from lower-working-class families who were forced into school for lack of employment. In that regard we find that these students, like their counterparts in the 1910 and 1920 cohorts, pursued their own ideas about courses and programs rather than the ideas of professional educators.

We remarked in Chapter 2 that a surprising number of working-class girls seemed to be taking a course regimen similar to that of white collar girls. This is illustrated clearly in Appendix B, Table B.10, where the distribution by curriculum track for these two groups is very similar in 1930. But it appears that the economic realities of the depression quashed the college aspirations of working-class girls, and the academic track share of their numbers plummeted. The college intentions of white collar boys, although much higher, seem to have been similarly affected by economic conditions, falling from nearly 60% to less than a quarter of this group. But they also seem to have been keeping their options open by following a general program rather than a vocational program.

In the wartime cohort, white collar girls followed a strong academic or commercial program, and blue collar girls cast their lot with a commercial program, with some looking toward sewing, cooking, or nursing. White collar boys took fewer academic courses than in the past but were not strongly attracted toward the vocationally oriented courses, while blue collar boys, many of whom were no doubt the first in their families to attend high school, were heavily concentrated in the vocational track.

In all, the data from Grand Rapids show that at least some of the national ideas and trends in curriculum planning took root in the system during the depression and the war. Academic courses, the great villain of progressive curriculum reformers, finally succumbed to the nearly 3 decades of concerted attack. Both the percentage of students in the college preparatory track and the overall share of academic coursetaking dropped markedly in this period. However, the expressed desire of curriculum reformers to also steer students away from vocational courses was not as successful. As we noted previously, in Rochester and elsewhere, students appeared to be taking clear stock of the economic situation before them and opted for more vocational courses, probably in an effort to make themselves more marketable. Nevertheless, the proportion of students in the general track also rose in this period, indicating that by the 1940s curriculum reformers were gaining the upper hand in transforming the high school into a more custodial institution and that students' coursetaking patterns were slowly falling into line.

CURRICULUM CHANGE IN THE STATE AND NATION: 1928–1945

Were these developments in Grand Rapids representative of changes in other school districts across the nation? In this section we consider information from a variety of sources—school-level data from Detroit, school accreditation reports in Michigan, material gathered from national studies of student coursetaking, and findings from several sociological case studies of communities in different parts of the country. Generally, all these data indicate that the curricular and coursetaking patterns we found in Grand Rapids paralleled trends in other school districts across the nation.

Detroit Coursetaking in Depression and War

Detroit is a superb site in which to assess the impact of the economic and educational factors we have been discussing. By the 1920s, as Grand Rapids' reputation for progressive curricular reform was waning, Detroit's was on the rise. By mid-decade, educational leaders viewed the Detroit Public Schools as one of the finest, most innovative school systems in the nation. Indeed, throughout the 1930s and 1940s, school officials from Detroit held prominent positions in every important educational organization concerned with curriculum and policy reform (Hampel, 1986; Mirel, 1984, 1993). In addition, Detroit served a large and increasingly diverse population of students, which allows us to examine how these reforms played out along racial lines.

　　In two earlier studies of Detroit, we found patterns of enrollment growth and change in student coursetaking quite similar to those we identified in Grand Rapids (Angus & Mirel, 1993; Mirel & Angus, 1986). For example, in Detroit, high school enrollments grew rapidly in the years *just prior* to the economic crash of 1929, rose sharply during the worst period of the depression (1929–34), but moderated somewhat as the economy improved (1936–37). These trends suggest that, in Detroit as in the other cities we've discussed, high school enrollments were strongly linked to the youth labor market. When that market weakened in the late 1920s, young people poured into high schools.

　　At the same time, the high schools increased their "holding power," since the rate of enrollment increase was higher for eleventh and twelfth grades than for tenth. Even more dramatic was the growth in high school graduates. While enrollments in grades 10 through 12 increased by about 150% between 1928 and 1940, the number of graduates increased by almost 240%, a development that may have been in part due to the easing of academic demands.[10] Clearly, during the Great Depression the custodial function of Detroit's high schools became more pronounced.

　　While we were unable to access student transcript data from Detroit,[11] we were able to track changes in coursetaking by calculating subject field enrollment distributions from end-of-semester class reports, available for each of the city's high schools.[12] Appendix C, Table C.1, displays the distribution of subject groupings during this period. Clearly, some, but not all, of the changes in curriculum policy described earlier influenced student coursetaking during the depression. By far the most successful effort was the one that steered students away from academic subjects. In 1928, over 76% of student coursework in Detroit was in the academic areas of English, foreign language, mathematics, science, and social studies. By 1939 that proportion had fallen to about 69% and by 1944 it was just over 65%. The percentages for foreign language and mathematics took the most severe hits, falling by almost a half and a quarter, respectively.

Enrollment shares rose in social studies and vocational classes. Commercial courses especially jumped from almost 13 to over 16% of the total courses taken. The increase in vocational coursetaking in the comprehensive high schools was paralleled, indeed outpaced, by the enrollment growth in the city's two magnet vocational schools, Cass Technical High School and Commercial High. Averaged together, the vocational high schools increased their enrollment a bit more than 100% over the 12 years compared with 68% for the comprehensive high schools. As in Rochester and Grand Rapids, it appears that many young people in Detroit responded to the depression by opting for vocational education to gain skills that might give them an edge in getting jobs in the tighter labor market. In all, these data highlight some important similarities between Detroit and Grand Rapids, particularly the fact that during the depression the academic share of coursetaking decreased sharply.

Our Detroit data also allowed us to carry the analysis into the World War II and postwar years, as high school enrollment decreased and as the employment picture for teens brightened considerably. During the period from 1940 to 1946, Detroit became "the arsenal of democracy," and thousands of migrants from the South, including large numbers of African Americans, crowded into makeshift housing and looked for high-paying jobs in the defense industries. Despite the population surge in the city generally, high school enrollments declined in this period due to the reopening of the labor market to teenagers and the lure of military service. The Detroit schools initially paid little attention to the enrollment decline as they focused their efforts on providing vocational education for young people and adults who were moving into the war industries.

This trend seemed to offer a golden opportunity to step back from the "life-education" policies advocated in the 1930s toward a more goal-oriented focus on vocational education. Indeed, Detroit's school leaders claimed that they had reorganized the curriculum according to the principle that all courses, "especially those in the eleventh and twelfth grades, must demonstrate their validity in terms of military pre-induction value, pre-employment preparation for employment in war industries, or civilian war service" (Bedell & Gleason, 1943, p. 86). As these school officials put it, the goal of these changes was the complete transformation of the curriculum "in favor of vocational education" (Detroit Board of Education *Proceedings*, 1940–41, p. 276; 1942–43, pp. 166–167; 1944–45, p. 2; 1945–46, p. 4).

Yet, much of this must have been smoke and mirrors. Despite these statements, there seems to have been little change in the subjects students studied in high school. Returning to Table C.1, we can see that there *was* an increase in the share of courses devoted to vocational subjects as predicted, but most of this occurred in the commercial department rather than in the vocational department that was more directly related to the war effort. Furthermore, this modest increase did not come at the expense of traditional academic courses such as English and science, but rather at the expense of the social studies, another area that was seen as more clearly related to the war effort than was literature or biology. Even the increase in commercial course enrollment share was probably more the result of a much higher dropout rate among young men compared with young women during the war years than of any deliberate shift in curriculum offerings. Males made up 44% of tenth graders but only 39% of twelfth graders in 1944. Also, males constituted 47% of graduates in 1939 but only 39% of graduates in 1944. Females held a large majority of the places in the city's two commercial high schools.

In all, perhaps the major consequence of the push for more "practical" education was the opportunity it provided school leaders to further degrade academic subjects. Beginning in 1942, with the blessing of the North Central Association, Detroit high schools permitted students in the academic tracks to substitute preinduction and vocational courses for academic courses required for graduation. In addition, as large numbers of students took after-school jobs, the board of education approved a plan to allow work experience to satisfy as much as one-fifth of the total class credits students could take each semester. Moreover, some school leaders used the war as a pretext to reiterate their condemnation of traditional (i.e., academic) courses. As the Michigan Assistant Superintendent of Public Instruction put it, "Many of the so-called cultural subjects, imbedded in the curriculum by right of tradition, were not fitting the average youngster to go out and earn a living" (*Detroit News*, 12/26/41, p. 3).

Besides providing opportunities for additional attacks on the traditional high school, developments in the 1940s appear to have had a decisive effect on the school experiences of Black students. The Black population of Detroit grew from 149,119 in 1940 to 303,721 a decade later, from about 9.0 to 16.4% of the city's total population (U.S. Bureau of the Census, 1943a, 1953). In the schools, the percentage of black students rose from approximately 5% in 1922 to 17% in 1946 (Detroit Commission on Community Relations Papers, 1946–47).

In sharp contrast to their rhetoric of emphasizing "practical, vocational training" during the war, school leaders dealt with the increasing numbers of Black students in exactly the same way they had approached the problem of the flood of White working-class youth in the 1930s, that is, by absorbing them into the general track. Reliable data on track placements in the high schools are rare. However, two reports (one by the Mayor's Committee on Youth Problems and the other by the Detroit Commission on Human Relations) indicated that between 1943 and 1946, the percentage of students in the general track jumped from 22 to 30% and that Black students were overrepresented in the general track (Detroit Commission on Human Relations Papers, 1946–47; Detroit Public Schools, Department of Guidance and Placement, 1943). The Detroit Commission on Human Relations report for the 1946 47 school year provides a rare glimpse of the racial distribution of students within the system of track placements (see Table 3.1).

The data dramatically illustrate the tendency to relegate Black students to the custodial general track rather than to the more purposeful academic or vocational tracks. Even in those four high schools that enrolled over three-quarters of the city's Black students, Blacks were to be found in the general track in much larger numbers than the White students who attended those schools. While African American students represented just under 12% of all high schoolers in that year, they made up 18% of those following the general track, an overrepresentation of 50%. In addition, Black students' access to the specialized high schools in the city also was limited and they made up only 9% of the enrollments of these schools (Detroit Commission on Community Relations Papers, 1946–47).

In a pattern similar to what we described in Chapter 2, the educational experiences of Black students were different in degree but not in kind from those of other students. World War II and the immediate postwar years saw little change in the curricular trends and patterns of student coursetaking that had begun in the 1930s. The push to downgrade academic courses and programs continued apace,

Table 3.1. Track Placements by Race, Detroit Public High Schools, 1946–47

		%			
		College		Technical and	
	General	Preparatory	Commercial	Vocational	*n*
All high schools[a]					
All students	30.0	26.7	29.5	13.8	38,686
Black students	44.4	19.4	27.6	8.6	4,642
Non-Black students[b]	27.1	28.1	30.2	14.6	34,044
Four high schools with more than 40% black students[c]					
Black students	50.8	21.7	24.4	3.1	3,482
Non-Black students	36.3	25.9	32.1	5.6	2,716

Source: Detroit Commission on Community Relations Papers.
[a]Includes the 15 comprehensive high schools, plus Cass Technical High School, Wilbur Wright Technical High School, Commercial High School, and East Commercial High School.
[b]Table identifies only Black students and total students.
[c]Miller, Northern, Northeastern, and Northwestern High Schools.

and the efforts of curriculum reformers to steer students to the amorphous general track were increasingly successful.

These trends were not limited to Detroit. In a 1979 interview, Kenneth Clark claimed that the deterioration of public education for urban Black children generally "started and accelerated around World War II." Clark noted that when he attended the New York public schools in the 1920s and 1930s the teachers "respected me enough to hold me to the standards by teaching me grammar, by teaching me arithmetic, music and other subjects that I would need to compete in this society. But in the 1940s something began to happen." As teachers became more concerned about protecting the self-esteem of poor or disadvantaged students (shielding these students from academic "embarrassment," as Clark put it), they started lowering standards. Moreover, he stated, some teachers began approaching Black "children with the assumption that because of their backgrounds, they cannot learn," a stance that introduced a "dangerous, catastrophic, self-fulfilling prophecy." As teachers increasingly assumed that Black students could not learn, Clark noted, they first stopped holding these students to high standards and then stopped holding them to any standards at all. Although his reflections focused primarily on the education of Black children, Clark argued that the deterioration of standards "cut across racial lines" (Jarrett, 1979, p. 6). He was correct in that assessment.

Michigan Course Enrollments

The available course enrollment data for the state of Michigan are quite rich and point in exactly the same directions as the data we analyzed for Detroit. From a combination of the state-level reports in the national data collections and a series of curriculum studies carried out by the North Central Association, we have compiled a data array that brackets the period of the depression and war with considerable precision. As Appendix D, Table D.1, shows, between 1925 and 1945, the academic share of course enrollments in Michigan high schools fell from 73% to 58%. The shift away from academic to nonacademic coursetaking was not even across the period, however. As youth unemployment deepened after 1925, and as high school enrollments grew, swelled by the entry of working-class students, the nonacademic share also grew at a rapid rate, from a 27% share to a 35% share in 5 years. This trend slowed during the trough of the depression, with the nonacademic share reaching 40% by mid-decade, and slowed again during the economically uneven years from 1935 to 1940, when it reached 43%. Surprisingly, during the war years when U.S. schools were dedicated to the war effort, and when educational rhetoric placed great emphasis on the need for vocational preparation, the academic proportion actually recovered slightly.

The decline of the academic proportion was not shared equally by all of the academic subject fields. English declined across all comparisons, but the total decline was modest, from 22 to 19%. Social studies showed the most uneven pattern, standing at a low of 13% in 1930, but maintaining roughly a 15% share over the period. Science also held its own at about 10% throughout. Math mostly declined, from a 14 to an 11% share, but it would have been lower had it not been for a wartime recovery of about 2%. The big loser, as it had been throughout the previous period, was foreign language, falling from a 13% share to a mere 4% of all course enrollments, less than music, less than industrial arts or household arts, and far less than physical education. As the United States assumed the mantle of world leadership at the end of World War II, it is nothing short of a national tragedy that the curriculum reformers, inspired by Progressive ideas, had virtually driven foreign language study from the field. Only a tiny minority of America's students were preparing to become fluent in the languages of those countries that had stood beside us in the war, let alone those we had defeated.

Changes in the relative shares held by the nonacademic subject fields were more surprising. Commercial courses, which had grown steadily in the previous period, peaked in 1930 at 15% of coursetaking, ahead of all the academic fields except English. These courses then began a slow decline to 12%, most of it coming in the war years. Michigan officials attributed the decline of commercial enrollments to the shortage of commercial teachers created by the war effort (Angus & Mirel, 1993). Both industrial arts and home economics grew slowly and modestly over the period; included in these enrollments were those that sometimes are classed as trade and industry, courses with a very narrow vocational objective. Agriculture, music, and art remained stable and modest across the whole period. The big gainer was physical education.

All told, the data we have analyzed from Michigan reveal that the trends we saw developing in Grand Rapids and Detroit also were occurring across the state. The decline in the academic share of coursetaking was both steady and dramatic. The ideas of curriculum reformers about reshaping high schools along less academic lines clearly came to fruition during the 1930s and 1940s. However, this decline in the academic share did not result in major increases in vocational education. As we noted, the big increases were in physical education, a subject area that fit quite nicely into the emerging custodial role for high schools by meeting youths' immediate needs in a nonacademic and nondemanding way.

National Course Enrollments

Many of the changes in the nature and function of a high school education that we have seen in Grand Rapids, Detroit, and Michigan were reflected across the nation. With respect to who went to school, we have found no longitudinal or serial cross-sectional data on the social class makeup of high school students other than the 1924 to 1930 data from Rochester that we discussed in Chapter 2. Although many of the depression era youth studies collected information on the class background of students, none except those involving Rochester did this in a way to permit analysis of change over time.[13] While it is true that not all cities experienced the same economic slowdowns in the late 1920s and the deep depression of the early 1930s that we found in northern industrial cities, we are convinced that generally the loss of jobs for teenagers, not curriculum reform, brought large numbers of children from lower-working-class homes into high school for the first time (see, for example, Anderson, 1988). The depression succeeded where curriculum reform and anti-child labor campaigns had failed. It moved the high school toward the degree and kind of social class, and to some extent racial, diversity that reformers had been claiming for years.

The quantitative record with respect to changes in coursetaking is more complete, even if not as detailed as we might wish. In 1933–34 and in 1948–49, the U.S. Office of Education (USOE) carried out studies of coursetaking in the nation's high schools. These studies are part of the series of reports on courses and coursetaking that we discussed briefly in Chapter 2. By 1928, these reports had become quite thorough in terms of the list of subjects and enrollments reported, and consequently provide a particularly useful collection of data for tracking trends. The major problem with these studies, however, is that the USOE conducted them irregularly, producing reports only for 1922, 1928, 1934, 1949, 1961, and 1973. Despite their infrequency, these studies offer us an increasingly detailed and trustworthy set of snapshots of high school course offerings and enrollments. These data form the basis for our analysis of whether the trends we have been describing are evident on the national level.

By comparing the findings for 1933–34 and 1948–49 with the studies done for 1921–22 and 1927–28, we can get an overall picture of curriculum change during the early years of the depression and the postwar period (see Appendix A, Tables A.2–A.4). Many of the main trends we have already seen in the cities and in Michigan appear in these data as well, particularly the drop in academic coursetaking. In 1928, over two-thirds of student coursetaking was in academic areas. Six years later this had fallen to just over 62%. Nationally, between 1928 and 1934, foreign language study declined from about 10 to 7% of all courses taken, continuing a trend that began about 1910. Mathematics, science, and English also declined slightly as shares of coursetaking, while social studies gained a bit.

In contrast to Rochester and Grand Rapids, all of the vocational areas remained quite stable during this period. This evidence supports neither the view that school systems made sharp cutbacks in vocational courses during retrenchment nor the view that students rushed into vocational programs to make themselves more marketable. It was likely true that students in urban systems such as Rochester, Grand Rapids, and Detroit had greater access to vocational programs than many of the other students represented in the national studies. In any case, in neither USOE study did enrollment in the showcase vocational programs (industrial arts, trade and industry, and home economics) exceed 8% of total coursetaking, a fact that provides further evidence (if any is needed) of the relatively small impact these courses had on student course choices nationally.

Despite the lack of movement in the vocational areas, the schools *did* report a sizable shift in the nonacademic share of all coursetaking during this period, rising from a 33% share to a 38% share. That is the most rapid shift in coursetaking of any time in the period covered by the USOE studies. It strongly supports our contention that the 1930s mark a turning point in the history of the American high school. By far the most important aspect of that shift corroborates what we observed in Michigan—the share of total course enrollments devoted to health and physical education rose dramatically from about 5% to over 11% in just 6 years, making these courses the fastest-growing segment of the nonacademic areas.

The USOE study of 1934 contains enough detail to permit a closer examination of some of the other trends we have highlighted in the cities. While the overall increase in high school enrollment reported by this study was from 2.9 million to 4.5 million, an increase of 55% in the 6 years, a number of individual course enrollments rose much faster than this and some courses failed to keep pace. In the social studies area, for example, such traditional offerings as ancient history, medieval and modern history, and English history were on the wane, increasing by only 1, 15, and 13% respectively, while enrollments in world history increased by 205%. Courses in civil government and community government also did not keep pace, perhaps as in Grand Rapids being moved downward into seventh and eighth grades. A course entitled Problems of Democracy, however, which was not listed in 1922 and which had tiny enrollments in 1928, increased by 415%. Among the English electives, all but dramatics grew apace, with journalism increasing by 371% and speech growing by 235%. But as we indicated above, the fastest-growing high school offering, in terms of course enrollments, was health and physical education, which showed a 423% increase, nearly eight times the rate of total enrollment increase. While in 1927–28 only 15% of all high school students were enrolled in a health and physical education class, by 1933–34 this had increased to over 50%.

As we have been arguing, enrollments in the showcase vocational courses, home economics and industrial arts, were not nearly as high as reformers had hoped or as historians have assumed. This is particularly surprising if, as we have noted, the social class makeup of the student body shifted sharply toward larger lower-working-class representation in these years. At the national level, in 1922, 26% of all girls were enrolled in a home economics class, in 1928 the figure was 29%, and by 1934 it was about 32%. For the boys, industrial arts enrollments were similarly modest at 23% in 1922, 26% in 1928, and 28% in 1934.[14] Carl A. Jessen, who compiled the 1933–34 report, also remarked that while one student in five was taking a shop course of some kind, four-fifths of those enrolled were taking one in which training for a specific occupation was *not* the primary motive (USOE, 1938).

We discuss the 1949 data in more detail in Chapter 4, but for the moment, these data provide us with a chance to assess the extent to which the overall coursetaking patterns followed the direction that the curriculum planners of the 1930s and 1940s had outlined. The 1949 data clearly indicate that high school coursetaking *was* moving in the direction that the educational leaders of this period had advocated. Specifically, the academic share of the curriculum fell to just over 59%, with foreign language dropping to only 4% of the total and math and science coursetaking declining as well. Only social studies gained. Among the nonacademic fields, between 1934 and 1949 the showcase vocational subjects rose slightly to just over 9% of enrollments, but during the same time commercial coursetaking slipped from over 11% to 10.5%. Health and physical education continued to rise, now accounting for over 12% of the total and more than doubling its 1928 percentage.

Historians have long argued that growth in physical education usually is related to wars and military buildups (Krug, 1960), but these data combined with the Michigan data prove otherwise. Health and physical education enrollments grew most dramatically in the late 1920s and early 1930s, a period in which military preparedness was simply not a national issue. Rather than resulting from threats by foreign powers, we see this trend as related to the development of the high school as a custodial institution. Indeed, probably no subject area better represents the great changes that overtook the high school in this period than health and physical education. Such classes fit perfectly into the life-education focus of the custodial high school. Classes that taught students about fitness and their bodies were clearly relevant, demanded no homework, were able to accommodate large numbers of students in a single class, often provided enjoyable opportunities for students to "let off steam," and were defensible in terms of addressing both the needs of students and the needs of the nation. These classes were all that supporters of life-education could ask for, and their increasing enrollments demonstrate how thoroughly the ideas of life-education had taken hold in American secondary schools.

Class and Curriculum

If the national coursetaking data support our argument about the changing nature of the high school, are there also data that sustain our contention that these curriculum and coursetaking changes were strongly related to social class and race? With regard to life-adjustment, Richard Hofstadter (1963) was convinced that there was strong class bias animating the "life-adjustment theorists." He believed that these programs were directed mainly at "children from unskilled and semi-skilled families who had low incomes and provided a poor cultural environment" (p. 344). But Hofstadter offered no data in support of that contention.

Two major sociological studies from this period, *Elmstown's Youth* by Hollingshead (1949) and *Who Shall Be Educated?* by Warner, Havighurst, and Loeb (1944), do provide some data demonstrating a relationship between class and curriculum quite similar to that we identified in Grand Rapids. Hollingshead, who looked at students in a "typical midwestern community," found that student enrollments in the three high school tracks—college preparatory, general, and commercial—were "related very significantly to class positions" (p. 168), with nearly two-thirds of the students from higher social classes in the college preparatory track and the majority of students from the lower social classes in the general track.

Warner, Havighurst, and Loeb found similar patterns in "Yankee City," the only community of the three they studied that had a high school with a clearly differentiated curriculum. They state that "[t]he evidence is clear that the class system of Yankee City definitely exercises a control over the pupil's choice of curricula" (1944, p. 61). Indeed, they found a linear relationship between class and curriculum, with the college preparatory track enrolling all of the upper-class pupils, 83% of the upper-middle-class students, 45% of the lower-middle-class students, 28% of the upper-lower-class students, and 26% of the lower-lower-class students. The students in the commercial and general tracks provided a reverse image of those in the college preparatory track, with only 12% of the upper-middle-class students in these tracks, but 55% of the lower-middle-class, 72% of the upper-lower-class, and 74% of the lower-lower-class students following these courses of study.[15]

In all, Warner, Havighurst, and Loeb (1944) presented a deeply critical vision of American education, particularly the modern high school:

> The educational system may be thought of as an enormous, complicated machine for sorting and ticketing and routing children through life. . . . Young children are fed in at one end to a moving belt which conveys them past all sorts of inspecting stations. . . . At a station labeled "high school" there are several types of inspection. The main belt divides into smaller belts which diverge slightly from each other. From some of the belts the children, now become youths, are unceremoniously dumped down chutes into the outside world, while the other belts, labeled "college preparatory," "commercial" or "vocational" roll steadily on. The young people are inspected not only for brains and learning ability, but also for skin color, pronunciation, cut of clothes, table manners, parental bank account. (pp. 49–50)

By the 1940s, then, it was becoming obvious to at least a few prominent social scientists that the Progressive plan for equal educational opportunity was sharpening rather than eliminating divisions along class and racial lines. These social scientists, however, offered few imaginative solutions to this problem. Indeed, so thoroughly did they accept the Progressive vision of the high school that Warner, Havighurst, and Loeb merely recommended improvements in the process of screening students from poor or minority backgrounds. It would remain for other scholars and researchers in the next decade to forcefully call this entire approach to secondary education into question.

SUMMARY

Without doubt, the most important event affecting the American high school during the second quarter of the twentieth century was the collapse and recovery of the youth labor market during the depression and war. Progressive curriculum theorists had always pointed toward the relation between secondary schooling and employment as an important argument in support of such reforms as the differentiated high school curriculum. But having in mind a smoothly efficient system in which high schools would funnel the youth of the nation toward their "probable destinies" in the work force, they were totally unprepared for either the collapse of the youth labor market or the storm of criticism that emerged in the 1930s over their failure to care about the "destinies" of students who dropped out of school.

Those two criticisms were among the factors that led New Dealers to sidestep the educational establishment and create alternative youth-serving institutions, the Civilian Conservation Corps and the National Youth Administration. These youth relief programs, designed to help counter the despair that threatened to overwhelm so many young people, produced a new and challenging vision of youth-serving agencies. This expansive vision, best articulated by leaders of the American Youth Commission, took in the whole youth-to-adult transition, and saw high schools playing an important but limited role in the transition to adulthood, sharing responsibilities with other tax-supported agencies.

The nation's educational establishment, represented by the Educational Policies Commission, reacted to this challenge with unremitting hostility, seeing the issue solely as a struggle for power and influence over the lives of youth and placing the issue entirely into the context of their desire for federal aid to education. Rejecting the idea that this was a vital debate about the best course for youth policy and development in a changing economic and social environment, they maintained that what was necessary was greater professional control over high school programs, the elimination of the competing New Deal youth agencies, and an adequate flow of funds.

At the end of World War II, still fearing that the youth relief agencies might be re-established, secondary educators pursued policies from their monopoly position that drew heavily from their response to massive youth unemployment and the floodtide of students. They shifted the entire thrust of secondary education away from what had been its purposes in the first quarter of the 20th century—preparation for either college or work—and replaced them with a far more nebulous purpose, keeping teenagers in school as long as possible. This shift in direction was driven not so much by the criticisms of the high school but rather by the abiding faith that most of the "newcomers" were incapable of doing high school level work, the loss of faith in the efficacy of vocational training, and a highly moralized commitment to universalizing high school graduation.

It remained for the educational establishment to prove that curriculum reform alone could restore high school enrollments to prewar levels and genuinely
meet the needs of all American youth. The nationwide life-adjustment movement,
which dominated educational thought between 1947 and 1953, was the first concerted effort to deal with those issues. Begun as an effort to meet the needs of the
"60%" of teenagers who they believed could not handle either college preparatory subjects or vocational training, life-adjustment education evolved into a hodge-
podge of relevant, undemanding courses that offered little preparation for future
adult roles or responsibilities. Further, this curriculum was increasingly legitimated
as a solid general secondary education appropriate for *all* students, not just the
60%. Not surprisingly, this banal educational vision would spawn waves of criticism over the next few decades, but it nonetheless came to be the dominant educational philosophy of the postwar period.

NOTES

1. Moreover, because of high unemployment in the depression years, the passage
of strong child labor laws, and the Supreme Court's upholding of the Fair Labor Standards Act, by 1940 child labor had declined to an all-time low of about one million workers aged 14–17 (David, 1942).

2. For a complete list of AYC publications, see *American Youth Commission* (1942,
pp. 298–299).

3. On the other hand, the Lynds reported that a 1931 analysis of 558 sophomores at
Central High School in Middletown found 36% of the students with IQ "scores of 90 or
less" (Lynd & Lynd, 1937, p. 225).

4. The National Survey of Secondary Education showed how leading thinkers in
the field of secondary education viewed the relationship between the intelligence level of
students, curriculum tracks, and equality of educational opportunity. The report declared
that "[t]he socioeconomic level of the different curriculum groups is somewhat in agreement with the intellectual levels. . . . That is, the academic and scientific curriculums have
larger proportions than the other curriculums from the upper levels; the household arts
and industrial arts curriculums have larger proportions from the lower economic levels
than the other curriculums . . . the commercial pupils in the comprehensive schools are
more nearly like the pupils in household arts and industrial arts curriculums than in the
academic curriculums" (Loomis, Lide, & Johnson, 1973, pp. 34–35).

5. One of the most disturbing aspects of this apparent acceptance of curricular differentiation by the AHA was the underlying elitism of the stance. The organization's defense of academic rigor in the social studies appears more like a defense of the college
preparatory courses rather than an effort to assert the rights of all students to the best possible instruction and content.

6. Cross-disciplinary courses such as Common Learning were one of the unintended
consequences of efforts by groups like the American Historical Association to end the

isolation of social science disciplines through the "correlation" or "integration" of studies. Although the 1934 AHA investigation of social studies concluded that the "program of social science instruction should not be organized as a separate and isolated division of the curriculum but rather should be closely integrated with other activities and subjects," the AHA believed in maintaining disciplinary integrity in this process. Educational leaders revised these ideas to produce courses such as Common Learning in which disciplinary integrity was lost and the problems addressed were often trivial, while citing the AHA studies as the justification for their efforts (American Historical Association, Commission on the Social Studies, 1934, p. 48; see also National Education Association, Department of Superintendence, 1936; Tryon, 1935).

7. The 1938 federal Advisory Committee on Education acknowledged that many students left school because of "poverty at home" but added that many dropped out because of the curriculum: "The curricular cause [of school leaving] consists simply in the failure of the school to provide a course of study that retains the interest of the pupil, or that appeals to him as at all useful or appropriate. The schools are not responsible for the loss of pupils through economic circumstances beyond their control, but they must accept a large measure of responsibility for an unsatisfactory curriculum" (p. 98).

8. Our reported graduation rate of 55% for boys in the 1940 cohort may seem too high, but part of the reason is that the Grand Rapids schools awarded 30 hours of academic credit for military service. If this brought a student's total above the 168 required for graduation, the diploma was awarded, in a few cases posthumously.

9. While student handbooks in Grand Rapids continued to refer to college preparatory, commercial, and vocational programs of study, we found no entries on the transcripts designating such programs. Thus, our definitions are somewhat arbitrary. Since we are focusing mainly on trends over time, this is a less serious objection than it would be if we were mainly concerned with the actual distribution. A similar procedure has been used in the recent transcript studies by Westat, Inc.

10. Similar trends can be seen across the country. In Seattle, for example, between 1930 and 1940 high school enrollment rose by only 13% but the number of graduates rose by 54%, due in part to an easing of academic demands as Seattle school leaders made a determined effort to increase access by new students to "such modern subjects as home economics, music, industrial arts, and physical education," a process the school leaders referred to as "equalization of opportunity" (Seattle Public Schools, 1940, p. 16; see also Seattle Public Schools, 1930).

11. The ordering of student transcripts on microfilm in Detroit made it impossible to draw random samples of entering student cohorts.

12. In lieu of recorded enrollments in physical education classes, we based estimates on how Michigan's physical education requirement applied to Detroit.

13. Bell's study of Maryland youth in 1938 found that just over 60% of high school students were from working-class homes (Bell excluded children of farmers and children whose parents' occupations were unknown). This compares with just under 50% for Pennsylvania in 1928 (Moore, 1933) and 52% for Wisconsin in 1923 (Uhl, 1925), which used the same assumptions.

14. Enrollments by gender were not provided in 1934. We have based our estimates on the assumption that the gender ratio in high school enrollments was at parity in 1934,

an assumption we think is warranted by both a continuation of the national trend line and the actual figures for lower-order places.

15. The small number of the Black high school students that Warner, Havighurst, and Loeb (1944) identified were in "Old City," the representative southern city in their study. The curricular situation for these students was quite different from that facing White students in either the North or South. Blacks in Old City did not get a high school until 1925, and like all Black schools in the South it was underfunded and unequal to the White schools in the community. Ironically, however, this underfunding and inequality meant that this school offered "a single curriculum which is academic—more so than the curriculum in the white high school. There is little vocational training" (Warner, Havighurst, & Loeb, 1944, p. 130; see also Siddle Walker, 1996). Nevertheless, Warner, Havighurst, and Loeb found the level of education in this school well below that of the White schools, and they argued that the overall educational inequality in the community played a major role in sustaining the subordination of Blacks by the White majority.

4

The Triumph of Curricular Differentiation, 1950–1964

IN THE 1950s, as the New Deal youth programs faded into memory and young people found entry into the full-time labor market increasingly difficult, the high school attained a virtual monopoly over the lives of Americans aged 14–17. By 1961 almost 10.5 million young people, over 87% of the 14–17-year-old age group, were in high school (National Center for Education Statistics, 1995). With that development, the high school became one of the defining institutions in the lives of American adolescents and a dominant institution in American life. But with that monopoly status came new challenges and controversies. As we noted in Chapter 3, during their campaign to abolish the New Deal youth programs, educational leaders claimed that with sufficient funds, increased professional guidance, and a relevant "life-based" curriculum, the comprehensive high school could serve all American youth and ameliorate their problems. In making these claims, educational leaders transformed virtually all discussions of youth problems into debates about educational and curriculum policy. Consequently, broad questions about who could best serve young people (including those not in school) and how to facilitate the school-to-work transition, questions that had dominated the 1930s, practically disappeared from policy debates. More important for our purposes, the belief that curriculum reform was the key to solving youth problems inspired a series of intense and often heated controversies about the nature and function of the high school.

These postwar debates seemed to evoke two polar opposite views of the high school curriculum. The first and clearly more dominant position argued that all school subjects were essentially equal in importance and emphasized expanding the curriculum to include more practical and "relevant" courses and knowledge. The second position maintained that a small number of essentially academic subject areas should have priority in the high school curriculum and that options for other courses of study should be drastically reduced. We associate these two views with *Cardinal Principles*, on the one hand, and the report of the Committee of Ten, on the other, although participants in the postwar debates rarely invoked these documents.

In this chapter and the next we examine the debates between the proponents of these two positions and their association with the national crises of the post-World War II years. Without doubt, the period between 1950 and 1975 was one in which a variety of critics directly challenged the educational status quo, and controversies about the high school curriculum intensified. Despite those controversies, however, we find that the coursetaking patterns of American high school students actually changed very little. Indeed, during this period the core beliefs of educational professionals—that most high school students were incapable of doing rigorous academic work, that curriculum differentiation was the key to equality of educational opportunity, and that the high school was primarily a custodial institution—gained even greater influence than before.

This chapter takes a somewhat different approach to these issues than we have used earlier. We begin with an analysis of the great debate of the 1950s and early 1960s, a debate that was strongly influenced by the growing fears about whether American public education could provide the kind of education necessary for the emerging postwar world. Because math and science coursetaking were central to that debate, we follow our analysis of what people said about the schools with a detailed look at national curriculum and coursetaking trends in those two areas. We reserve our discussion of national trends and developments in other subjects and in Detroit and Grand Rapids until the next chapter, which expands on the idea that the period between 1950 and 1975 witnessed the triumph of curricular differentiation.

THE HIGH SCHOOL AS A NATIONAL ISSUE

As we have noted, beginning in the mid-1930s a small but growing number of scholars, including Mortimer Adler, William Bagley, Robert Hutchins, and Isaac Kandel, routinely denounced the new curricular trends in American schools as both anti-intellectual and undemocratic. Throughout this period, educationists usually dismissed these critics as vestigial elitists whose days were numbered. By the late 1940s, however, these critics were joined by a number of other commentators, including school board members, professors outside of colleges of education, some politicians, and the editors of leading newspapers in major cities. Indeed, such papers as the *Atlanta Constitution*, *Chicago Tribune*, *Detroit Free Press*, and *New York Daily News* had been publishing exposés about the deteriorating quality of public education, particularly high school education, for some time (Knight, 1953). In December 1946, for example, the *Free Press* ran a series asking, "Are our schools failing in their job of preparing youth to earn a living in business and industry?" (*Detroit Free Press*, 12/8/46). The series concluded that for the most part the answer was yes and that the failure was due largely to the schools' abandoning "the fundamentals" and replacing drill and intellectual rigor with "socialized" education (*Detroit Free Press*, 12/10/46).

The press and politicians were not the only critics of the changes in school curricula. Early in 1950, for example, a group of Minneapolis parents presented the board with a petition condemning the system's life-adjustment-style programs for failing to teach students basic, academic subjects and for usurping the educational role of families. The parents declared that they "would like the privilege of teaching their own children, at home, such things as When should we go steady?, How to plan a party?, or How can we become popular?" (Franklin, 1982, p. 26).

Despite such criticisms and protests, throughout the late 1940s and early 1950s, most school leaders deftly deflected criticism of life-adjustment-style programs by firmly repeating the conventional wisdom of their profession. The Detroit superintendent, for example, explained away the problems identified above by claiming that as enrollments increased so did the number of less capable students who needed life-adjustment education (*Detroit Free Press*, 12/14/46). Similarly, the Minneapolis superintendent reminded the protesting parents that the "traditional curriculum" had not met the "modern needs" of the students (Franklin, 1982, p. 26).

Usually such statements of professional certitude quieted the waters. If the criticism grew too sharp, however, prominent educational leaders attacked their critics as right-wing cranks, "fascists," or simply "enemies of the public schools" (Courtis, 1939, p. 52; Ravitch, 1983, p. 71). In 1947, for example, Harold Rugg of Teachers College lumped Adler, Bagley, Hutchins, and Kandel with religious "Fundamentalists [and] the defenders of private enterprise" (p. 605) as opponents of progressive efforts in politics and education.

Such shrill cries grew worse following the publication in 1949 of Mortimer Smith's *And Madly Teach* and Bernard Iddings Bell's *Crisis in Education*. For the first time in many years educators began to fear that a "counterrevolution" actually might be possible. Over the next 10 years, these works were followed by a host of widely discussed speeches, articles, and books that also vehemently denounced "modern" curricular trends (for a sample, see Scott, Hill, & Burns, 1959). Indeed, during the 1950s and early 1960s, controversy about American education generally and the high school curriculum specifically generated more national attention than at any previous time in history.

Many historians have provided accounts of this "great debate" (e.g., Church & Sedlak, 1976; Cremin, 1961; Krug, 1972; Ravitch, 1983; Rudy, 1965; Spring, 1972; Tozer, Violas, & Senese, 1993) and we do not wish to repeat their work. However, we do want to focus on three aspects of this debate that explicitly relate to themes we identified and discussed in earlier chapters. First, in many ways these debates revived the earlier conflicts between professors of academic disciplines and their colleagues in schools and colleges of education (and to a lesser extent the conflict between educators and lay boards of education) over who should control the high school curriculum. Second, the progressive concept of equal educational opportunity (particularly as it related to the high school curriculum) was central to these conflicts. Third, despite the withering criticism directed at educationists and their new high school program, the education establishment and the differentiated high school emerged from these debates stronger than they had ever been. In order to assess these themes, we will examine three main events in this debate—the attack on life-adjustment led by Arthur Bestor and others, the impact of Sputnik and the subsequent writings of Hyman G. Rickover, and, finally, the reassertion of differentiation as the solution to the problems of the high school as embodied in the writings of James B. Conant.

Lost in the Educational Wasteland

Of all the new critics of the American high school, individuals such as Bernard Iddings Bell, Albert Lynd, Hyman Rickover, and Mortimer Smith, none could bring to their critiques of progressivism the wealth of experience or knowledge of Arthur E. Bestor, Jr. (Bell, 1949; Bestor, 1953/1985; Lynd, 1953; Rickover, 1959; Smith, 1949). In 1953, when he published *Educational Wastelands*, the book that brought him national recognition, Bestor was a professor of history at the University of Illinois. But that fact tells little about the background that prepared him to level so trenchant a critique of progressive high schools. His father was the director of the Chautauqua program in New York, one of the most important adult education efforts in American history. As a young man, Bestor attended the Lincoln School in New York City, a showcase progressive high school attached to Teachers College. Later, in the late 1930s, while he was completing his Ph.D., he taught at Teachers College (Cremin, 1961). In presenting his critique of progressive education, therefore, Bestor was not speaking as an uninformed outsider but as someone who had experienced the best of the progressive educational tradition. From that perspective, he argued that progressivism had fallen far short of its original ideals (Bestor, 1953/1985; Cremin, 1988).

In making that argument, Bestor (1953/1985) re-examined the idea of equal educational opportunity and emerged with a vision of that idea that was remarkably close to that of the Committee of Ten. Bestor forthrightly declared that "[g]enuine education . . . is intellectual training" (p. 3) and that "schools exist to teach something, and that this something is the power to think" (p. 10). He was equally adamant that teaching students to think meant that schools must concentrate on "the scientific and scholarly disciplines" (p. 18), areas of study that could be learned only in a sustained, systematic way. Like the Committee of Ten, Bestor believed that teaching these disciplines was the raison d'être of schooling and that classes in these subject areas were more important than any other educational aspect of schooling. As he put it, "Only a firm conviction of the importance of fundamental intellectual training, and a stern insistence upon subordinating all other activities to this one, can enable teachers and administrators to preserve the educational system from utter chaos" (p. 73; see also p. 162).

Above all, like the Committee of Ten, Bestor maintained that virtually all students in high schools should follow such a program. Thoroughly rejecting the idea that the increasing democratization of high school enrollments meant that most of the new students were incapable of rigorous education, an idea that, as we have seen, had become conventional wisdom among educationists, Bestor declared, "To assert that intellectual capacity decreases as one reaches down into lower economic levels of the population is to deny, point-blank, the basic assumptions of democratic equalitarianism" (p. 36).[1]

The failure of leading professional educators to take that idea seriously provoked Bestor's most scathing arguments, his assessment of life-adjustment. Focusing on the Prosser Resolution, Bestor argued that contrary to its claims of promoting educational democracy, the Resolution embodied a philosophy of education that "asserts that the public schools must 'adjust' a majority of our children—three-fifths or some other proportion—to the bitter fact that they are good for nothing but undesirable, unskilled occupations, and that intellectual effort is far beyond their feeble grasp" (pp. 82–83). Although his description of the life-adjustment courses in Illinois was leavened with humor, beneath his discussion of units about "the problem of selecting a 'family dentist'" (p. 86) or "how the last war affected the dating pattern in our culture" (p. 100) was outrage at the general direction of secondary education in this country. Life-adjustment, he argued, was education designed to teach the majority of high school students to recognize their modest place in society, "to keep it, and to be content with it" (pp. 82–83).

Having identified the problem, Bestor turned to attack its source. Where, he asked, "did these preposterous educational notions come from?" His answer was, the "interlocking directorate of professional educationists" (pp. 101–102), a coterie that included professors of education, school administrators, and bureaucrats in the state departments of education and the U.S. Office of Education. In attacking this interlocking directorate, Bestor renewed the battle for control over the high school curriculum that pitted educators in the academic disciplines against those in the educational establishment, a battle that, as we noted earlier, began with the report of the Committee of Ten.

The great change that had taken place in the educational world during the 60 years that separated the report of the Committee of Ten from *Educational Wastelands* was the rise of schools and colleges of education. From these beachheads within the universities, Bestor argued, professors of education had gained enormous influence over public education by articulating a fairly coherent ideology about schooling and professional control of education, by inculcating that ideology in leading school administrators and educational bureaucrats in the nation, and by training an increasing number of American teachers. As long as education professors dealt with matters of school administration and methods and materials, there was little in these efforts to fault. However, Bestor argued, during their rise to power, many professors of education began to shift their research and policy interests from identifying and promoting the best *methods* to educate America's children to determining the best *curriculum* for these children, thereby usurping the rightful role of other important curricular stakeholders, namely, scholars in academic disciplines, school boards, community members, and parents. As he put it, professors of education "are deciding not merely how subjects should be taught in the public schools, but also what subjects should be taught. Under the guise of improving the methods of instruction, they have undertaken to determine its content as well" (p. 43). In calling for a restoration of the academic ideal in American high schools, Bestor urged universities to abolish schools and colleges of education and return control of decisions over curricular content to more appropriate (and competent) groups and individuals within universities and communities.

Educational Wastelands quickly became a rallying point for people concerned about the condition of public education. Members of the "intelligentsia" applauded the book, particularly its attacks on professional educators, and such magazines as *Life*, *Time*, and *U.S. News and World Report* gave it extensive coverage (Cremin, 1961; Rickover, 1959). Moreover, Bestor's powerful arguments against watered-down high school programs, particularly life-adjustment, were quickly taken up by other prominent critics. In 1956, Bestor and Mortimer Smith joined the board of directors of the Council for Basic Education, dedicated to the belief that "schools exist to provide essential skills in language, numbers, and orderly thought, and to transmit in a reasoned pattern the intellectual, moral, and aesthetic heritage of civilized man" (quoted in Cremin, 1961, p. 346; see also Smith, 1956).

By the late 1950s, debates inspired by Bestor's critique raged in school systems across the country. Early in 1957, for example, the president of the Detroit board of education denounced the high school program in his system as an "educational cafeteria" that offered little of educational substance to most students. In a statement that clearly echoed Bestor, he railed at the widely held belief among educators that "mass education necessarily means mass mediocrity." The local high schools, he concluded, were neither producing "proficient technicians" nor "ordinary citizens equipped with the fundamentals necessary for living in a scientific age" (*Detroit Free Press*, 4/5/57; see also 4/9/57).

By Spring 1958, such criticisms were so widespread that they began to shake the confidence of some school leaders. A Gallup poll of 1,100 high school principals found that a large majority believed that "high schools today demand far too little work of students," that "there are far too many easy courses and too much 'automatic promotion,'" and that there is "too little emphasis on reading and too much emphasis on extra-curricular activities such as athletics" (*Detroit Free Press*, 4/6/58).

However, many other members of the education profession responded to the increasingly intense criticism with anger and alarm. Some educationists labeled Bestor and his supporters as "congenital reactionaries," while others claimed that their criticisms of the high school were part of sinister campaigns to cut school budgets, campaigns that threatened public education itself (Cremin, 1961; Mirel, 1993; Rickover, 1959). Other professional educators, such as Myron Lieberman, called for a counterattack. Flatly rejecting the demands by Bestor and other critics for greater lay and "academic" control over the school and curriculum, Lieberman argued that professional educators, including for the first time teachers as well as education professors and administrators, should have the final say in all schools. Disparaging lay governance of local schools as a scheme that had "outlived its usefulness," Lieberman declared, "A genuine profession of education would not accept any lay determination either local, state, or federal, of what to teach and how to teach it" (quoted in Rudy, 1965, p. 333). Central to this effort was the strengthening of teachers' unions, organizations that a decade later would emerge as powerful new members of the interlocking educational directorate.

Beyond that call for empowering teachers, prior to 1957 these rancorous national and local controversies about high school curriculum really amounted to much ado about nothing. However, in October 1957, after the Soviet Union launched Sputnik, the situation changed drastically. As the Russian satellite ominously traced its orbit around the earth, Americans seriously began considering whether the crisis in education *had* contributed to our failure to be first in space. Suddenly, questions about the quality of the high school curriculum became part of an urgent debate about national security.

The Schools and National Security

Throughout late 1957 and all of 1958, a torrent of criticism swirled about American education, much of it focusing on the high school curriculum (Scott, Hill, & Burns, 1959). Typical of these criticisms was a four-part series by the *Detroit Free Press* that appeared in March 1958. Asking, "What is a high school diploma worth?" the series featured interviews with personnel managers from major corporations who uniformly declared the diploma practically worthless because of the schools' "cafeteria-style" education and low standards. Evidence of the accuracy of those perceptions came from such sources as the Wayne County Government, which reported a failure rate of 90% for high school graduates taking the civil service test for entry level clerical jobs, a test of verbal and arithmetic skills set at the seventh-grade level. In addition, after comparing transcripts of current graduates from one prominent high school with transcripts of graduates in 1933, *Free Press* reporters found that the 1958 students took 12% less English, 10% less history, 40% less mathematics, and 40% less science. Indeed, general track students in 1933 took almost the same amount of academic work as did students in the college prep track of 1958 (*Detroit Free Press*, 3/18/58).[2]

School leaders across the state responded to such attacks by strongly reaffirming their faith in the efficacy and fairness of differentiated secondary education. When asked for an opinion on these criticisms of the high schools, the registrar of Michigan State University defended the current high school program by invoking the twin specters that had been haunting school leaders for half a century—the traditional high school curriculum and the potential dropout. The registrar claimed that misguided critics wanted the progressive high schools to "go back to the curriculums of the past." He continued:

> There's a battle going on between those who want only to teach college preparatory courses and those who want a well-rounded program. It's true we could solve many of our problems today in educating the slow learner by going back 20 years to a course of study which would rid the schools of that type of student. But courses in shop and the like are essential if we are to prepare the non-college student for outside life. (*Detroit News*, 4/1/58)

Detroit's assistant superintendent for secondary education echoed these views, declaring, "We are trying to keep the dropout rate down and keep youngsters in school as long as possible by offering interesting, attractive and constructive courses" (*Detroit News*, 4/3/58). Several months later, a report by several professors of education working as consultants for a citizens' advisory committee on school needs for Detroit articulated these ideas even more clearly. Echoing the ideology that had undergirded progressive thought for decades, they revealed just how deeply intertwined the principle of curricular differentiation, the idea of equality of educational opportunity, and concerns about the dropout had become for educational professionals:

> There are some laymen (and a few teachers) who . . . express the wish that many of these students now in high school and in the general curriculum would join this dropout group. "Good riddance" they say. This is a denial of equality of educational opportunity which is one of the basic freedoms that this country and other democratic societies have subscribed to . . . *Identical education does not provide equal educational opportunity. It denies it.* The school must offer all types of courses to do for each what a limited narrow program will do for a few. (Detroit Board of Education, 1958a, pp. 99, 100; emphasis in original)

Indeed, educational leaders were so thoroughly committed to offering "all types of courses" that when the president of the University of Michigan requested a report on the amount of math and science coursetaking by Michigan high school students, the director of the university's bureau of school accreditation replied, "It seems to me that it is not the amount of science and mathematics offered, nor the diversity of science and mathematics offered, that poses a problem. . . . As a matter of fact, in analyzing 668 schools and programs, the areas of the curriculum that tend to be slighted are not mathematics or science but the following and in this order: 1. Art; 2. Orchestra and string work; 3. Boy's vocal work" (Leach, 1957).

In the past such comments and assurances by leading educators might have defused the crisis. However, the launch of Sputnik inspired an unprecedented wave of national soul-searching that quickly threatened to overwhelm the educational establishment. Probably no individual in these years seemed to represent this new challenge to the "interlocking educational directorate" more than did Hyman Rickover. At a time of crisis in national defense, his views about education received an enormous amount of attention due in large part to his position as a vice admiral of the U.S. Navy and the head of the navy's atomic submarine program. He claimed that his interest in education began in the late 1940s as he interviewed men for the submarine program. As a result of these interviews, he became gravely concerned about the quality of American education, particularly what he saw as the failure of schools to teach students "fundamental principles . . . [and] the ability to think independently" (1959, p. 23; see also Plath, 1996). As work on the program proceeded, his concerns deepened. In the mid-1950s, Rickover began giving speeches on the woeful state of education in the United States. Requests for such speeches increased dramatically after Sputnik and he was soon one of the leading figures in the great debate. Rickover compiled these talks into *Education and Freedom*, which appeared in 1959.

In many ways, the criticisms Rickover leveled at public schools paralleled those articulated by Bestor and Smith. Like them, Rickover denounced educational professionals as arrogant and narrow-minded, condemned the absurdities of life-adjustment education, and called for more rigorous, academic work in high schools. But in a number of fundamental ways, Rickover differed quite dramatically from some of those earlier critics. Like most of them, Rickover urged high schools to adopt higher academic standards generally, but unlike critics such as Bestor, Rickover's primary focus was curricular and programmatic reform for elite students. As he put it, "Talented children are this nation's reservoir of brain power. We have neglected them too long" (1959, p. 208). Indeed, like John Tildsley in the 1930s, Rickover seemed more concerned about how the deterioration of the high school curriculum had affected education for the talented rather than how it had affected schooling for the majority of students. In the 1950s, this emphasis on elite education was inspired by Rickover's fear that inadequate education for gifted students endangered national security. Whereas Bestor sought to ensure the future of American democracy through a well-educated electorate, Rickover was concerned mostly with maintaining American military superiority over the Soviets, a position that in his view depended on a steady flow of brilliant, well-trained leaders in engineering and the sciences.

According to Rickover, the greatest obstacle to the education of such leaders was not so much arrogant educationists, bad curriculum, or even an ill-conceived philosophy of education (although these factors certainly contributed to the problem). Rather, he maintained that the very structure of American secondary education, particularly the commitment by educators to the comprehensive high school, undermined efforts to adequately train this intellectual elite. Finding the roots of the comprehensive high school in "the post-Jacksonian upsurge of democracy" that sought to bring diverse students under one roof, Rickover argued that the founders of the institution never realized the deleterious effect such a policy would have on superior students. In their haste to bring all the children of a community together in a single, common school, the founders of American education failed to acknowledge "the incontrovertible fact that children are unequally endowed with intelligence and determination and that it is impossible to educate the slow, average, and fast learners together if by educating we mean the capacity to think, to understand, and to make wise decisions" (p. 134). For Rickover, the consequences of such heterogeneous groupings were obvious:

> There is ample evidence that in any class which includes slow and fast learners the slower group sets the pace and receives more attention from the teacher. The above-average children are kept from advancing at the speed appropriate to their ability, with the result that some lose interest in learning as such, others develop sloppy habits, and a few build up a false sense of superiority which convinces them that they are so smart that they will never need to apply themselves to anything. (p. 117)

Indeed, Rickover traced almost all the current problems of American education to this commitment to "comprehensives," citing, for example, "the abandonment of standards of excellence" (pp. 135–136) in order to increase the holding power of the high schools. He saw such actions as damaging the education of talented youth because declining standards for the many eventually meant declining standards for the gifted.

The policy implications of these ideas were clear. If comprehensive public high schools were the problem, separate public high schools for elite students were the solution. He pointed approvingly to such institutions as the Bronx High School of Science and urged policy makers to establish more of these kinds of schools. However, the model Rickover embraced most enthusiastically was European, not American, in origin. Throughout *Education and Freedom* and in the books that followed, Rickover routinely applauded European-style education in which educators rigorously culled the talented and gifted students from the masses (Plath, 1996). "European educators have had much more experience with the capabilities of talented children," he wrote, "something which is lacking in this country" (p. 116). In his 1962 testimony before the U.S. House Appropriations Committee, which later was published as *Education for All Children: What We Can Learn from England* (1962), Rickover urged the members of Congress to help set up academic high schools similar to those in Europe.

Throughout the late 1950s and early 1960s, Rickover's dogged pursuit of these policies made him a major figure in the debate about the nature and function of the American high school. Thoroughly disdainful of the educational establishment, Rickover "got under the hide of many of the nation's educational administrators and professors of education more thoroughly than Bestor had ever done" (Rudy, 1965, p. 335). Nevertheless, with his attack on the comprehensive high school, his adulation of European forms of high school organization, and his emphasis on education of the gifted and talented, Rickover inadvertently played directly into the hands of educational leaders. However angry they may have been at his criticism, Rickover presented arguments that educationists had been contending with for years. In attacking the comprehensive high school, "democracy's high school," Rickover appeared to be challenging one of the finest achievements of American education, an institution that they claimed provided equal educational opportunities for all students through its vast range of curricular options. Educators pointed out that early in this century Americans had carefully considered European models of secondary education and found their class-based elitism unworthy of emulation. In the end, Rickover could be easily dismissed as an educational aristocrat who cared nothing for average students. As one wag put it, Rickover's recommendations amounted to a policy of "[e]ducate the best and shoot the rest" (quoted in Plath, 1996, p. 79). Moreover, in calling for greater attention to gifted and talented students, Rickover (unlike Bestor) endorsed the educationists' fundamental belief in differentiation.[3] Indeed, in both aspects of his attacks, questioning the comprehensive high school and supporting gifted and talented education, Rickover paved the way for a resolution of the great debate about American high schools. The person who would provide that resolution was James B. Conant.

Differentiation Reaffirmed

In many ways, James B. Conant was perfectly suited for the role he would play in the great debate about the high school curriculum, a role that called for someone who could appeal to supporters of all the major positions in the controversy. As a distinguished scientist and past president of Harvard University, Conant had such strong academic credentials that even the most "traditional" critics of American secondary schools were assured of his commitment to rigorous, discipline-based education. Moreover, having served from 1953 to 1957 first as the High Commissioner and then ambassador to West Germany, a nation on the front line of the Cold War, Conant was a public figure who could rival Rickover in firsthand knowledge about what America needed educationally to confront the Soviet threat. Finally, as we noted in Chapter 3, during the 1940s Conant had served on the Educational Policies Commission of the National Education Association. In that position, he had won the respect of leading educationists who saw him as a man whom they could trust and with whom they could work. This breadth of appeal, combined with the substantial support Conant received from the Carnegie Corporation and the media, enabled him to shape the history of the American high school for decades to come. His report, *The American High School Today* (1959), essentially ended the raging debate about the high school curriculum in the 1950s and determined how the institution would respond to the challenges of the 1960s and early 1970s (Hershberg, 1993; Preskill, 1984; Teicher, 1977).

Well before he stepped down as ambassador to West Germany, Conant had arranged with the Carnegie Corporation to fund a major study of American high schools (Conant, 1959; Preskill, 1984). Upon returning to the United States, he assembled a team of researchers who between September 1957 and July 1958 investigated over 100 high schools in 18 states. Members of the team spent these months interviewing educators, assessing programs, and completing surveys that asked a broad range of questions about curricula, facilities, and student course-taking. Conant analyzed these data and rapidly produced the final report.

Quickly dubbed "the Conant report," the study benefited from a carefully planned media blitz. Major stories on the report appeared in *Life*, *Look*, *Newsweek*, *Time*, and *U.S. News and World Report* (Preskill, 1984). All of these media outlets trumpeted Conant's key finding that "no radical alteration in the basic pattern of American education is necessary in order to improve our public high schools" (Conant, 1959, p. 40). The book became a best seller.

On one level, the Conant report reads like a direct response to Hyman Rickover. Conant focused his research exclusively on the comprehensive high school, the institution that Rickover identified as the source of the educational crisis. Unlike Rickover, however, Conant gave the institution a ringing endorsement. In the opening section of the report, Conant (1959) declared, "I think it is safe to say that the comprehensive high school is characteristic of our society and further that it has come into being because of our economic history and our devotion to the ideals of equality of opportunity and equality of status" (p. 8). Indeed, Conant devoted most of the opening two sections of the report to explaining why Americans rejected a European-style system of separate vocational and academic schools, the type of educational structure that Rickover had so strongly endorsed. He argued that because the comprehensive high school gave students a vast range of opportunities for discovering their potential (thereby ensuring "equality of opportunity"), and because it gathered all the students of a community into the same institution (thus ensuring "equality of status"), it stood in marked contrast to the segregated, class-bound nature of European secondary schools. With this argument, Conant attacked the weakest points in Rickover's position by presenting them as elitist and essentially un-American. In making these claims, Conant reiterated the arguments that educational professionals had been mouthing about the comprehensive high school for almost half a century, namely, that it was "democracy's high school" and that attacks on it were tantamount to attacks on democracy itself.

But Conant's rejection of a European-style structure for American secondary education masked his more fundamental agreement with Rickover on important educational policies. Like Rickover, Conant gave lip service to the need for higher standards for all high school students, but ultimately his main concern was also the education of the gifted. His positive assessment of public high schools largely centered on the degree to which they offered a range of options to the majority of students, not on their skill in educating the gifted and talented. "If the fifty-five schools I have visited, all of which have a good reputation, are at all representative of American public high schools," he wrote, "I think one general criticism is in order: The academically talented student, as a rule, is not being sufficiently challenged, does not work hard enough, and his program of academic subjects is not of sufficient range" (p. 40; see also Greer & Harbeck, 1962). In fact, in a confidential memo to his staff early in 1959, Conant admitted having serious reservations about his positive assessment of American high schools generally, noting that if he was going "to be really frank about the public school situation, he would have to say that the vast majority of the schools he visited were badly neglecting the education of the most gifted students" (Preskill, 1984, p. 284).

In short, education of the gifted and talented students was as central to Conant's thinking as it was to Rickover's. The only difference between the two was where programs for these students should be housed. Conant believed that the current structure of comprehensive high schools, based as it was on the principle of differentiated instruction for diverse ability groups, could easily handle upgraded programs for the gifted and talented while remaining true to the "democratic" mission of the institution.

Not surprisingly, therefore, Conant's recommendations for improving public secondary schools concentrated mainly on strengthening differentiation. One of his top priorities, for example, was eliminating small high schools (those with graduating classes of 100 or less) because such schools could not differentiate their programs adequately. Lacking sufficient numbers of academically talented students to justify special programs and lacking the resources to offer vocational programs, such schools, Conant argued, shortchanged all the pupils enrolled. Beyond that general suggestion for change, Conant presented 21 specific recommendations for improving public high schools, almost two-thirds of which focused on fine-tuning the processes of differentiation and many of which focused on improving the quality of education for the gifted. These recommendations included strengthening the counseling system to more precisely identify students' abilities and, returning to a theme that he had addressed in the 1940s, to override the demands of overly ambitious parents and steer mediocre students toward appropriate, lower-level courses; individualizing students' programs of study; increasing ability grouping; diversifying "programs for the development of marketable skills"; providing special programs for "very slow readers"; adopting new programs for the "academically talented"; identifying and cultivating extremely gifted students (the top 3% of students) early; creating an academic inventory "to provide meaningful statistics about the education of the academically talented"; tightening prerequisites for advanced academic courses; publishing a list of academic, commercial, and vocational honors students; expanding the options for additional foreign language instruction, especially for superior students; and providing a greater range of science courses appropriately divided between courses for students with strong and weak math skills. Even some of Conant's recommendations designed to encourage common educational and social experiences for all students wound up strengthening differentiation. For example, he qualified his recommendation that schools require a body of core courses for all students by urging school leaders to divide the mandated courses in foreign language, math, and science into two tiers, one of which would "maintain high standards" for high-ability students while the other would hold students of lesser ability to "another standard" (p. 48).

In all, the Conant report was a masterful example of educational and political duplicity, hiding elitist policies under a smoke screen of democratic and egalitarian rhetoric. At the same time that he was defending the "democratic" character of the comprehensive high school, Conant specifically rejected the idea proposed by critics such as Bestor that *all* students should receive an equally high-quality education. In rejecting that idea Conant directly opposed a growing trend among American parents, namely, the increasing desire to send their children to college. A 1958 Gallup poll found that almost two-thirds of the parents surveyed believed that everyone should have a chance to attend college and that the government should provide either loans or income tax deductions to make that possible (*Detroit Free Press*, 4/10/58). Unlike Conant and his educationist allies, these parents defined equal educational opportunity as access to higher education, not as the opportunity to be channeled into low-level courses. Obviously they were the very people Conant had in mind when he urged counselors to hold firm against parents of mediocre students who demanded their children be placed in college preparatory classes.

Rather than boldly challenging the educational status quo, Conant embraced it. By making recommendations that barely diverged from conventional educational philosophy and practice, he helped restore the shaken confidence of school leaders and gave them a plan of attack that could effectively neutralize local critics. Conant's endorsement of programs for the gifted and talented was a policy that most educationists supported, and in some cases even acted upon, well before the report was issued.[4] In all, Conant arrived on the educational scene like a white knight who lifted the siege against the embattled public schools. Combined with the passage in 1958 of the National Defense Education Act (NDEA), which provided federal funds for additional high school mathematics, science, and foreign language instruction, and the efforts of the National Science Foundation (NSF) to create new and exciting curricula, the Conant report played a major role in ending the great debate about the nature and function of the American high school (Ravitch, 1983). Indeed, by the mid-1960s the great debate was a fading memory. In its wake, however, many commentators and later many historians assumed that curricular offerings and patterns of student coursetaking had changed substantially.

In order to assess the accuracy of those perceptions, we will turn to a brief look at two of the most important subject areas in this controversy, mathematics and the sciences, to try to assess the impact these controversies had on curriculum and student coursetaking.

ENROLLMENTS IN MATHEMATICS AND
THE SCIENCES, 1948–1964

Educational historians frequently have claimed that the great educational and social controversies of the 1950s and 1960s inspired major changes in curriculum and coursetaking in American schools by breaking the grip of life-adjustment principles on the high schools and shifting the institution back toward greater academic seriousness. Robert Church and Michael Sedlak (1976), for example, state that "the fifties and sixties saw as profound a shift in thinking about education as had been seen since the Progressive Era. The schools refocused on subject matter and intellectual discipline" (p. 407; see also Cremin, 1988; Ravitch, 1983; Spring, 1972; Tozer, Violas, & Senese, 1993). But are those perceptions accurate, and if they are, were the changes uniform or vastly different in various subject areas, and did those changes touch all students equally or were some more favored by certain reforms than others?

No group of subjects is better suited for answering such questions than math and science, given the centrality of these subjects to the great debate of the 1950s. During this period the U.S. Office of Education (USOE) conducted several studies of coursetaking in these areas, which allow us to assess the impact of the controversies on high school education. The USOE interest in coursetaking in math and science actually predates the great debate. In 1948, concurrent with its endorsement of the life-adjustment movement, the USOE carried out a small-scale national survey of the teaching of science in public high schools. This was followed by a similar survey of mathematics teaching in 1952 and joint surveys of math and science in 1954, 1956, and 1958. In 1961, the USOE calculated from its general study of course enrollments a selected survey of math and science offerings. In addition, tables on math and science enrollments continued to be published in the *Digest of Educational Statistics* until at least 1965.

Two different rationales provided the impetus for this series of studies. "As our society depends increasingly on science and technology," the author of the 1956 report stated, "it is important that all citizens have an understanding of the nature of science and mathematics. The continued security and growth of the United States in this age of technology require steady increases for many years to come in the Nation's supply of high quality engineers, scientists, and teachers of mathematics and the sciences" (USOE, 1956, p. ii). These rationales, the need for greater scientific literacy for "all citizens," and the need for increasing the supply of "engineers, scientists, and teachers of mathematics and the sciences" were exactly the themes that dominated the debate about science and mathematics in the 1950s, distinguishing Bestor, who supported the former position, from Rickover and Conant, who supported the latter.

However, a careful reading of the reports from those years reveals that the USOE was itself far from neutral in this debate, demonstrating time and again that like Rickover and Conant it was more concerned with training an elite corps of scientists and mathematicians than with improving scientific literacy throughout the general population. The office fully accepted Rickover and Conant's premise that algebra, geometry, trigonometry, and calculus were appropriate subjects for some students but inappropriate for most. Indeed, the USOE showed little genuine concern for the role of science and math in the general education of citizens. Rather than supporting the efforts of such critics as Bestor to bring greater rigor into high school education for all, the tone of the reports was more critical of the critics than of the high schools.

Nothing revealed more clearly the USOE's deep commitment to the idea of the differentiated high school than its analysis of the transcripts of a national sample of the graduates of 1958 (Greer & Harbeck, 1962). Carried out in the wake of the Sputnik scare and evidently prompted by the great debate, the study sought to learn what programs were being followed in the high schools by "pupils of various abilities." Throughout the study, USOE researchers characterized groups of students as "academically able," "typical," or "less able," based solely on their IQ scores. Because the "able" pupils enrolled in college preparatory curricula at a higher rate, ranked higher in their graduating classes, accumulated slightly more high school credits, and took more mathematics and science than their "less" able counterparts, the researchers affirmed that high schools generally were on the right track in terms of student coursetaking. But they took the view that high schools were not as sharply differentiated by ability groups as they ought to be. Even the most ardent life-adjuster probably would not have placed as much faith in the power of IQ to determine the track placement of high school students as did these USOE staffers. With that bias in mind, we can turn to the data that the USOE presented in its series of reports.

The data displayed in Table 4.1, which lists the percentage of students in grades 9–12 enrolled in science and math courses between 1948 and 1963, highlights the increases in these two subject areas that took place during these years. On first blush, it appears that the great debate did indeed have an impact on student coursetaking. Overall, math enrollment rates rose from about 55% of students in grades 9–12 taking a math course in 1948 to about two-thirds of students in 1963. However, these were extremely modest gains, given the passion of the great debate, and the gains in science were even more modest. In fact, enrollments

Table 4.1. Percentage of Students Enrolled in Mathematics and Science Courses in Public Secondary Schools in Grades 9–12, United States, 1948–49 Through 1962–63

Subject	1948–49	1952–53	1954–55	1956–57	1958–59	1960–61	1962–63
Mathematics	54.8	50.7	59.0	60.3	65.2	63.8	67.0
General math, elem.	12.0	11.6	12.2	13.4	13.1	12.5	12.1
General math, adv.	0.8	0.5				4.9	
Algebra, elem.	19.3	17.6	18.3	20.8	22.6	19.6	21.2
Algebra, int. and adv.	7.5	5.6	6.6	6.6	8.2	9.8	10.1
Plane geometry	11.1	8.7	13.6	10.8	12.5	11.7	14.5
Solid geometry	1.7	1.6	2.2	2.2	1.4	2.1	0.7
Trigonometry	2.0	1.7	2.6	2.7	2.8	3.0	2.0
All other math	1.5	3.4	3.5[a]	3.8	4.6	0.3	6.4
Science	54.5	—	—	56.9	59.6	59.7	59.9
General science	19.9	—	—	21.8	20.2	22.2	18.2
Biology	18.4	—	9.7	20.5	21.4	21.7	24.7
Chemistry	7.6	—	7.3	7.5	8.4	9.1	8.5
Physics	5.4	—	4.6	4.4	4.8	4.9	4.0
All other science	3.2	—	—	2.7	4.8	1.8	4.5

Sources: Adapted by the authors from U.S. Office of Education, 1964, tab. 17, p. 29; U.S.Office of Education, 1965, tab. 16, p. 27; Brown, Ellsworth, and Obourn, 1957.

[a]This figure is an extrapolation. Actual enrollments were not reported.

in other subjects, such as health and physical education, which were not central to the great debate, jumped from about 69% of students in grades 9–12 in 1948 to over 102% in 1960, over three times the increase of mathematics.

The explanation for these increases has less to do with Sputnik or the great debate than with the fact that high school enrollments generally were on the rise in this period. Consequently, there were large increases in the numbers of students, and small, uneven increases in the rates of enrollment in such rigorous courses as algebra, geometry, trigonometry, biology, and chemistry. In all, however, as Appendix A, Table A.2, shows, the share of math and science coursetaking remained virtually unchanged between 1948 and 1960.

However, a closer look at the data reveals a more disturbing trend. The most dramatic enrollment increases were not in the most rigorous courses but in the lower-level "practical" courses. The author of the 1952 report was the first to acknowledge this trend, stating that "enrollments in mathematics for general education have increased, but the enrollments in college-preparatory mathematics have not kept pace with the growth of the high schools" (Brown, 1953, p. 40). The author of the report comparing 1948 with 1960 found little change in that pattern despite the enormous amount of attention given to math and science in the great debate. The author noted, "Courses of a practical nature continued to proliferate [between 1948 and 1960]. . . . In mathematics such courses as consumer mathematics, economic mathematics, mathematics for modern living, refresher mathematics, and terminal mathematics were reported. Science offered household biology, science for modern living, everyday physics, and consumer science among others" (Wright, 1965, pp. 19–20). In other words, the overall trends in math and science enrollments appeared unchanged by the great debate. Rather, movement toward what one commentator at the time called "split level" education continued apace, with increases in enrollments in rigorous science and mathematics courses matched, and in many cases outpaced, by enrollments in less intellectually challenging courses (Latimer, 1958).

The massive USOE and NSF curriculum projects of the 1960s provide an excellent case in point. Developed in the wake of the Sputnik scare, the NSF projects set out to develop new and more challenging curricula in the sciences, mathematics, foreign language, and the social studies. Mainly taking the form of new teaching materials designed to replace traditional textbooks, these experimental approaches were adopted by many high schools in the early 1960s. Despite the substantial amounts of money spent on these projects and the considerable publicity they received, the NSF projects boosted enrollments only modestly at best and they appear to have had no lasting impact. At the same time that high schools showed modest increases in some of the more rigorous math courses such as calculus, they also continued to show increases at the other end of the difficulty spectrum, in the remedial and applied mathematics categories. Between 1960 and 1972 modest declines in chemistry and physics were offset by increases in lower-level general science courses such as physical science and earth/space science.

In the late 1960s, as we shall discuss in Chapter 5, this trend was influenced by the shift in national priorities from the Cold War to domestic social problems such as poverty and inequality. But the trend also was caused by the way in which high schools adopted the NSF curricula. Schools targeted these curricula to high-performing, college-bound students who probably would have taken all the advanced mathematics and science courses the schools offered regardless of the curricular revisions.

As we argued in the previous chapter, probably the most important factor shaping curriculum changes in this period was the continued growth of high school enrollments to over 15.1 million in 1972. Educators responded to these new students, as they had in the past, by assuming that increased enrollments inevitably meant increasing numbers of low-ability students. Believing that these students were incapable of mastering difficult course material, educators expanded the less demanding general courses for them. Thus, whether one looks at the sciences or mathematics, the dominant trend was toward rising enrollments in less challenging classes. As the authors of the report comparing 1960 with 1972 noted, "The emphasis on making a high school education available for every youth, as noted in the [1960–61] study, has continued, with added attention given to the lower ability groups. . . . Graduation requirements were relaxed in many schools and elective courses became more common" (Osterndorf & Horn, 1976, p. 22).

In all, these data indicate that claims that high schools in the 1950s and 1960s refocused on subject matter and intellectual discipline are quite wide of the mark at least as far as math and science courses are concerned. The math and science coursetaking trends demonstrate the persistence and indeed the strengthening of policies regarding differentiation, not a revitalization of rigorous academic coursetaking for high school students generally. If the great debate about the high school curriculum in the 1950s had any effect, it was in the reaffirmation and revitalization of the policies of "split level" education. From that perspective, James B. Conant did not just end the great debate, he won it.

SUMMARY

Educational historians frequently characterize the 1950s and early 1960s as a period in which two powerful philosophies of education battled for the loyalties of American educators. The metaphor these historians often employ is that of a swinging pendulum in which educational policy and practice move away from child-centered programs, such as life-adjustment, toward more curriculum-centered programs, such as those proposed by Arthur Bestor. The consensus is that by the early 1960s, life-adjustment education had been routed and rigorous academic courses once again held sway over the high school curriculum (Angus & Mirel, 1993). Yet, as we have demonstrated, despite the enormous attention and passion directed at American education in this period, very little changed in terms of student coursetaking in the two curricular areas central to the great debate, math and science.

The reason for this lack of change is simple. Most of the major participants in the debates of the 1950s and early 1960s accepted the philosophy of education that had guided American high school policy and practice since the Progressive Era, namely, that serving the needs of youth through a differentiated curriculum was the key to educational progress and equality of educational opportunity. Certainly neither Hyman Rickover nor James B. Conant challenged the idea that schools should offer substantially different programs for students of varying abilities. They quarreled only over how that process should be carried out.

Among the participants in the great debate, only Arthur Bestor and his allies proposed a revolutionary change in the nature of high school education. Reaffirming the principles of the Committee of Ten that all students had the right to high-quality academic education, these "conservatives" generated much controversy but little action. Few people within the educational establishment took their ideas seriously and by the mid-1960s they were all but forgotten as the nation moved on to other problems with its schools.

Only a rhetorical pendulum moved during this period. Differentiation remained triumphant in the years immediately following World War II. In the next chapter, we examine whether that philosophy of education was able to withstand the far more powerful assaults of the late 1960s and early 1970s, more powerful because they were deeply rooted in the massive social and political changes of those years.

NOTES

1. Bestor (1953/1985) was quite aware of the fact that different students had different mental abilities, talents, and capabilities, but unlike most educationists he did not think that such differences demanded separate curricular tracks. Rather he argued that most students of "lower mental ability. . . can be brought at a slower pace along the same route" (p. 37).

2. The *Free Press* claimed that the situation was actually even worse than these figures indicated, because the figures took no account of "the watered-down standards or the damage done by the Detroit school system's policy of automatic promotion," or of the fact that a grade of "D" once meant that the course had to be repeated, but was now considered a passing grade (*Detroit Free Press*, 3/18/58, p. 18; see also Angus, 1991; *Detroit News*, 3/31/58).

3. In fact, as early as 1956 the Educational Policies Commission had moved toward Rickover's position with its publication of *Manpower in Education* (1956). The EPC specifically called for cultivating the diverse but latent talents of all the nation's youth (Angus, 1965).

4. For example, the director of the University of Michigan's accrediting bureau stated that if problems with math and science did exist, they were found in the failure of the high schools to differentiate sufficiently to meet the needs of the "gifted child" (Leach, 1957).

5

The Triumph of Curricular Differentiation, 1964–1975

IN THE EARLY 1960s, as the nation emerged from the great debate about public education, it was still possible to describe the United States as a country with a strong central core of shared values. "The American way" and "the American dream" were phrases that carried meaning, and many citizens still looked to the American comprehensive high school as an institution that would help their children realize those values and aspirations. Between 1964 and 1975, the nation changed to such an extent that historians and political scientists have characterized it as the "unraveling" or "fragmenting" of America. Such cataclysmic events as the assassinations of John Kennedy, Martin Luther King, Jr., and Robert Kennedy; the massive and often violent opposition to the war in Vietnam; the dramatic changes wrought by the civil rights and women's movements; the riots in major cities; and the Watergate scandal and resignation of Richard Nixon all contributed to the sense that during this period the country's social and political life underwent a radical transformation (Gitlin, 1987; Matusow, 1984; Polenberg, 1980).

Education unquestionably played a major role in this tumultuous era. The nation's schools were often the center of important political movements, the sites of demonstrations, protests, and occasionally violent outbursts (Gitlin, 1987; Matusow, 1984). Moreover, during the late 1960s and early 1970s, a host of political leaders, commentators, and social activists called for radical changes in American public education, changes that they hoped would prompt a revolution in American society generally. This outpouring of revolutionary and reform literature, coupled with the dramatic events that took place in and around schools, has led many scholars to argue that this period was one of the great "turning points" in the history of public education (e.g., Bowles & Gintis, 1976).

In this chapter we question these claims, particularly with regard to secondary education. We do so largely because the underlying philosophy that guided most of the criticism of public schools and the subsequent policies enacted in those schools in this period continued to draw much of its intellectual sustenance from ideas that in one way or another supported differentiated curricula. Given the source of some of the most important criticisms of public schools in this era, that argument may seem surprising. How, for example, could the civil rights or the women's movement, which existed in order to secure equal rights and treatment for *all* Americans, provide support for educational policies that historically had contributed to second-class education for minorities and women? The answer to that question lies in how educators who were committed to the differentiated high school used that philosophy and the structure of the institution to absorb and at times co-opt the demands made by leaders of these movements. Indeed, educators found many of these demands quite compatible with the structure of the comprehensive high school, which proved to be capable of absorbing challenges and institutionalizing change. The key to that capability was differentiation.

In making this argument we again return to our examination of coursetaking and curriculum data from Grand Rapids, Detroit, Michigan, and the nation. However, in this chapter we introduce some changes both in how we present our quantitative data and in the type of data we analyze. As in Chapter 4, we do not have individual student data from Grand Rapids. Therefore, in analyzing developments in that city we must rely on school-level data that we gathered from various sources. The only available data for Michigan during this period are derived from three national studies, so we will discuss state-level developments only briefly. Finally, in previous chapters we have seen that shifts in the ratio of academic to nonacademic courses and shifts in the relative share of coursetaking by subject families were firm indicators of the progress of curriculum reform. In the years from 1964 to 1975, the most striking finding from our national and local data is the degree to which these ratios remain stable. In this chapter, therefore, we focus more closely on coursetaking changes *within* specific subject areas.

HIGH SCHOOLS AND SOCIAL UNREST

In the early 1960s, education and schooling moved near the top of the national political agenda when Lyndon Johnson enlisted educators as troops in the War on Poverty, a campaign whose dominant strategy seemed to be that with enough funds and goodwill America could "school" people out of poverty (Graham, 1984). During these years, federal and state funds flowed into public schools and colleges of education at unprecedented levels. But poverty proved to be a particularly intractable problem and, after early (and often premature) evaluations declared that many school-based antipoverty programs were failures, a deep gloom settled over the field of education. Compounding this gloom was the changing nature of criticism about public education. Whereas criticism in the early 1960s argued that specific changes in schools were necessary for them to continue their traditional role of curing the ills of society, by the 1970s critics declared that not only couldn't the schools solve those ills, but in many cases the schools were as much a cause of the problems as were other "establishment" institutions (Ravitch,

1983; Spring, 1976). These attacks produced what might be termed an institutional paralysis. As a 1973 report on secondary education put it:

> The American high school has become a beleaguered institution. Everyone agrees that the high schools are in difficulty, but there the agreement ceases; even before they arrive at proposals, experts find themselves arguing about what is wrong and about the source and size of the trouble. While educators ponder the problem, the high school environment deteriorates further. (National Commission on the Reform of Secondary Education, 1973, p. 8)

The critics of education generally and the high school specifically were many and varied in the 1970s, and it is difficult to capture all the nuances of these criticisms within a few categories, but we think it is useful to identify three broad visions or movements that played point-counterpoint with each other during the fragmenting decade: the "Black Power" movement, the "humanistic education" movement, and the "neo-efficiency" movement. Unlike other educational historians who have analyzed these movements (e.g., Ravitch, 1983; Spring, 1972), our purpose is to focus on the specific impact each had on high school curricular reform and the effect, if any, each had on student coursetaking.

Of the three efforts, the Black Power and humanist critiques of American education had the most in common. Certainly, both groups viewed American schools as part of the problem rather than part of the solution to the crises in American life, and both argued that schools served the interests of the powerful far more than they served the interests of the masses. Proponents of both schools of thought argued for more "power to the people" in terms of greater parental and community participation in educational governance (and, conversely, less power for educational professionals), greater attention to the main issues of the day (i.e., racism, the war in Vietnam, poverty), greater choice for students in terms of coursetaking, and, ironically given later political developments, greater choice for parents concerning their children's schools through the use of educational vouchers (Gross, 1971). Both schools of thought believed that American public education was characterized by too much structure, too many rules, and too little respect for the innate goodness and natural curiosity of children, and both believed that planning the curriculum had been usurped by professional educators from the only groups with a natural right to plan it, the parents and the children themselves. While these groups often echoed progressive ideas of an earlier time, their hyperbole was unique, utilizing such phrases as "death at an early age" (Kozol, 1967), "cultural homicide" (King, 1967), and the "total mindlessness of the schools" (Silberman, 1970).

The third initiative, the neo-efficiency or, as it was called at the time, the accountability movement, advocated a series of changes that echoed those of early-twentieth-century reformers who emphasized educational efficiency (Callahan,

1962). Supporters of this movement called for such innovations as the development of middle schools, management by objectives, competency-based teacher education, performance contracting, and career education. Their common theme was that the trouble with American education was its failure to establish clear and explicit goals and to organize itself efficiently for the pursuit of those goals. Although many of the aims of this movement seem to directly challenge those of the two movements discussed above, the consequences of the three were surprisingly similar.

The Black Power Movement

Gaining equality of educational opportunity for Black children was one of the guiding forces of the civil rights struggle during both its "Freedom Now" and its "Black Power" phases. Although these two aspects of the movement differed greatly over goals and tactics, both agreed that high-quality education for Black children was vital for racial progress and the creation of a truly egalitarian society. Both efforts thus had the potential for making dramatic changes in American high schools, particularly in terms of boosting the number of academic course offerings available to Black youth and in raising the proportion of academic coursetaking by Black students. During the 1960s and 1970s, however, neither appeared to have such an effect.

Ever since 1898, when the U.S. Supreme Court asserted in *Cummings v. Richmond* that the separate but equal doctrine did not extend to providing high schools for Black students, securing quality secondary education became an important part of the battle for equal rights (Du Bois, 1903/1982; Kluger, 1975). In the first half of the twentieth century Black communities in both the North and South vigorously fought to establish or improve Black high schools, often against implacable White opposition (Anderson, 1988; Siddle Walker, 1996). Certainly, the most dramatic and widely watched school integration effort in the 1950s took place on the secondary level, the attempt to integrate Little Rock Central High School (Beals, 1994; Ravitch, 1983).

Curricular and coursetaking issues generally were subsumed within the larger quest for integration, but there is no question that battles such as those in Little Rock were predicated on the belief that the only way to ensure that Black students would receive the same curricula, courses, and textbooks as Whites was for Black children to attend the same schools and follow the same courses of study as Whites. From this point of view, racial and educational progress had to be measured not only in the numbers and percentages of Black and White students attending integrated schools but also by the numbers and percentages of Black students getting the best possible education in *all* schools. With that in mind, Martin Luther King, Jr., noted with satisfaction in 1967, "In the schools more Negro students are demanding courses that lead to college and beyond, refusing to settle for the crude vocational training that limited so many of them in the past" (p. 11).

Unfortunately, by the mid-1960s, many African Americans had become increasingly frustrated and angry as Whites effectively blocked housing and school integration, especially in the supposedly more liberal North. Over the next few years, as the battle over school desegregation deteriorated into furious battles about forced busing, mainstream civil rights groups seemed to lose their focus on how best to improve the quality of education for Black children. Moreover, as these battles raged, skepticism increased among some African Americans about whether integration actually would improve race relations, secure racial progress, or improve the education of Black youth. At the same time, a number of Black leaders began looking closely at school policies and practices and unearthing extensive evidence of institutionalized racism in both integrated and predominantly Black schools (Cohen, 1990; Mirel, 1993; Stolee, 1993). The Black Power critique of the schools arose out of all these trends.

By far the most powerful expression of these sentiments appeared in *Black Power* by Kwame Ture (Stokely Carmichael) and Charles Hamilton (1967/1992). Ture and Hamilton began with the proposition that "black people in this country form a colony, and it is not in the interest of the colonial power to liberate them" (p. 5). Thus, White-dominated institutions in the Black community clearly did not and could not work in the interests of Black people. Public schools figured prominently in this analysis. As Ture and Hamilton argued, "[T]he American educational system continues to reinforce the entrenched values of the society. . . . [The] values of this society support a racist system; we find it incongruous to ask black people to adopt and support most of those values" (pp. 37, 40).

These ideas led to two main objectives in education, one political, the other curricular. Politically, Black Power advocates demanded an end to White control of Black schools. As Ture and Hamilton put it, "White decision-makers have been running those schools with injustice, indifference, and inadequacy for too long; the result has been an educationally crippled black child turned out onto the labor market equipped to do little more than stand in welfare lines to receive his miserable dole" (p. 159). Extending the critique of educational professionals that began in the 1950s, Ture and Hamilton denounced White teachers and administrators for the damage their polices and practices had wrought on Black schools:

> Control of ghetto schools must be taken out of the hands of "professionals," most of whom have long since demonstrated their insensitivity to the needs and problems of the black child. These "experts" bring with them middle-class biases, unsuitable techniques, and materials; these are, at best, dysfunctional, and at worst destructive. (p. 166)

"Black parents," Ture and Hamilton continued, "should seek as their goal the actual control of the schools in their community; hiring and firing of teachers, selection of teaching materials, determination of standards, etc." (p. 167).

The second objective (which Black Power advocates believed would flow naturally from the successful implementation of the first) focused on transforming the curriculum. Recoiling at the "traditional, irrelevant" (p. 167) White-dominated curricula used in ghetto schools, Black Power advocates demanded that schools serving Black children reorient their programs to reflect the history, culture, and contributions of Black people. In the early 1960s, Malcolm X had argued that the traditional school program was part of a deliberate attempt to hide the Black man's true role in history, and Black Power advocates sought to thoroughly revise school programs to recover that lost history and culture and immerse Black students in it. Indeed, by 1967, even critics of Black Power, such as Martin Luther King, Jr., denounced "history books which have completely ignored the contribution of the Negro in American history" (King, 1967, p. 48). King demanded an end to what he termed "cultural homicide" (p. 50). These demands went beyond just revising history or literature courses. They quickly extended into calls for transforming all facets of the curriculum from textbook illustrations to teaching methods.

Both of these objectives of Black Power advocates had the potential for challenging the reigning educational orthodoxies in Black secondary schools, particularly the policies and practices that had led to large numbers of Black students receiving a second-rate education in urban high schools. Supporters of community control believed that if they had the power to replace racially biased White educators with Black principals, counselors, and teachers, they could put an end to such racist practices as assigning large percentages of Black students into the meaningless, dead-end high school programs, such as the general track. Similarly, they believed that if the curriculum were thoroughly revised to accurately portray the lives, culture, and history of Black people, if new materials and methods were created that would give schoolwork immediate relevance for Black children, then these children would naturally strive for higher levels of achievement and greater academic success. But, like the mainstream civil rights movement, whose efforts for greater educational equality in this period got sidetracked and eventually overwhelmed over the issue of busing, the Black Power movement produced few great changes in secondary education.

Three main factors account for this failure. First, like many mainstream civil rights leaders, as Black Power advocates entered the political arena, *means*, such as gaining community control of schools, often tended to become *ends*, and the original goal, in this case improved education for Black children, faded into the background. The deterioration of the community control experiment in Ocean Hill–Brownsville into a pitched political battle provides perhaps the best example of that phenomenon. In this struggle, the educational issues that inspired the attempted changes virtually disappeared from the debate as Black militants, community members, and the United Federation of Teachers fought over school governance (Ravitch, 1974).

Second, throughout this period neither mainstream civil rights nor Black Power organizations really questioned the basic structures of secondary education, particularly the differentiated curricula. Thus, efforts to replace White principals, teachers, or guidance counselors with Blacks in order to get fairer access to programs or better track placements for Black students addressed only a symptom rather than the source of educational problems in ghetto schools.

Third, school leaders easily could accommodate many of the curricular changes proposed by Black Power advocates, such as courses in Black history or literature, by simply approving these courses as appropriate for fulfilling graduation requirements. More important, some of the key educational ideas espoused by Black Power leaders were rooted in the same Progressive philosophy that had dominated educational thinking since the 1920s. While White educators might have questioned some of the new content being demanded, they were often in agreement with the basic premises that supported Black Power arguments. These premises included the beliefs that (1) the primary function of the schools is to meet the "needs" of young people; (2) the keys to meeting these "needs" are relevant courses and curriculum materials; (3) different students need different types of curricular materials and courses; (4) learning about oneself and one's local community is a prerequisite to learning about the wider world; and (5) promoting positive self-images and self-esteem is a central goal of education. Only the addition of subject matter designed to specifically strengthen *racial* identity and self-esteem distinguished these curricular reforms from ones rooted in Progressive philosophy. Rather than being revolutionary, Black Power advocates actually articulated ideas that were quite conventional, ideas that did not threaten the fundamental principles upon which modern secondary education had been built.

One particularly striking example of this latter trend can be found in Detroit in 1967. In June of that year, Rev. Albert Cleage, Jr., the most militant Black leader in the city, came before the Detroit board of education and called for a radically new curriculum in Black schools, a curriculum stressing positive self-images for Black children, relevant courses such as Black history and Black culture, and a new emphasis on the arts, dance, and creative writing. The report declared that "the curriculum for inner city schools must differ markedly from the curriculum of the outlying schools" (quoted in Angus & Mirel, 1993, p. 203). In a sense, Cleage simply put a new racial spin on an idea that had animated secondary education since early in the century, the idea that identical education does not further equal educational opportunity, but denies it (NEA, 1908). The hope that increasing numbers and percentages of Black students would take ever greater shares of academic courses was pushed aside, as it had been in the past, by demands that schools serve the "needs" of youth.

The Humanistic Education Movement

While the Black Power critique of American education drew some but by no means all of its educational ideas from Progressive philosophy and practices, the humanistic critique was a conscious reassertion of Progressive ideology. It differed from earlier versions of progressivism mainly in its apparent resolution of the two dominant but conflicting streams of Progressive thought, social reconstructionism and child-centeredness. The humanistic educators of the 1960s resurrected and sharpened the critique of public education first voiced by social reconstructionists of the 1930s by tearing away what they believed was the facade of neutrality and democratic idealism that obscured the real function of schools, namely, to serve the interests of the ruling elite. As Theodore Roszak, an intellectual leader of the counterculture, argued in 1969, "We call it 'education,' the 'life of the mind,' the 'pursuit of the truth.' But it is a matter of machine-tooling the young to the needs of our various baroque bureaucracies: corporate, governmental, military, trade union, educational" (p. 16). Furthermore, like the reconstructionist thinkers, many of the humanistic educators of the 1960s believed that a social revolution could begin in the schools. They parted company with the reconstructionists, however, in that they saw child-centered education (which George Counts had denounced in the 1932 speech that launched the reconstructionist critique) as the path to that revolution.

The revitalization of these ideas actually began in the late 1950s with the eloquent, often impassioned writings of Paul Goodman. In *Growing Up Absurd* (1960) and *Compulsory Mis-Education* (1966), Goodman joined such critics as David Riesman and William Whyte in condemning the stifling conformity and vapidity of American middle-class life. In these books and in a flood of essays, Goodman focused on how public education slowly but certainly destroyed the intellectual, emotional, and spiritual vitality of American adolescents. These works sounded what would become some of the major themes of the humanistic education movement, themes that seemed to promise a new, powerful assault on the status quo in secondary education. Like earlier critics, Goodman blasted the inanities of life-adjustment education, seeing it as the utter betrayal of progressive education. Moreover, Goodman (1960) also denounced James Conant's narrow vision of who should be well educated and the idea implicit in Conant's work that public schools "are, effectively, to be used as apprentice training grounds for the monopolies and armed forces" (p. 95). With growing urgency he called for education that would ennoble the human spirit, cultivate the mind, and encourage the development of morally courageous individuals.

As the 1960s wore on, Goodman (1966) argued that such educational reform had to begin by breaking the power of the professional educators, "school-monks: the administrators, professors, academic sociologists, and licensees with diplomas who have proliferated into an invested intellectual class" (p. 7). However, unlike Arthur Bestor, whose arguments these paralleled, Goodman rejected the idea that scholars in academic disciplines were better suited to guiding American education than the "school-monks." Indeed, Goodman saw scholars in those disciplines as deeply implicated in creating the technocratic society that he believed was devouring the soul of the nation. Moreover, given the prevailing situation in high schools, Goodman believed that a return to rigorous academic standards in high schools would result in an educational disaster since so many students were angry and alienated within the institution.

Rather, Goodman argued that compulsory schooling itself was the major source of America's educational problems, particularly in the post-World War II years when it appeared that the sole purpose of high schools was to "warehouse" reluctant adolescents. During that period he noted that "An important function of the schools began to be baby-sitting and policing" (1966, p. 145). The only re- form that he believed would improve the situation was a form of "deschooling" in which compulsory high school education was abolished and young people were freed to discover themselves and their life work through such activities as appren- ticeships. In short, Goodman advocated a more radical form of curricular differ- entiation than educationists had ever considered—a differentiated program in which schooling itself became an elective. While such ideas were never fully re- alized, they contributed to the spawning of alternative schools in the 1960s.

In making these appeals, Goodman believed that changes in education and society were possible, even imminent. He concluded the preface to *Growing Up Absurd* by declaring, "One has the persistent thought that if ten thousand people in all walks of life will stand up on their two feet and talk out and insist, we shall get our country back" (1960, p. xvi). By the mid-1960s, the civil rights move- ment, the growing youth counterculture, and the escalating protests against the Vietnam War impelled far more than 10,000 people to take to the streets to "get their country back." Transforming American education was a key goal for many of these protesters who saw the public schools as a bulwark of the oppressive "establishment" and a promoter of many of the nation's gravest ills, including racism, sexism, militarism, and the glorification of technocracy. As Herbert Kohl (1969) put it, "[F]or most American children there is essentially one public school system in the United States, and it is authoritarian and oppressive. Students every- where are deprived of the right to make choices concerning their own destinies" (p. 12). Yippie leader Jerry Rubin (1970) stated simply, "High school students are the largest oppressed minority in Amerika [*sic*]" (p. 214).

To a considerable extent, these negative ideas about public education, so widely discussed and so immensely popular in the late 1960s and early 1970s, were reactions to the excessive rhetoric and expectations of the previous decade. At the beginning of the War on Poverty, for example, Lyndon Johnson had claimed that "the answer for all our national problems comes down to a single word: edu- cation" (quoted in Bowles & Gintis, 1976, p. 19). Yet the enormous sums that flowed into Great Society educational programs and the public schools seemed to have little impact on the problem. Increasing numbers of Americans, particularly university professors, began to suspect that this focus on education diverted people's attention away from more pressing issues or even worse, strengthened the schools' real mission, which was to support capitalist domination of society and reproduce social inequality (Bowles & Gintis, 1976; Katz, 1971).

Similarly, the ideas put forward by Rickover and Conant in the late 1950s, that schools must play an integral part in what John Kennedy had called "our long, twilight struggle" with international Communism by training scientists, engineers, and patriotic citizens, became in the late 1960s damning indictments of the institution. As the bloody conflict in Vietnam escalated, protesters reinterpreted the relationship of public education to national defense by labeling schools as core components in the "military/industrial complex." The angry rhetoric of these critics reached a fevered pitch when Jonathan Kozol (1975) claimed the soldiers who participated in the horrendous massacre at My Lai owed their training less to the military and more to the public schools. "It is essential that we be precise," he wrote. "It is not the U.S. Army that transforms an innocent boy into non-comprehending automaton in six months. . . . Basic training does not begin in boot camp. It begins in kindergarten. It continues with a vengeance for the subsequent twelve years" (p. 54).

Such statements, augmented by the equally impassioned criticism of the schools by Black militants, had a profound impact on ideas and demands for educational change in the late 1960s and early 1970s. These ideas and demands, however, were not limited to mere changes in curriculum as were reform efforts in the past, but rather pointed to vast changes ranging from deschooling, to creating alternative "free schools," to adopting the philosophies and practices of the British "infant school," to creating "open schools" or "open classrooms" that allowed children the maximum amount of freedom to learn and discover. In all, these initiatives sought to utterly change the nature and structure of public education (Featherstone, 1971; Kozol, 1972; Ravitch, 1983).

The implications for high schools of this rhetorical firestorm were simple and straightforward. Reawakened, the progressive spirit immediately identified and attacked its old enemies—the traditional school, the traditional classroom, the traditional curriculum. In terms drawn virtually intact from the progressive lexicon, radical educators rejected teacher-centered classrooms, denounced lockstep educational processes, and vilified academic content areas. John Bremer, director of the Parkway Project, an alternative high school in Philadelphia, put the matter succinctly: "It is not possible to improve the high school; it has reached the end of its development" (quoted in Silberman, 1970, p. 349).

Long associated with the traditional, "authoritarian" high school, academic subjects came in for particularly sharp criticism in part because Progressives had targeted them so routinely in the past, but also because Cold Warriors had presented them as vital to national security during the great debate of the 1950s. Subjects such as mathematics, science, and foreign language were tainted by their association with the American "war machine." Given these attitudes, it was not surprising to find such humanistic critics as Neil Postman and Charles Weingarten

(1969) announcing their desire to "[d]issolve all 'subjects,' 'courses,' and 'especially course requirements,'" to compel "every teacher who thinks he knows his 'subject'" to write a book on it so "he will be relieved of the necessity of inflicting *his* knowledge on other people particularly his students," and to make every class an "elective" and pay teachers only if students attended their classes (pp. 138–139). Unlike the demands of earlier periods, the stakes were much higher. Amid the violence and upheaval of the late 1960s and early 1970s, many protesters and critics believed that changing the schools was the first step toward transforming the nation.

Gradually the protesters and critics developed a fairly consistent list of changes that they believed would utterly transform American secondary education. As summarized in 1971 by Ronald Gross, one of the leading popularizers of these efforts, the changes included the following:

1. Students, not teachers must be at the center of education.
2. Teaching and learning should start and stay with students' real concerns, rather than the artificial disciplines, bureaucratic requirements, or adults' rigid ideas about what children need to learn.
3. The paraphernalia of standard classroom practice should be abolished: mechanical order, silence, tests, grades, lesson plans, hierarchical supervision and administration, homework, and compulsory attendance.
4. Most existing textbooks should be thrown out. (p. 23)[1]

However, rather than being new and revolutionary, these ideas generally were warmed-over reassertions of fundamental progressive principles, albeit spiced with the belief that such changes could subvert the reigning racist, sexist, and militaristic establishment. Thus, as with the Black militant critique, educational leaders had little trouble accommodating most of these demands to their fundamental philosophy of education and then implementing them within the existing structure of American secondary education.

Nothing more clearly demonstrates how well educational leaders accommodated the humanistic demands than the response to Charles Silberman's bestselling book *Crisis in the Classroom* (1970). Like the Conant report of a decade earlier, Silberman's book was funded by the Carnegie Corporation and served as a vehicle for both voicing and absorbing criticism of the schools. Although Silberman did not give comprehensive high schools the same ringing endorsement, which, given the temper of the times, would have been impossible, he nonetheless performed exactly the same service for educationists—he gave them a way to respond to the vehement criticism of the high school that utilized and strengthened the basic structure of the institution. The key, once again, was curricular differentiation.

Beginning his book with what had become a routine castigation of American education, Silberman (1970) declared, "It is not possible to spend any prolonged period visiting public school classrooms without being appalled by the mutilation visible everywhere—mutilation of spontaneity, of joy in learning, of pleasure in creating, of sense of self" (p. 10). As impassioned as other humanistic critics about these conditions, Silberman pointed to a different villain. Rather than attributing these educational horrors to the demands of the military/industrial complex or the insidious designs of a racist, sexist society, Silberman argued that what ailed American education was "mindlessness . . . [the failure] to think seriously or deeply about the purposes or consequences of education" (pp. 10–11). In many ways, mindlessness was the perfect villain because throughout the book Silberman skillfully avoided identifying its source and thus could recommend reforms without attacking the people who would play a role in carrying them out. Indeed, unlike most other humanistic critics, Silberman pointedly did *not* single out school administrators and teachers as the cause of the nation's educational crisis. He thus ensured that *Crisis in the Classroom* would get a respectful hearing among educators.

This is not to say that Silberman pulled his punches. Secondary schools, he declared, "tend to be even more authoritarian and repressive than elementary schools; the values they transmit are values of docility, passivity, conformity, and lack of trust" (p. 324). Moreover, he argued that the high school program that most students found utterly irrelevant had strongly contributed to the mood of alienation and rebellion of American youth. Unlike deschoolers, however, Silberman was not prepared to scrap the high school altogether. He maintained that with major changes in the program and culture of the institution, the high school could be transformed from a source of alienation to a center for youthful self-discovery and educational growth.

Silberman envisioned high schools as places where young people's quest for identity and self-realization could be broadened and deepened through interaction with what Matthew Arnold termed "the best that has been thought and known in the world" (quoted in Silberman, 1970, p. 326). Yet in making that argument, Silberman specifically rejected the approach to that knowledge offered by Arthur Bestor, declaring that the academic regimen Bestor would have required was too simplistic. Silberman argued that forcing all high school students to take history, for example, still did not answer "the history of what? Taught how, with what emphases, and with what relation to other subjects or disciplines?" (p. 328). Silberman claimed that the same questions also could be asked of all disciplines, including mathematics and the sciences. Indeed, given what he believed was the state of flux in scholarly disciplines generally, Silberman argued that requiring all students to have a strong disciplinary background really gave no direction whatsoever to curriculum planners. "In short," he concluded, "there is, and can be, no one curriculum suitable for all time, or for all students at a given time" (p. 332).

How then could high schools teach "the best that has been thought and known" if they did not require all students to take a core set of courses that imparted the knowledge and skills of the great traditions? Although Silberman was not terribly clear on this point, it appears that he wanted high schools to organize their structure and curricula along Deweyan lines in which students were free to discover their identities and in the process draw on the great disciplinary traditions as they were appropriate to that search. Silberman declared that the high school "does this by helping students develop the knowledge and skills they need to make sense out of their experience—their experience with themselves, with others, with the world—not just during adolescence, but for the rest of their lives" (p. 336). To implement this process, Silberman argued that schools had to provide these young people with more freedom than previous generations of students had.

Unlike Conant, Silberman did not make a series of specific recommendations about how to reform the American high school, but *Crisis in the Classroom* clearly endorsed a number of changes in policy and practice that would significantly change the institution. These included such "[m]odest changes in school regulations" as the abolition of dress codes, "[s]omewhat bolder attempts to humanize schools as a whole—for example by cutting the number of required classes, leaving students with a third or more of their time unscheduled, to be used for independent study, taking more electives, for fulfilling some course requirements outside the classroom, or for relaxation and leisure," and lastly, "[r]adical experiments involving changes of the most fundamental sort—reordering the curriculum and indeed the entire teaching–learning process, and in some instances broadening the very concept of what constitutes a school" (p. 337).

Two things stand out from these recommendations. First, despite his insistence that high schools must "bring the young into contact with, and possession of their culture" (p. 334), Silberman's recommendation that students have greater freedom, choice, and unstructured time in high school hardly ensures that such a development would take place. Indeed, given the degree of youthful rebellion against the larger culture in the late 1960s and early 1970s and the often daunting prospect of mastering academic disciplines, it was more likely that students would have used their increased freedom to avoid contact and possession of their culture, unless one meant by *their* culture, sex, drugs, and rock 'n' roll. Second, telling educators that the way to transform and humanize high schools was by offering students more curricular choices and electives was preaching to the converted. As we have seen, the idea of improving high schools by expanding educational options for students had been part of the professional educational mantra since *Cardinal Principles*. The one dramatic change that Silberman introduced, using nonschool or out-of-school experiences for course credit, was an option that educators could easily accept since it directly related to the ever-present progressive attempt to link education to life itself.

Facing pressure from young people in upper-middle-class suburbs, the most powerful proponents of the youth counterculture, educators quickly adopted key aspects of Silberman's recommendations. Dress codes vanished almost overnight. Similarly, educational leaders increased the number and the range of course offerings, often by abolishing two-semester sequences of courses and allowing students to choose from a wide array of options to fulfill graduation requirements. By far the most dramatic changes came in the creation of schools-within-schools or alternative high schools designed to accommodate the demands of the most vocal parents and students for nontraditional education that could still meet the requirements for admission to prestigious colleges and universities. Like the showcase progressive schools of the 1920s, the media attention given to these humanistic alternatives was way out of proportion to the numbers of students enrolled. Indeed, only a tiny fraction of high school students ever participated in these experiments, and by the mid-1970s these alternative schools increasingly began to resemble mainstream high schools.

The Neo-Efficiency Movement

The neo-efficiency or accountability movement of the late 1960s and early 1970s had few charismatic leaders, utilized none of the hyperbole, and captured little of the media attention accorded to either the Black Power or humanistic critiques of the schools. Nevertheless, its effects on the schools and in particular on the high school curriculum were somewhat deeper than those of either of the two other movements. Part of the reason for this impact is that neo-efficiency reformers used the term "accountability" as a metaphor for what they sought, leaving the precise meaning of the term vague enough so it could act as an umbrella under which many ideas could be gathered. At the core of the neo-efficiency campaign was a "results-oriented, problem-solving, pragmatic perspective which is variously called technology, management, engineering" (Mecklenburger, 1972, p. 2). Fitting comfortably under the accountability umbrella was a conglomerate of old and new reform ideas: programmed instruction, individualized instruction, differentiated staffing, behavioral or performance objectives, competency-based instruction, teaching machines, instructional systems, computer-managed instruction, team teaching, behavioral modification, performance contracting, and career education. Ironically, like the Black Power and humanistic critiques of American education, many of these ideas also had their roots in Progressive Era reforms, but in the initiatives of individuals such as David Snedden and Jesse B. Davis, whom historians have described as "administrative progressives" or "social efficiency educators" (Kliebard, 1986; Tyack, 1974).

The strength of the accountability movement lay in its ability to rally support from multiple sources of discontent and in its capacity to gloss over differences between these different groups. Some of its main supporters, for example, were Black parents who were outraged over the apparent inability of professional educators to design and implement effective programs to narrow the achievement gap between Black and White children. Other supporters—suburban parents, business leaders, disgruntled taxpayers—were concerned about the rising costs of public education and the lack of a commensurate increase in student performance on standardized tests. These diverse groups supported such reforms as statewide testing programs to collect systematic evidence on student performance, to distinguish between effective and ineffective districts, schools, and teachers, and to relate performance to costs (Center for Statewide Educational Assessment, 1973).

While most of the accountability programs were aimed at students in the elementary or junior high school grades, probably the most widespread and influential of all these efforts focused on high school-aged youngsters, namely, career education. In many ways, career education was the most ambitious of all the accountability reforms. In a 1973 speech, Robert M. Worthington, U.S. Office of Education (USOE) Associate Commissioner for Adult, Vocational and Technical Education, claimed, "Career Education is a revolutionary approach to American education based on the idea that all educational experiences, curriculum, instruction, and counseling should be geared to preparing each individual for a life of economic independence, personal fulfillment, and an appreciation for the dignity of work. . . . It is directed at changing the whole educational system to benefit the entire population" (quoted in Bailey & Stadt, 1973, p. 270).

Career education was the centerpiece of President Nixon's Commissioner of Education Sydney P. Marland's term of office. Announcing the USOE's commitment to career education in a speech to the American Association of Secondary School Principals in January 1971, Marland claimed the program would enable the high schools to finally reach their two most important goals, preparation for college or preparation for what career educators called "the world of work." In his 1971 report to Congress, Marland declared, "We must eliminate anything in our curriculum which is unresponsive to either of these goals, particularly the high school anachronism called the 'general track,' a false compromise between the college preparatory curriculum and realistic career development" (quoted in Spring, 1976, p. 234).

Like other efforts to transform the high school, career education arose in response to a series of pressing national concerns, including the "stagflation" of the 1970s, that is, slow economic growth coupled with inflation, lack of growth in the nation's productivity, a substantial increase in the nation's foreign trade deficit, and rising unemployment among college graduates. These economic problems, taken together, were the first signal to the average citizen that the age of the "global economy" was upon us. The Nixon administration tried to respond to these economic problems by reorienting the population toward the virtues of hard work and by convincing young people to spend more time planning and preparing for their future in the labor market. The basic idea of career education was that education at all levels should be reoriented to focus on preparation for work (as we have noted, a similar vision animated the efforts of Jesse B. Davis almost 6 decades earlier). According to this idea, American education historically had taken preparation for citizenship to be the primary goal of public education, even if honored more in the breach. Supporters of career education, however, were committed to shifting work preparation to that primary position without actually dislodging any of the schools' other goals (see Hoyt, 1976). The movement had a strong coherence with other accountability efforts because it focused on the results or outcomes of the educational process and pointed to specific measures of success, such as the immediate employability of all high school graduates as a "performance objective" (Bailey & Stadt, 1973).

Although Marland promoted and popularized career education—indeed he devoted virtually all of his discretionary funds to it—the true voice of the movement was Kenneth Hoyt of the University of Maryland, who became the first Director of the Office of Career Education in 1974. More than anyone, Hoyt clarified and refined the concept of career education. At the same time, he held career education activities to a high standard of performance and was one of the movement's keenest critics (Hoyt, 1974, 1976, 1977). Prior to Hoyt's arrival, career education activities were largely limited to sponsoring conferences and "exemplary" projects whose purpose was to stimulate state and local career education initiatives. By the end of 1973, half the states had appropriated funds to support career education projects and five states had passed laws mandating its adoption in the schools (Herr, 1976). But with Hoyt's appointment the movement entered a new phase.

In 1974, Congress allocated $7 million for grants to encourage all states and local educational agencies to "carry out a program of career education," whose purpose was to ensure that "every child should, by the time he has completed secondary school, be prepared for gainful or maximum employment and for full participation in our society according to his or her ability" (U.S. Congress, 1974, n.p). During the next 2 years, career education boomed. Hoyt wrote that "the concept has swept the country," and that "never has a call for educational change been adopted so fast in so many places with so few Federal dollars. In this sense, career education has truly broken all records" (Hoyt, 1976, p. 1). However, one reason for that success was the USOE's strategy of "curriculum infusion," which made it difficult to know what, exactly, was being implemented. The idea behind curriculum "infusion" was that career education should not enter the curriculum in the form of new courses or subjects, but rather that *all* courses and subjects should be refocused on their career development aspects (Hoyt, 1977).

By the end of the 1976–77 school year, the mood in the USOE had shifted. Hoyt knew that it was time to move beyond demonstration projects and models, but this could not be done without major federal and/or state appropriations. These were not forthcoming. He wrote, "The day of reckoning for career education is fast approaching. . . . Like any other movement, career education will—and should—be judged more by its deeds than by its words. Good intentions are a poor substitute for effective action" (Hoyt, 1977, p. 6).

Furthermore, Hoyt knew that there was little hard evidence that career education was having the desired effect. In 1977, responding to unduly optimistic assessments of the decade's social programs generally and programs like career education specifically, Hoyt reported soberly that between 1964 and 1974, the nation had invested over $14 billion in "various kinds of manpower programs," with no appreciable declines in such areas as the high school dropout rate or the levels of youth unemployment. He added, "[I]f anything we have witnessed, in the occupational society, an increase in a variety of indicators of work alienation" (Hoyt, 1977, p. 1).

By the end of the decade, career education had run out of steam. Ironically, given the way it tried to avoid the label of vocational education, its chief legacy was the growth of regional vocational/technical high schools or skills centers, which often had the further ironic effect of reducing vocational programs in the comprehensive high schools. While Marland's successors endorsed the concept of career education, it was never as high a priority in later administrations. Congress did not substantially increase its support when the initial 3-year funding was reauthorized, and by 1982 career education money was folded into block grants.

From the beginning, career education, like the Black Power and humanistic movements, appeared to have the potential to radically reform the high school curriculum. But in fact, it failed to realize its revolutionary potential (Hoyt, 1976). Part of the explanation for this apparent failure lay in the fact that "infusion" was more feasible in the elementary school, with its essentially integrated curriculum, than in the highly departmentalized high school. Moreover, career education never could quite shake allegations that it was just a ploy to expand vocational education, allegations that gained credence after many of the movement's promoters claimed that their program was going to end once and for all the college preparatory emphasis of the high schools. Despite the fact that some of the movement's more thoughtful advocates saw career education as a means for improving basic academic skills, it eventually became just another voice in the chorus demanding a reduction in what remained of the academic emphasis in American secondary education (see, for example, Bailey & Stadt, 1973; Lederer, 1976). Over the years, the most trenchant critics of the movement saw it as at best a new approach to vocational education and at worst a subterfuge for limiting the occupational and social mobility of minority youth (Grubb & Lazerson, 1982; Herr, 1976).

Although many of the initiatives pursued by advocates of neo-efficiency were unlike and even contradictory to those sought by the Black Power and humanistic critics, in several important ways, all three efforts shared a common outlook. Like supporters of the other two movements, supporters of neo-efficiency believed that their efforts would utterly transform American education by restoring power to disenfranchised groups, in this case, concerned citizens and taxpayers worried about accountability. Moreover, advocates of career education strongly believed that their movement would reduce youthful alienation by guiding young people toward satisfying and productive adult careers. But perhaps most important, none of the leaders of these movements challenged the underlying principle of the comprehensive high school, curricular differentiation. Thus, it mattered little whether Black militants demanded more attention to Black history or literature, or suburban hippies demanded courses on ecology or Zen Buddhism, or career educators sought to infuse their concerns into all subject areas; educational leaders could easily respond in time-honored fashion, adding alternative programs or adapting curricula. This is not to say that high schools were not sorely challenged during these years, but rather that these challenges revealed the remarkable resiliency of the institution.

The Educators Respond

One of the best examples of that resiliency can be found in the report of the National Commission on the Reform of Secondary Education. Established in the early 1970s by the Charles F. Kettering Foundation, the commission included leaders of the American Association of School Administrators, the National Association of Secondary School Principals, and the North Central Association; the president of Smith College; the dean of the College of Education of the University of South Carolina; the state superintendent of Michigan; and two high school students. The commission members saw their mission as akin to that of the 1918 Commission for the Reorganization of Secondary Education (CRSE) in seeking to reconceptualize secondary education in response to rapidly changing social, economic, and cultural realities (National Commission on the Reform of Secondary Education, 1973).

Like the more widely publicized critiques of education discussed earlier, the report began with a sense of crisis, noting that the "American comprehensive high school today must be viewed as an establishment striving to meet the complex demands of a society in the throes of social change, at a time when the school system has become too large as an institution and is literally overrun with a mix of young people from inconsistent social backgrounds" (p. 10). Echoing Silberman, the commission argued that many of the problems facing the high school were rooted in its lack of clarity regarding its mission and goals, a situation strongly related to the numerous efforts by political leaders to use the schools for such campaigns as "advanc[ing] achievement in science and mathematics" after the Sputnik crisis, "eliminat[ing] poverty and racial discrimination" (p. 34) during the War on Poverty, or pursuing other policy initiatives as the mood of the country shifted. Expressing full support for the comprehensive high school, the commission offered a new set of goals for secondary education and a series of recommendations for realizing those goals.

Compared with the CRSE's *Cardinal Principles*, which the commission explicitly cited as its point of departure, the new goals appeared to be far more concerned with academic content than was the earlier document. While *Cardinal Principles* had only one vague reference to academic knowledge ("command of fundamental processes"), the first section of the new goals listed seven "Content Goals" such as "Achievement of Communication Skills," "Achievement of Computation Skills," and "Attainment of Proficiency in Critical and Objective Thinking" (pp. 32–33). Unfortunately, when these goals were defined more carefully, the desired achievement levels proved to be minimal at best. Adequate communication skills, for example, were "reading and writing to a level of functional literacy" and computational skills were those "sufficient for the management of household responsibilities" (p. 33). These Content Goals were balanced by a series of "Process Goals" that seemed to be a marriage of the life-adjustment and counterculture themes. These included "Knowledge of Self," "Appreciation of Others," "Ability to Adjust to Change," and "Clarification of Values" (pp. 33–34).

While these goals *were* an improvement on *Cardinal Principles*, the curricular recommendations that the commission offered as ways of implementing them rested on the basic assumptions embodied in the 1918 manifesto, namely, that the best education possible consisted of meeting the needs of diverse students through an ever-expanding and differentiated curriculum. Indeed, the recommendations were a laundry list of curricular reforms that represented as many suggestions for change from as many different sources as the high school could possibly bear. Some of these recommendations were thoughtful and long overdue, such as removing textbooks that contained negative stereotypes of minorities and women. But others, generally in response to demands of the humanistic critics, were simply trendy. For example, the commission called for easing compulsory attendance laws (to make high schools less custodial); providing "alternative paths to high school completion" so students could design individualized programs of study; giving academic credit for life experiences; allowing for alternative schedules for students and teachers to work together in the evening, on weekends, and over holidays; eliminating class ranks for all high school students; and ending the requirement that students be in good academic standing in order to participate in extracurricular activities. To meet the calls for change from the proponents of neo-efficiency reforms, the commission urged schools to implement career education and integrate "career awareness" throughout the curriculum, expand career opportunities for students, and provide job placement services for students. In short, the commission recommended that high schools become even more expansive in their curricular offerings and options.

Given the enormous attention high schools received in this era, the depth of passion about the various reform proposals, and the determination of political and educational leaders to use schools to solve major social problems, we would expect that the 1960s and early 1970s were a period of substantial change in the curriculum and coursetaking in the nation's high schools. We now turn to our analysis of data on Grand Rapids, Detroit, Michigan, and the nation in order to assess what impact these movements and reform efforts had on coursetaking in the nation's high schools and on the educational experiences of students.

TURBULENCE AND STABILITY IN GRAND RAPIDS

Grand Rapids serves as an excellent illustration of the capacity of progressive school systems to adapt to waves of critical attacks while avoiding fundamental change. Grand Rapids in this period was not among the national leaders as it had been in an earlier era, but it experienced all the reform pressures described above, and it eagerly embraced several of the "innovations" that were prompted by these reforms. For example, the percentage of African American students in the district rose sharply from about 6% in 1950 to 22% in 1970. Recognizing that these students were concentrated in schools with the lowest achievement levels in the city, school officials initiated compensatory programs well before federal funds became available. In addition, the school board appointed a Citizens Committee to investigate racial imbalance in the schools and to recommend changes, which were implemented. Consequently, in the early 1970s, when African American parents charged the board in Federal District Court with deliberate and unlawful segregation, Judge Albert J. Engel ruled that the district was *not* guilty of the charges; this decision was later upheld by the Court of Appeals. The basis for the ruling was the numerous steps the district had taken to respond to the special problems of Black students.

Another example was the establishment in 1970 of an educational park, partly in response to heightening racial conflict but also in response to charges by some students, parents, and younger teachers that the school system was too bureaucratic and impersonal, echoing the humanistic critics. Grand Rapids' educational park, however, did not take the form of a large central "campus," served only secondary students, did not preempt the district's commitment to neighborhood schools, and had no effect on racial balance. It was essentially a curricular arrangement in which certain classes not available in the regular curriculum of the comprehensive high schools were offered in specified high schools or the junior college, with transportation provided by the district. It created a way to greatly expand curriculum offerings and to satisfy demands for such courses as Russian, Swahili, parapsychology, and ballet without making major alterations to the regular high schools.

The neo-efficiency movement was given its due as well. When the U.S. Office of Economic Opportunity funded a major study of performance contracting in 1971–72, Grand Rapids was one of 18 sites selected nationwide (Comptroller General of the United States, 1973). Long after the experiment had been labeled a failure by most observers, Grand Rapids continued to operate a number of private firm contracts, believing that disadvantaged children progressed further under the contracted services than they would have without the extra help (Webster, 1973). Grand Rapids was equally responsive to the career education movement, backing the establishment of the regional Kent Intermediate Skills Center in 1972 and opening a second center, the College Avenue Skills Center, in 1975.

All these "innovations" had one thing in common: They promoted the expansion of the high school curriculum and provided ways to further differentiate the student body. They were therefore fully in accord with the basic philosophy of secondary education that the district had adopted so vigorously by 1910. In fact, only for a brief period was there any flagging of the commitment to expansive secondary schools. Between 1940 and 1950, Davis Technical and Vocational High School was closed and the total number of different courses offered in the high schools declined from 87 to 57. By 1960, this number had risen back to 76; with the establishment of the educational park, it rose to 139 courses. With the addition of the skills centers, the number of different courses rose to 172 (see Appendix B, Table B.11).

In 1971, 38 courses not available in the comprehensive high schools were offered in the educational park, and of these, 27 had never been offered previously. The offerings at the skills centers added another 20. By 1975, the educational park courses numbered 63 and the skills centers' courses numbered 30. In the academic subject fields, English courses included creative writing, children's literature, and writing to publish; new science courses included astronomy, aviation, natural resources, field biology, and ecology; the educational park offered calculus and computer math; advanced levels of certain foreign languages were offered when demand at any one of the comprehensive high schools was too low to justify the offering. But the most vigorous field for curriculum experimentation was social studies. Eleven courses not otherwise available were offered, including several that reflected the influence of the counterculture and the humanistic critique of the schools. These courses were death and dying, world religions, anthropology, American Indians, exploring behavior, exploring childhood, philosophy, humanities, urban studies, women's studies, and man, mysticism, and magic. The skills centers offered occupational preparation in a wide range of fields, including advertising, air conditioning, food service, industrial mechanics, institutional housekeeping, residential construction, retailing, upholstering, and welding. The educational park also offered vocational training opportunities such as automotive repair, electronics, welding, graphics, child care, and cosmetology, and such other personal development courses as modern dance, jewelry, weight training, gymnastics, musical form and analysis, guitar, and voice.

While this amazing array of course offerings illustrates the district's response to reform pressures, the relative stability of subject field enrollments illustrates the other side of the coin. During the decade of the 1940s, the period of course reduction, the academic share of course enrollments rose dramatically from 50 to 60%. It rose another four percentage points during the period of life-adjustment education and Sputnik, but it remained stable through the remainder of the 1960s and 1970s. Partly, this was because the educational park course offerings covered all the subject fields, but even more, it was because most of these courses were offered in one or two sections and total enrollments were low. In 1971, for example, the 48 educational park courses drew only 2,002 student registrations, compared with a total of 34,705 registrations for the high schools as a whole. Skills center course registrations were smaller still, numbering only 365 in 1975, compared with 1,378 educational park registrations and total registrations exceeding 30,000. In these turbulent times, the vast majority of students stayed in their "home" high schools, following much the same curriculum regimens that their parents and grandparents had followed (see Appendix B, Table B.12).

Throughout this entire period, graduation requirements were kept low. In 1964, they were just what they had been in 1950—3 years of English, 3.5 years of social studies (specifically, 1 year each of civics, world history, and American history, and a half-year of government), 1 year each of mathematics and science, and 2 years of physical education. The total "units" required for graduation were 160 (10 equaling one course for 1 year), of which about 60 were electives. Students also were required to accumulate two majors and two minors; a major consisted of 3 years of courses in the same subject field, and a minor of 2 years. By 1975, the requirements had been made slightly easier by dropping the world history requirement (see Appendix B, Table B.3).

In the case of mathematics, the 1-year requirement could be met with any form of math offered in ninth grade, such as general math, business arithmetic, or shop math. A *minor* in mathematics could consist of 1 year of business arithmetic and 1 year of bookkeeping. Many students, more than half, took ninth-grade mathematics as their one and only exposure to secondary mathematics. Enrollments in more advanced mathematics courses in 1957, 1960, and 1964 ranged from 12 to 20% of the students in the grades in which they were offered. The sciences fared a bit better. Many students, two-thirds to three-quarters, completed a science minor by combining ninth-grade general science with tenth-grade biology or with twelfth-grade physiology. Enrollments in chemistry dropped off to less than half of those in the eleventh grade, and in physics to less than a quarter of those in the twelfth. Furthermore, enrollments in both these fields declined between 1957 and 1964, in chemistry from 42 to 30% and in physics from 23 to 14%. The only science to gain in popularity was twelfth-grade physiology, rising from an 11% share of twelfth graders in 1957 to a 38% share in 1964. By 1971, physics enrollments had fallen so low that it was offered only as an educational park course and was not available as a regular course in the comprehensive high schools.

Yet, small signs of change were in the wind. In 1972, for example, the board of education adopted a new "philosophy of education" whose top three priorities were getting students to "acquire the basic skills," "apply rational intellectual processes to the identification, consideration, and solution of problems," and "develop a comprehension of a changing body of knowledge of the various disciplines" (Bureau of Accreditation and School Improvement Studies Archives). Other objectives included learning good health and safety habits, acquiring a marketable skill, and becoming a citizen who has a sense of self-respect. That same year administrators at Creston High School issued a set of "objectives" for the school that placed "upgrading of the academic climate [of] our school" as the most important goal for the upcoming school year. To do this, "academic subjects indicated by student and parental requests are being brought back into the base school" (e.g., physics and advanced placement English). Also cited were improvements in the English program, "through re-organization by semester, with emphasis placed on the mechanics of English at all levels and yet provid[ing] built in meaningful electives for students" (Bureau of Accreditation and School Improvement Studies Archives).

Grand Rapids, in the third quarter of the century, experienced and responded to all of the significant social and political developments of the era by making small, marginal changes in structure and curriculum, leaving the "center" intact. It maintained extremely low graduation requirements; it established an educational park and two skills centers to offer a host of special courses that appealed to small numbers of discontented students, teachers, and parents; and it maintained a relatively undemanding but conventional curriculum in the comprehensive high schools. In contrast to Detroit, African American enrollment share never exceeded one-quarter and there was never a demand to develop a distinctively African American curriculum.

RACE AND CURRICULUM IN DETROIT

While Detroit experienced all the major educational debates and developments of the 1950s, by the mid-1960s only one issue dominated its educational politics, race (Mirel, 1993). Yet, despite a huge racial shift in its population and considerable racial conflict and protest over educational policy, there was surprisingly little change in curriculum offerings or student coursetaking. Indeed, the period from 1950 to 1975 was, with respect to course offerings and registrations, a period characterized mostly by continuity and stability.

The degree to which the high school curriculum in Detroit withstood all assaults can best be seen by looking, first, at how educational leaders addressed the demands of the city's Black community for equal education, and second, at how Black leaders themselves came to define equal education. During the late 1960s and early 1970s, Detroit played a pivotal role in the nation's debates about race and education with its involvement in the *Milliken v. Bradley* desegregation suit and its experiment with decentralized school governance (Mirel, 1993; Wolf, 1981). In addition, the pattern of actions taken by both school leaders and community leaders with regard to curricular issues and the consequences of those actions paralleled developments across the nation.

Black Detroiters had been protesting the poor quality of secondary educa-tion in their community since the 1930s. By the late 1950s, during the national debate about secondary education, Black Detroiters redoubled their efforts. In 1958, for example, Remus Robinson, the first Black member of the Detroit school board, decried the fact that courses in predominantly Black high schools "were 'watered down' so that students were hampered in college or failed to measure up to college entrance requirements" (*Michigan Chronicle*, 3/12/58). Groups of Black parents also denounced the poor quality of education in their children's schools, particularly the lack of college preparatory courses and the failure of teachers to encourage students to meet high standards. Despite sympathetic words from the superintendent, virtually nothing was done to address these demands. A typical response to these protests came from a school administrator who declared that "better students" *were* getting more rigorous courses but the "mediocre students," who he claimed were the vast majority in this case, were getting what school per-sonnel deemed best for them (Angus & Mirel, 1993, p. 199; see also *Michigan Chronicle*, 4/12/58).

The fact that policies of curricular differentiation had a particularly negative impact on poor and African American students was amply demonstrated several years later in Patricia Cayo Sexton's 1961 study of Detroit's public schools. Using data from 1957, Sexton found that more than one-third of Detroit's stu-dents were in the decidedly unchallenging general track and that most of these students were from "lower-income" schools. Since Blacks accounted for perhaps 45% of Detroit students in 1957 and constituted the largest segment of poor chil-dren in the district, probably far more than a third of Black children were in the general track of the Detroit high schools (Sexton, 1961).

This pattern continued into the mid-1960s. In 1964, the Detroit Urban League found that the predominantly Black high schools had "larger numbers of students enrolled in the 'general' courses than in college preparatory or trade-oriented curriculum." Even in Mumford High School, probably the most academically oriented integrated school in the city in 1967, 22% of Black students were in the general track compared with only 2% of Whites (Angus & Mirel, 1993).

In April 1966, a massive walkout by the students from Northern High School dramatically focused the attention of the city on these issues. While the decline in academic quality was emblematic of problems in all the Black high schools in the city, they were particularly poignant at Northern, which was "THE outstanding high school in Detroit in the 1920s, 1930s, and 1940s." As the racial composition of the school changed in the postwar years, Northern became "primarily a custodial institution . . . and was only on the surface an institution where systematic learn-ing took place" (Gregory, 1967, p. 29).

The catalyst for the walkout was the decision by the school principal to ban an editorial in the school newspaper that denounced "inferior education" at Northern. The editorial decried the lack of adequate college preparatory courses at the school, the low academic standards, and the policy of social promotion, and it compared Northern unfavorably with a predominantly White school in the northwest section of the city. While it is doubtful that the editorial writer had more than anecdotal evidence for his comparison with the White high school, Table 5.1 supports his contention, showing clearly a relationship between a school's racial composition and the level of its "mathematics" offerings.

The suppression of the editorial quickly escalated into a school boycott to protest the principal's leadership. Initially, community leaders greeted the protest with amazement and approval. As one observer put it, "Did you ever hear 1,000 kids cheering at the idea of a good algebra class? They did" (Angus & Mirel, 1993, p. 201). Despite such initial enthusiasm and support for the walkout, over the next few weeks the focus of the controversy shifted from concerns about raising educational standards to demands that the White principal be replaced with an African American. In that sense, it foreshadowed what would be the pattern of educational politics in the city for the next decade, as personnel issues—often with

Table 5.1. Percentage Distribution of Enrollment in Mathematics Courses by Level of Course and Racial Composition of High School, Selected Detroit High Schools, 1946–47 and 1966–67

School	African American Percentage of Student Body	Mathematics Level		
		Honors	Regular	Remedial and General
1946–47				
Northern	69.3	0.0	60.0	40.0
Northwestern	42.0	0.0	75.0	25.0
Pershing	8.8	2.7	83.8	13.5
Chadsey	4.2	10.5	80.2	9.3
Southeastern	1.1	0.0	94.8	5.2
Mackenzie	0.0	5.7	88.9	5.4
Denby	0.0	0.0	96.6	3.4
1966–67				
Northern	98.6	0.0	48.6	51.4
Northwestern	99.6	2.2	77.5	20.4
Pershing	47.6	6.8	85.7	7.5
Chadsey	51.5	3.6	65.1	31.3
Southeastern	79.4	2.7	68.0	29.4
Mackenzie	56.4	1.7	69.2	29.1
Denby	2.9	6.3	75.1	18.6

Sources: Detroit Commission on Community Relations Papers; Bureau of Accreditation and School Improvement Studies, folders for Detroit public high schools.

strong racial overtones—dominated discussions of education while debates about improving educational standards or increasing academic coursetaking virtually disappeared. When curriculum issues did become part of the debate, they invariably focused on efforts to introduce what later would be called "Afrocentric education," such as Rev. Albert Cleage's initiative that we noted earlier (Angus & Mirel, 1993).

Nothing demonstrates better the disappearance of concerns about improving academic standards than the 1968 report of the High School Study Commission. Created in the aftermath of the Northern High School boycott to investigate the problems of secondary education in the city, the commission noted problems of track placement, social promotion, and the generally low level of academic achievement by Black students, but ultimately determined that greater community involvement and decentralization were the best approaches to improving the system. Indeed, the report never addressed directly such issues as ending social promotion or eliminating the general track (Detroit High School Study Commission, 1968).[2]

What do the data we have been able to collect on student coursetaking in Detroit tell us about the effects of the Black struggle for better schools? Before addressing that question, it must be noted that, due to a variety of factors, such as White flight and a high Black dropout rate between 1950 to 1975, high school enrollment in the city did not parallel that in the nation. Detroit high school enrollments, grades 10–12, rose from 42,000 in 1950 to a peak of 56,000 in 1963, but then declined throughout the period of rising racial militancy to 47,500 by 1973. Over this period, African Americans became the majority of students in the Detroit public schools, with the Black enrollment share rising from 17% in 1946 to 50% in 1963 and reaching 75% by 1975 (Mirel, 1993).

With those enrollment trends in mind, we can turn to the coursetaking data to assess how students responded to the changes and turmoil that engulfed the Detroit schools between 1950 and 1975. Appendix C, Table C.2, suggests that at the broadest level of analysis there was virtually no change in the relative importance of various subjects in the curricular experience of Detroit high schoolers across the whole era. The trends that characterized Detroit high schools in the 1930s and 1940s—the dramatic decline in study of foreign languages and mathematics and the increase in social studies, vocational subjects, and other nonacademic offerings—ended by the early 1950s and despite the racial turmoil of the postwar decades, changed little thereafter. In light of these data, the life-adjustment movement appears to have legitimated changes that had already taken place a decade earlier, solidifying these changes and making them relatively impervious to the attacks that would occur in the 1950s and 1960s.

On first glance, the data on the distribution of subject field enrollments in Detroit high schools present a picture of slightly increasing emphasis on academic subjects.[3] However, as in Grand Rapids, there may be less here than meets the eye. In both cases, changes in course offerings and enrollments *within* subject families prove to be more important and revealing than shifts between subject families. In Detroit, as in other cities, the values of educational leaders in regard to the curriculum were most clearly expressed in the requirements for graduation and in the courses offered. The values of students and/or their parents were expressed in the choices they made within these larger constraints, and these are revealed at least partly by the kinds of course enrollment data we have been analyzing. Given this, it is surprising how little Detroit's graduation requirements changed between the early 1950s and the middle 1970s, and how weak they were. As shown in Appendix C, Table C.3, there were only two changes, an increase in English from 3 years to 4, and the specification in 1957 that the one year required in science be in physical science, biology, chemistry, or physics. Even these modest changes were largely without effect because the vast majority of students took 4 years of English anyway and the high schools continued to offer general biology and general chemistry, nonlaboratory versions of these subjects for the noncollege-bound.[4] Moreover, most students took 2 years of math and/or science instead of the required 1 year in order to meet another graduation requirement. In the case of math, this extra year could be taken in business math or shop math, a point that we will elaborate later.

Overall, little changed between 1956 and 1961 except for a slight shift from English and social studies toward foreign language and science. The 2.2% increase in the science share between 1956 and 1961 resulted from additional sections of nonlab biology and chemistry. The Sputnik scare does seem to have resulted in at least a small increase in the taking of science classes by the noncollege-bound. In 1966, the distribution was much the same.

In 1966 and 1967, the school board began to hear angry but disparate demands by African American leaders. On the one hand, the leaders of the Northern High School boycott called for a stronger academic curriculum with more emphasis on college preparatory courses. On the other hand, leaders of the Black Power movement called for a distinctly African American curriculum for predominantly Black schools. What do the data show? First, there was a significant increase in the academic share of coursetaking between 1966 and 1975, from 58 to 62%. English remained the same, foreign language and science declined slightly, social studies increased, and mathematics showed a big increase. At face value, this would seem to support the notion that the Northern boycott had some effect. But a closer look at curriculum changes during the period casts that claim into doubt.

Focusing on curriculum changes *within* subject fields, the theme was modest expansion in all fields except English, where curriculum *explosion* would be a better descriptor. In the English departments, most offerings in 1966 were simply labeled "English," although it is clear that the various sections of English were ability tracked, with several different systems of designation in use at different high schools.[5] Speech, journalism, debate, and drama also were offered, although enrollments were very small. A few high schools offered creative writing, great books, and humanities, also with extremely small enrollments. By 1975, the big change was in the development of a long list of new literature courses, such as courses in the short story, mystery story, science fiction, American literature, women in literature, film literature, Bible literature, poetry, mythology, and Afro-American or Black literature. Consistent with national trends, most of these were semester-long rather than year-long courses, and were offered largely to eleventh- and twelfth-grade students. Speech courses expanded to include radio/TV speech, mass communications, mass media, and broadcasting. For those needing remediation, a single course in reading improvement in 1966 was joined by basic skills, grammar and usage, developmental reading, extending skills, and introduction to literature. Yet, in the face of this massive expansion of titles the English share of total enrollments remained the same precisely because the vast majority of students had been taking English every semester anyway. The effects of this course expansion on the amount and quality of learning in the language arts are open to question, but it is clear that the change played no role in shifting the overall pattern of coursetaking.

In the other academic fields, developments were more modest. In mathematics in 1966, all schools offered general math, algebra, geometry, advanced algebra, and refresher math, as well as business arithmetic and shop mathematics, which could be taken to fulfill the 1-year graduation requirement. A few schools offered math improvement and/or senior math, while only one offered precalculus. By 1975, the curriculum expanded slightly on both ends of the difficulty spectrum, with prealgebra and precalculus offered by all schools. Only one high school offered calculus and only three offered some form of computer math. Behind this modest expansion in offerings was another, far more significant change, one that explains the apparent increase in math enrollments and indeed accounts for most of the increase in the academic share generally.

In 1966, enrollments in business arithmetic and/or business math, courses overwhelmingly offered in commercial departments, had a combined enrollment of 4,895, representing 16.3% of all commercial enrollments (see Table 5.2).[6] Shop math, taught by industrial arts teachers, had a combined enrollment of 1,648, or 16.2% of industrial arts enrollments. Since individual high schools varied widely in the ratio of business math enrollments to total commercial enrollments, and even more in the ratios of shop math to industrial arts, we conclude that these courses were not merely providing appropriate mathematics for commercial or vocational majors but were also providing some students with an easy way to meet the district's 1-year mathematics graduation requirement.[7] However, by 1975, combined enrollments in these two forms of mathematics fell to 3,331, while enrollments in the new prealgebra classes amounted to slightly over 4,000. Total enrollments in all forms of mathematics together remained virtually unchanged. In other words,

Table 5.2. Percentage Distribution of Enrollment in Mathematics Courses in High Schools Grouped by Racial Composition of School, Detroit, 1966–67 and 1975–76

	Business Arithmetic	Shop Math	Below Algebra	Alg./Geom. & Above	Refresher Math
1966–67					
Five Black high schools[a]	22.1	6.9	22.7	44.0	4.4
Four White high schools[b]	16.0	5.8	4.7	67.8	5.8
Four swing high schools[c]	22.8	7.6	11.6	52.3	5.6
Southwestern High School[d]	29.3	4.5	10.3	42.1	13.8
All high schools	22.2	7.5	9.8	54.8	5.6
1975–76					
Five Black high schools	8.4	1.6	43.5	40.8	5.8
Four White high schools	12.6	4.4	14.7	62.7	5.5
Four swing high schools	15.4	3.9	23.7	52.3	4.8
Southwestern High School	0.0	1.2	27.2	67.2	4.4
All high schools	11.3	2.9	22.4	57.7	5.6

[a]Central, Eastern (King), Northeastern, Northwestern, Southeastern, all nearly 100% African American in both years.

[b]Denby, Ford, Redford, Osburn, all less than 5% African American in 1966–67 and less than 25% African American in 1975–76.

[c]Cooley, Mackenzie, Mumford, Pershing, all less than 60% African American in 1966–67 and more than 60% in 1975–76.

[d]Southwestern was the only high school with a lower percentage of African Americans in 1975–76 than in 1966–67.

what appeared to be a large increase in mathematics enrollments was in fact a policy change to encourage students to take prealgebra to meet the 1-year math requirement rather than business or shop math.

Science changed less than mathematics. The pattern of offering biology and chemistry in both laboratory and nonlaboratory versions continued. Other science courses included physics, physical science, earth science, physiology (offered in a few schools), and small numbers of unique courses such as those developed by the National Science Foundation. At the same time, the number of sections offered in physics declined sharply from about three sections per high school to one. Foreign language enrollments continued to be largest in Spanish and French, offered by all schools, while some schools continued to offer Latin and/or German, and one or two offered Italian or Russian.

In social studies, several important changes occurred: World history was restored as a graduation requirement, to be taken in ninth grade; civics was replaced by a 1-semester course in government; and such electives as psychology, Afro-American (or Black) history, and ethnic studies joined world geography, economics, sociology, and contemporary affairs. As the percentage of African American students in the system continued to grow throughout the 1960s and 1970s, the demand for a distinctively African American curriculum appears to have had some effect. In 1966, seven of the 17 comprehensive high schools offered a few sections of "Negro history" with a combined enrollment of 611, and one offered a section of "Negro literature" with 26 students enrolled. By 1975, all the high schools but two offered Afro-American history and all but four offered Afro-American literature. The enrollments were 2,009 and 1,085, respectively, substantial increases to be sure but still a very small share of total coursetaking. Afro-American history represented less than 6% of social studies enrollments, and Afro-American literature represented less than 3% of English enrollments. Of course, a more distinctively African American focus may have been infused into standard U.S. history or American literature courses, a development stimulated not only by the temper of the times but also by the increasing share of African American teachers and administrators in Detroit during this period (Mirel, 1993).

Given the dominance of the issue of race in Detroit during the 1960s and 1970s, it is important to explore how the distributions of coursetaking differed among high schools with different racial compositions. Five of Detroit's high schools had virtually a 100% African American student body in 1966 and continued to have the same in 1975. Four of its high schools were predominantly White in 1966, with less than 10% non-White students. Three of these continued to have less than 10% in 1975, while one of them had less than 25%. A third group of four high schools had from 40 to 60% African Americans in 1966 and increased these percentages to 60 to 90% over the next 9 years. We will refer to these groupings of schools as Black high schools, White high schools, and swing high schools (see Table 5.3).

When we compared these groupings of schools on variations in average subject field distributions, we found, with one exception, that the differences were exceedingly small. For example, many authors have suggested that African American students were tracked into vocational programs while White students were encouraged to take college prep classes. As we noted earlier, during the 1940s and 1950s, Black students were placed in the dead-end general track rather than the more promising vocational tracks (see Angus & Mirel, 1993). However, by 1966, that situation had changed somewhat, with the combined vocational share of coursetaking in the Black schools averaging 2.2 percentage points higher (24.7%) than the White schools (22.5%). By 1975, the situation had reversed once again, with the Black high schools and the swing high schools showing a lower vocational share (18 and 19% respectively) than the White schools (21.4%).

Similarly, in the average share represented by the academic fields combined, the Black high schools (at 55.7%) averaged 4.5 points lower than the White schools

Table 5.3. Percentage of Course Enrollment in Selected Subjects in High Schools Grouped by Racial Composition of School, Detroit, 1966–67 and 1975–76

	1966–67			1975–76		
	5 Black	4 White	4 Swing	5 Black	4 White	4 Swing
Foreign language	3.3	5.2	5.0	3.7	4.1	3.5
Science	11.9	10.4	11.4	10.3	9.3	10.0
Commercial	16.2	13.7	15.2	8.6	12.4	10.7
Industrial arts	4.1	5.6	5.7	5.2	5.0	4.4
Home economics	4.4	3.2	3.0	4.2	4.0	3.9
Health & phys. ed.	12.6	12.7	12.3	15.0	12.0	12.8
Total academic	55.7	60.2	57.7	62.1	59.9	63.0
Total vocational	24.7	22.5	23.9	18.0	21.4	19.0

Note: High school groupings are the same as in Table 5.2.

(60.2%). However, by 1975 this situation was reversed, with the Black schools increasing their academic share to an average of 62.1%, while the White schools remained about the same at 59.9%. The changes in both the academic and vocational shares are best explained by what happened in the commercial field. The most dramatic shift we encountered was the sharp drop in the commercial share average for the Black schools, from 16.2% in 1966 to 8.6% in 1975. This relates directly to the change in enrollments in business arithmetic discussed above and can best be seen in how mathematics coursetaking was distributed at the two time periods. Table 5.2 summarizes these differences from the viewpoint of the racial composition of high schools.

Table 5.2 makes clear that the use of business arithmetic or shop math to meet the district's 1-year mathematics graduation requirement was more prominent at high schools with large numbers of Black students. While all high schools reduced or eliminated this practice within the next 9 years, the shift from business arithmetic to prealgebra was most dramatic in the Black high schools. It is also clear that although the share of mathematics enrollments represented by algebra, geometry, advanced algebra, precalculus, and senior math remained relatively stable between these two points in time, the share for the Black high schools was consistently and significantly lower. Providing further evidence that mathematics course enrollments were a function of race is the fact that Southwestern High School, the only high school to have fewer Black students in 1966 than in 1975, all but eliminated business and shop math while increasing college preparatory math enrollments from 42.1% to over two-thirds.

In all, during the period from 1950 to 1975, Detroit maintained relatively weak graduation requirements, participated in the national trend of course proliferation in English and social studies during the 1960s and early 1970s, continued to offer a "split level" education in science, and struggled to find forms of mathematics in which students poorly prepared at lower levels could succeed for at least 1 year. Despite all of these apparent changes, the coursetaking data mostly demonstrate a relatively stable pattern across the period. This was in the face of sharply rising African American enrollments and a growing Black militancy from the mid-1960s on. Had we information on changes in course *content* over this same period, more radical change might be evidenced, but probably only in English and social studies. Given the massive social changes that engulfed the city and its schools during these years, the most remarkable feature about high school education in Detroit was its stability.

COURSETAKING TRENDS IN MICHIGAN AND THE NATION

As we have seen, during the third quarter of the twentieth century Michigan played an important role in the civil rights struggle and participated in all the major educational trends of the era. Unfortunately, the data we have for Michigan for this period are less comprehensive than the data we have found for any other era, but, as Appendix D, Table D.2, demonstrates, they do point to some interesting developments.[8] On the surface, the coursetaking data show a substantial shift in favor of academic courses, with most of the growth concentrated in English registrations. Yet, given the explosion of English offerings we saw in Grand Rapids and Detroit, this change must be approached with skepticism.

Shedding some light on the *quality* of English teaching in the state at the time is a 1962 study of high school curriculum content by John N. Wales, a British researcher. Wales (1962) found that despite "conspicuous variation among local communities" in the funding and size of schools, the "educational content" of Michigan high schools was "surprisingly similar" and to be what he bluntly called "mental pablum" (p. 39). Concentrating on English courses, Wales found state-approved textbooks largely constructed around life-adjustment themes and topics. Tenth-grade English texts, for example, devoted considerable time to lessons on "Taking Part in Conversations" or "Courteous Listening" and suggested student assignments on such topics as whether 14-year-olds should get driver's licenses or whether parents should be less strict. Even the more skills-oriented portions of the texts focused on things that students should have mastered in elementary schools, such as "Using the Dictionary," "Using the Library," and "Building Sentences" (pp. 42–46).

The national trend data on this period are considerably more interesting. The long-running efforts by the U.S. Office of Education to trace changes in the nation's high schools by collecting cross-sectional data on course enrollments ended with the study done in 1972–73.[9] There are thus three national data collections that can be used to characterize changes in coursetaking in the period roughly from

1950 to 1975, the collections of 1949, 1961, and 1972, each of which reported course enrollment data for each state as well as for the nation as a whole. In addition to these, we have located four studies of coursetaking based on the transcripts of graduating seniors spanning the years from 1958 to approximately 1976, which we analyze below.

Cross-Sectional Data

What is immediately striking about the national data (see Appendix A, Tables A.2–A.4), given the dramatic debates over the nature and function of the high school of the 1950s and the sweeping social and political changes occurring in the 1960s and early 1970s, is, again, the profound *stability* of high school coursetaking patterns over the period. The ratio of academic to nonacademic courses shows a swing of only about 2%. The combined totals of mathematics, science, and foreign language, subjects receiving extraordinary attention in the 1950s and early 1960s, were exactly the same in 1961, 23.5%, as they were in 1949, and by 1972 had fallen by 0.4%. English and social studies combined were 35.8% in 1949 and 36.3% in 1972, having dipped by about 2.0% in the interim. On the nonacademic side, the combined totals of all vocational subjects declined from 20.9% of all course enrollments to 15.4%, with business courses representing about two-thirds of this decline and the other fields one-third. These losses were counterbalanced by gains in the "personal development" areas of art, music, and health and physical education, mostly the latter, which increased its share of total coursetaking by 40%, the only really dramatic change evidenced by these data.

Another reason for surprise at the stability of these coursetaking data is that this was a period of tremendous enrollment increase. National aggregate high school enrollments increased from about 6.4 million in 1950 to a peak of over 15.6 million in 1975, a rate only somewhat less than the phenomenal growth rates of the early part of the twentieth century (see Appendix A, Table A.1). By 1975, 91% of 14–17-year-olds were in high school. Since that time, the rate has remained between 91 and 93% of the age group (National Center for Education Statistics, 1988). This growth meant that while critics of the schools such as Arthur Bestor could argue that the academic seriousness of the nation's high schools had been profoundly undercut, as indicated by the *percentage* decline in academic coursetaking, defenders of the high schools could respond by pointing out that the actual *numbers* of young people studying academic subjects were rising dramatically (Hand, 1958). For example, while foreign language study remained relatively constant at 4% of all courses taken, the actual numbers of students taking a foreign language course increased from 1.2 million in 1949 to 3.7 million in 1972 due to substantial aggregate enrollment increase. However, enrollment growth also meant that substantially larger numbers of students also were enrolled in low-level, less demanding courses.

The national cross-sectional studies also provided the percentage of all students in grades 9 through 12 who were actually enrolled in, for example, an English or a mathematics course during each data collection year. Looked at in this way, some of the trends are consistent with those we noted in earlier chapters, for example, the rise in enrollments in health and physical education, but others appear to be quite different. The data suggest that the Sputnik reforms did increase student exposure to science, math, and foreign language courses, but, as we discussed in Chapter 4, they do not reveal the "split level" nature of those increases.[10] Moreover, the growth in percentage enrollments in these subjects reversed over the next decade, the very period in which the new math and science curriculum designs sponsored by the National Science Foundation were being implemented in many of the nation's high schools (Weiss, 1978). Also, the relative *share* of these subject fields remained constant.

Another surprising finding is that in three subject areas, English, social studies, and health and physical education, the percentage of students taking such courses rose above 100%. According to the USOE data, 140% of students were taking an English course in 1972–73. In other words, all students were taking one English course and nearly half were taking two. However, we believe these increases are partly artifacts of the way the USOE data were tabulated, since every course enrollment, regardless of the length of the course, was counted as a unit. This means, for example, that a high school that offered a series of 1-semester English courses, as Grand Rapids and Detroit began to do in the 1960s, appeared to have twice the enrollments in English of a high school that offered only year-long courses such as English 1, English 2, English 3, and English 4. Thus, subject fields in which many year-long courses had been divided into semester-long or shorter courses with different titles, such as English and social studies, are shown to have somewhat exaggerated enrollments compared with fields, such as foreign language and mathematics, in which these divisions had not occurred.

This also explains the increase in course enrollments per student shown in Table A.2. When this figure is recalculated counting semester-long enrollments at half value, the figures are 5.94 for 1960–61 and 5.93 for 1972–73, or virtually unchanged. Nonetheless, a significant percentage of year-long courses had been split into semester-long offerings over those years, a trend we see as driven by the influence of the humanistic education movement on the English and social studies teachers in the late 1960s and early 1970s, and representing an effort to create courses that had greater interest and relevance for students. Not only was there a trend toward shorter courses (see Table 5.4), but this development was quite uneven across the subject fields, with English and social studies leading the way in the academic subjects, and home economics and health and physical education leading in the nonacademic subjects.

The USOE reports provide opportunities to examine some trends at a finer level of detail than that of aggregate enrollments in subject families. Comparing

Table 5.4. Ratios of Enrollments in Year-Long Courses to Enrollments in Semester-Long or Shorter Courses by Subject Field in Public Secondary Schools for Grades 9–12, United States, 1960–61 and 1972–73

Subject	1960–61	1972–73
English	93/7	63/37
Foreign language	100/0	95/5
Mathematics	90/10	91/9
Science	97/3	89/11
Social studies	81/19	58/42
Commercial	88/12	75/25
Industrial arts	78/22	67/33
Home economics	84/16	49/51
Trade and industry	90/10	81/19
Agriculture	96/4	89/11
Health and phys. ed.	75/25	59/41
Music	100/0	79/21
Art	68/32	66/34

Sources: Wright, 1965; Osterndorf & Horn, 1976.

the 1960–61 survey with that of 1948–49, for example, in English, we find significant increases in enrollments in developmental and remedial reading and a fivefold increase in creative writing and advanced composition. In social studies, ancient, medieval, and modern history ceded the field to courses in U.S. history and world history, while proportionate enrollments in civics, government, and such other courses as economics and sociology were stable. In science, biology moved from tenth grade to ninth, a few more schools offered a second year of chemistry and/or physics, and, most important, there was a substantial growth in enrollments in advanced general science, physical science, and earth science, courses often intended for the noncollege-bound. A small increase in the share of students sticking with a foreign language for a third year of study also was reported. In the arts, instrumental music showed substantial growth, and the enrollment in general art courses was five times what it had been in 1949. Consistent with the life-adjustment philosophy, enrollments in vocational courses for skilled or semiskilled occupations fell from 7% to 4% of the pupils in grades 9–12.

Summarizing the report for 1961, the author sounded a familiar refrain:

Intensification of the drive for a high school education for every youth, which has been characteristic of the years since 1949, brought with it the problem of providing a worthwhile educational program for pupils of increasingly divergent abilities. Considerable attention was necessarily directed to the lower ability groups, since a larger proportion of the high school population was coming from that segment of the population. . . . A tremendous growth occurred in enrollments in courses of a remedial and skill nature in the field of English. . . . Courses of a practical nature in everyday living continued to proliferate. . . . The English field provided courses in practical English, language orientation, oral communication, and fundamental grammar, in addition to the remedial ones. In mathematics, such courses as consumer mathematics, economic mathematics, mathematics for modern living, refresher mathematics, and terminal mathematics were reported. Science offered household biology, science for modern living, everyday physics, and consumer science, among others. (Wright, 1965, pp. 19–20)

The authors of the 1972–73 study found that these trends toward lower-level educational offerings continued apace:

> The present survey has shown a sizable increase in the number and types of courses being offered in the nation's public secondary schools and the number of pupils enrolled in these since the 1960–61 study. The emphasis on making a high school education available for every youth, as noted in the earlier study, has continued, with added attention given to the lower ability groups. This has resulted in considerable experimentation with course offerings and the introduction of many new courses. Remedial courses were offered to one segment of the student population; another segment had access to advanced and college-level courses. Courses of a practical nature proliferated. . . . Graduation requirements were relaxed in many schools, and elective courses became more prominent. As a result, in most of the subject areas a *drift away from the basic courses was noted.* (Osterndorf & Horn, 1976, p. 22, emphasis added)

Transcript Data

Another type of data that indicates changes in high school coursetaking during the third quarter of the twentieth century comes from transcripts of graduating students. Two studies reported the average numbers of high school credits earned in specific courses or subject families for different cohorts of graduating seniors, a USOE study of 1958 graduates and an analysis of data on the high school class of 1969 and the classes of 1975 to 1981, prepared by Clifford Adelman for the National Commission on Excellence in Education (Adelman, 1983; Greer & Harbeck, 1962). To these can be added a calculation by Osterndorf and Horn (1974), included in their report of the 1972–73 cross-sectional study, of what the average high school graduate had studied. Appendix A, Table A.8, presents these data, which offer a very different picture from that revealed by the cross-sectional studies.

The main reason for this difference is that these distributions are based on *credits* rather than course enrollments, and thus are not artificially inflated by the splitting of year-long courses into shorter courses. The credit distributions show a consistent and significant decline of the academic share over the period, from

74% of credits to 60%, a decline similar to that of the pre-World War II years. Within the academic category, the share held by mathematics, science, and foreign language combined held steady between 1958 and 1969 at 30%, then fell to 26%. The share represented by English and social studies fell sharply between 1958 and 1969 from 43 to 37%, then fell further to 34%.[11] What is particularly disturbing about this trend is that it reflects the educational experience of high school *graduates*. We assume that if the credits reported included the experiences of students who dropped out, the picture would be even worse, since school officials probably steered "potential" dropouts to even less rigorous courses and programs.

As we have noted, the losses in academic subjects were matched not by gains in vocational fields, but rather by gains in the personal development fields, particularly health and physical education. The increase in credits earned in health and physical education was greater than the increase in enrollment share, simply because more high schools granted more credit toward graduation for courses in this subject field. The share of credits earned in art and music also showed substantial gains over most of this period, rising from 8% in 1958 to 14% in 1969 and to nearly 20% in 1973, a larger share than all of the vocational fields combined. This also reflects greater generosity on the part of school officials in granting full credit for courses that earlier had been granted only partial credit. Another trend that we saw clearly in our Grand Rapids and Detroit data was the tendency for increasing numbers of courses to be offered 5 days a week. In the prewar period, and even in 1958, it was common for courses in physical education, health, art, and music to meet 2 or 3 periods a week instead of 5. They could be scheduled to share the same time period with other, similar classes and thus provide greater opportunity for students to take electives. By the mid-1970s, virtually all courses met 5 periods a week, expressing the prevailing educational philosophy that all high school courses were of equal value.

Taken together, the various data on high school curriculum developments in America in the third quarter of the twentieth century illuminate one common theme. If graduation requirements were soft in the 1950s and softer still in the mid-1970s; if the number of courses offered in the nation's high schools continued to increase; if the main emphasis of curriculum developers was on expanding practical, remedial, interesting courses for the "lower-ability groups"; if the great debate touched off by Sputnik had little effect on the exposure of ordinary high school students to rigorous mathematics and science, then one conclusion seems inescapable—in the face of raging arguments and massive social upheavals, the American high school continued to follow the pattern of curricular reform and student coursetaking that had been charted in the Progressive Era. Although educational professionals altered and refined those original progressive ideas in response to the Great Depression, the postwar efforts to lure high school students back to school, and the eventual "universalization" of high school enrollments in the 1950s, the fact remains that the basic Progressive theme, that a differentiated curriculum was the key to educational progress and equality of educational opportunity, continued to drive policy and practice. Our data indicate that the dramatic changes in the period from 1950 to 1975 that other historians have identified were either ephemeral or simply did not have much influence on student coursetaking. Indeed, we find little evidence that *any* of the great, competing movements to change the meaning and purpose of secondary education had an important impact on curriculum or coursetaking. Rather, what appears to have been happening was a long, slow working out in practice of the philosophy of differentiation, a philosophy almost as old as the century itself.

Despite or perhaps because of that stability, in the mid-1970s two USOE researchers found some evidence of public dissatisfaction with the effectiveness and even the general tone of American secondary schools:

> Recent developments in measuring academic achievement may indicate the need to shift back to the basic skills with renewed emphasis on real life needs and the ability to get a job after graduation. Recent findings in the National Assessment of Educational Progress of shortcomings in writing, science, and mathematics, and declining test results for the past 12 years on the College Entrance Examination Board's Scholastic Aptitude Test and the American College Test are causing many educators to reevaluate learning at the secondary level. (Osterndorf & Horn, 1976, p. 22)

As we show in the next chapter, such sentiments helped launch a new reform effort that shook the very foundations of American high schools in the 1980s.

SUMMARY

Historians generally have described the period from 1960 to 1975 as a time of tremendous change in American education. They maintain that the angry protests and movements of the 1960s and early 1970s had a profound impact on the schools. During this period historians claim that curriculum policy shifted dramatically due to the impact of such developments as civil rights protests, the counterculture, or economic change (Angus & Mirel, 1993). Yet in this chapter, both in our examination of the debates themselves and in our analysis of data on curriculum and coursetaking, we have found such a construction to be misleading. Despite the rhetoric and the dramatic changes many of the protests and movements brought to American society, high schools were islands of stability in terms of the philosophy that guided their policies and the nature of student coursetaking.

The idea that high schools must meet the needs of youth through increasingly differentiated programs dominated virtually every important policy decision involving American high schools. Yet, nothing indicates more clearly the utter vacuousness of that idea than the fact that almost every critic of American education during this period, including Paul Goodman, Black militants, countercultural gurus, and proponents of neo-efficiency reforms, was driven by the belief that the educational establishment had failed to address the needs of youth as each group defined them. Virtually all these critics argued that greater curricular differentiation was the key to meeting those needs, whether such differentiation meant an infusion of Black history and culture, alternative pathways to skills and knowledge, course credit for life experiences, or career education. Professional educators were only too happy to oblige. It is hardly astonishing, therefore, that despite an explosion of new courses, programs, and reform initiatives in the 1960s and early 1970s, our analysis of the data reveals the underlying and fundamental stability of patterns of student coursetaking rather than great change.

In short, *Cardinal Principles* remained triumphant. The National Commission on the Reform of Secondary Education (1973) reported that as late as 1966, a survey of American teachers found that 85% of them agreed that *Cardinal Principles* were "a satisfactory list of the goals of education today" (p. 28). When asked about revising the national goals for secondary education, one administrator claimed that "most educators believe that this was answered for all time with the formulation of the Cardinal Principles so many years ago" (p. 29). As late as 1975, that appeared to be an accurate assessment of the state of thinking among secondary education leaders. *Cardinal Principles* and a more refined policy of differentiating the curriculum had proven to be powerful tools for deflecting or co-opting the waves of harsh criticism that bombarded the schools from all sides during this turbulent era.

NOTES

1. In addition to these recommendations, Gross included a number of items that today are mainstays of the "conservative" educational agenda. These include abolishing certification requirements for teachers, ending legal restrictions that "impede the formation of new schools by independent groups of parents," and breaking the "schools' monopoly on education" by giving "every consumer a voucher for him to spend on his education as he chooses, instead of increasing allocations to the school authorities" (Gross, 1971, p. 24).

2. Several of the individual high school reports recommended increasing the mathematics requirement for graduation from 1 year to 2 years, but the idea did not survive the debates that produced the final, city-wide report, and the mathematics requirement was not increased until the early 1980s.

3. Because tracing changes in the coursetaking of Detroit high school students presents some difficulties related to incomplete and ambiguous records, we selected the 1966–67 and 1975–76 school years as providing the best available data.

4. This practice dated from the 1930s when enrollments grew much faster than additional schools or the requisite science labs could be built (Mirel, 1993). It was still the policy in the 1990s.

5. One of these systems used X for upper track students, Y for regular sections, and Z for the lowest track. These designations dated from the early 1920s when Detroit's "X–Y–Z system" was nationally recognized for the tracking of all students on the basis of intelligence tests given during the kindergarten year (see Williams, 1986).

6. The lack of access to quality mathematics courses had dire consequences for Black students. During this period, Black youth in Detroit were blocked out of the construction trades apprentice programs run by the trade unions. The unions defended the almost total absence of Blacks in these programs by citing their low scores on the qualifying exams, a large portion of which were devoted to basic mathematics. Ironically, only the Black youths who were in the academic track were likely getting enough mathematics to qualify for skilled trades training (see Phillips, 1971).

7. Nationally, in 1961, business arithmetic accounted for only 6.4% of business course enrollments, and shop math was only 0.4% of industrial arts enrollments, far below the levels in Detroit.

8. The only available data for Michigan during this period are derived from the three national cross-sectional studies.

9. Taking note that this shift in study design brought to an end a valuable historical record, the USOE contracted with Evaluation Technologies Incorporated to develop a method of transforming the high school transcript data into estimates of coursetaking data that would be consistent with the earlier studies and would extend the series to 1982. Unfortunately, the samples for 1972–73 and 1981–82 are not precisely similar (see West, Diodato, & Sandberg, 1984).

10. It is possible for the *proportion* of students enrolling in a particular subject to increase, while the proportionate share of enrollment in that subject remains the same or declines only if the total number of courses elected is rising. It was, from 5.61 courses per student in 1948–49 to 6.42 per student in 1960–61.

11. This decline in relative share held by English and social studies is masked in the cross-sectional enrollment data for the reason we discussed relative to Appendix A, Table A.2. Splitting a 1-year English course into two semester-long courses would double the apparent enrollment in English courses given the way the USOE tabulated its data, but it would not alter the number of credits given in English. The actual decline in the English and social studies share of total credits signals not that students were taking smaller amounts of such courses, but that more credits were being granted for such courses as music, art, physical education, and health.

6

The Restoration of the Academic Ideal? Upheaval and Reform, 1975–1995

FEW PERIODS IN THE history of American education have seen such dramatic developments and such contentious debates as the 1980s and early 1990s. During this period the nation witnessed the first major changes in urban school governance since the Progressive Era in such cities as Chicago, Miami, and Rochester; a politically powerful campaign to transform public and private school funding through the use of vouchers and parental choice; the creation of state-supported academies for academically gifted students; the proliferation of charter schools freed from state regulations in order to experiment with innovative programs; a concerted effort involving dozens of professional and civic organizations to develop national educational standards in major subject fields; and a furious debate about our national character as reflected in controversies about curriculum content in such areas as history, literature, and science (Ravitch, 1995). Indeed, struggles over educational issues have become so pervasive that even such seemingly benign questions as what is the best approach for teaching reading have led to bitter, politically charged debates (Gursky, 1991).

Transforming high schools and the high school curriculum has been central to many of these controversies and reform campaigns. Perhaps the most striking thing about recent efforts to reshape secondary education has been the degree to which many participants voice themes similar to those articulated in the 1950s, particularly themes sounded by such critics as Arthur Bestor. *A Nation at Risk*, the widely cited federal manifesto that galvanized many of these reforms, specifically targeted secondary schools as one of the weakest components of a grossly deficient educational system. "Secondary school curricula have been homogenized," the report declared, "and diffused to the point that they no longer have a central purpose. In effect, we have a cafeteria-style curriculum in which the appetizers and desserts can easily be mistaken for the main courses. Students have migrated from vocational and college preparatory programs to 'general track' courses in large numbers" (National Commission on Excellence in Education, 1983, p. 18). But unlike the 1950s, when such criticism came mostly from isolated commentators who vainly challenged the "interlocking educational directorate," during the 1980s and early 1990s, the people demanding change included such influential leaders as the U.S. Secretary of Education and the president of the American Federation of Teachers.

Perhaps nothing better indicates the breadth of these reform efforts than the unprecedented gathering in September 1989 of President George Bush and the nation's governors (lead by then governor of Arkansas Bill Clinton) in which the assembled leaders pledged to revitalize American public education. Their vehicle for this revitalization was a set of "clear national performance goals, goals that will make us internationally competitive" (Weinraub, 1989, p. A10). Two of these goals focused specifically on curriculum. Goal Three declared, "American students will leave grades four, eight, and twelve having demonstrated competency in challenging subject matter including English, mathematics, science, history and geography; and every school in America will ensure that all students learn to use their minds well, so they may be prepared for responsible citizenship, further learning, and productive employment." Goal Four states that "U.S. students will be first in the world in science and math achievement" (U.S. Department of Education, 1991, p. 3). In some ways these two goals hearkened back to the objectives of the Committee of Ten by demanding that all students pursue a strong academic course of study and by asserting that some academic subject areas are inherently more important than others.

But have these efforts actually had an effect on high school curricula and student coursetaking? Could they be just another series of political and educational storms similar to the ones we described in the 1950s and 1960s, portentous and dramatic outbursts promising major changes but passing quickly over the high school with little real effect? Are educationists once again paying lip service to the shifting national moods while still pursuing policies and practices that maintain the educational status quo? Or could it be that we are witnessing a true restoration of the academic ideal in American secondary education and a profound reinterpretation of the idea of equal educational opportunity? This chapter examines these questions.

We undertake this analysis with a great deal of caution, in part because as we write, this reform effort still has not run its course. Its strength and direction remain uncertain. For example, there have been impressive national gains in the academic share of high school coursetaking but the factors that have caused these gains and the degree to which these gains actually represent important shifts in student behavior, rather than simply changes in course titles and content, are considerably less clear. Consequently, our analysis in this chapter takes a somewhat different form than in previous ones. Since we do not know the ultimate outcome of the current effort to reorient the American high school, it would be foolish to claim that specific factors clearly contributed to various changes. We will, therefore, touch only briefly on the major factors that appear to be influencing current trends related to high school curriculum and coursetaking. We mainly focus our analysis of data on an examination of what has actually happened in this period. We will, however, shift the order of our analysis by first considering the widely discussed national trends in coursetaking. We will focus on several national studies of high school transcripts commissioned by the National Center for Education Statistics as well as a number of other, smaller studies that highlight trends in student coursetaking. We will follow that discussion with an examination of trends in Michigan, Grand Rapids, and Detroit, to get a more precise view of what was actually happening on the state and local level and to see the degree to which trends in these contexts paralleled those in the nation.

CHALLENGING THE EDUCATIONAL STATUS QUO, 1975–1990

Efforts to reform the American high school could not have begun at a more propitious time than the mid-1970s and the early 1980s. During this period, Americans from every walk of life were facing challenges and problems that led them to question virtually every major institution in the country. As the nation wrestled with the divisive legacy of the 1960s and struggled with what seemed to be a declining economy, the national mood ranged from skepticism, at best, to cynicism, at worst. Increasingly, many Americans questioned the quality of leading political and economic institutions and rejected the pat assurances of politicians and experts who asserted that the country was still on the right track (Dionne, 1991; Lasch, 1995; Matusow, 1984). Public education was not immune from these events. Indeed, as a highly prized institution that was, at least theoretically, sensitive to the changing attitudes of parents and local communities, public education may have felt the effects of these events sooner and more directly than did other institutions.

Amid growing doubts and concerns, a series of developments coalesced in the 1980s to create a national awareness and, it appears, a national effort to transform at least some important aspects of the American high school. Four things stand out about this most recent campaign to transform secondary education. First, this campaign marks the first serious challenge to the very idea of the differentiated high school in the history of the institution. As we have demonstrated in previous chapters, despite the great rhetorical battles fought between 1930 and 1975, the comprehensive high school remained virtually impervious to fundamental change. Beginning in the late 1970s, however, the campaign for reforming the high school directly targeted the differentiated curriculum as a central problem in American education. Leaders of this campaign called for curricular and coursetaking changes that essentially demanded an end to or a severe limitation of differentiation. Second, this challenge to differentiation drew support from a broader and more diverse constituency than did any previous effort. Buttressed by a series of widely publicized reports about the dismal condition of public education, this campaign included professors from academic disciplines who reasserted the types of criticism offered by Bestor and others; some prominent educational leaders who took a new perspective on the idea of equality of educational opportunity; left-wing scholars who directed their fire at the class, race, and gender biases of tracking; business leaders worried about the educational quality of the work force; feminists and civil rights leaders outraged about the unequal education provided to women and minorities; and, above all, parents deeply concerned about the quality of their children's education. Third, this broad constituency successfully convinced politicians in almost every state to enact legislation mandating more rigorous, academic high school graduation requirements, laws that forced educational policy makers to dramatically limit the curricular options available to high school students. In short, these new state policies compelled a retreat from differentiation. Finally, despite the vehement defense of the differentiated high school curriculum by members of the "interlocking educational directorate," it appears that for the first time in history their arguments are falling on deaf ears. More important, educationists seem to have been less successful in stopping or subverting the political and policy changes that challenged differentiation. We will briefly examine all these factors.

Concern and agitation about the condition of American education had been growing throughout the late 1970s. In November 1977, for example, *Time* magazine ran a cover story that declared, "[T]he health of U.S. education in the mid-1970s—particularly that of the high schools—is in deepening trouble" (Swan & McGrath, 1977, p. 62). Focusing on suburban and small-town high schools rather than those in inner cities, the article highlighted a series of problems that increasingly would dominate discussions of the high schools: the decline of student performance as revealed by falling Scholastic Aptitude Test (SAT) scores; the breakdown of civility and order within the schools, particularly the dramatic rise in violence; the growing rates of student absenteeism; the trend toward taxpayer revolts against rising educational costs (especially when those rising costs coincided with declining student achievement); and community anger about the increasing militancy of teachers' unions. In addition, the article noted growing alarm among parents and educators about the post-1960s explosion of courses and the "pathetic" state of graduation requirements that granted students full credit for such courses as "Great Sleuths, Exploring the Occult, and Contemporary Issues," as well as "the American Teenager and Interior Decorating." As one teacher put it, such courses amounted to little more than "education by entertainment" (pp. 65, 72).

By the early 1980s, these problems clearly had touched a national nerve. An April 1981 *Newsweek* cover story bluntly titled, "Why Public Schools Are Flunking," presented the results of a Gallup poll in which "nearly half the respondents say schools are doing a poor or only fair job—a verdict that would have been unthinkable just seven years ago, when two-thirds in a similar poll rated schools excellent or good. Fifty-nine per cent believe teachers should be better trained; more than 60 per cent want their children taught in a more orderly atmosphere; and *almost 70 per cent call for more stress on academic basics*" (Williams et al., 1981, p. 62; emphasis added).

Some leading scholars and educators were coming to similar conclusions. One year later, Mortimer Adler published a widely discussed educational manifesto, *The Paideia Proposal*, that presented the most forceful critique of curricular differentiation in American high schools since Arthur Bestor. Adler (1982) declared simply: "We should have a one track system of schooling, not a system with two or more tracks, only one of which goes straight ahead while the others shunt the young off onto sidetracks not headed toward the goals our society opens to all" (p. 5). Denouncing curricular differentiation as undemocratic, Adler stated: "All sidetracks, specialized courses, or elective choices must be eliminated. Allowing them will always lead a certain number of students to voluntarily downgrade their own education" (p. 21). That same year, David Kirp (1982) argued that public schools had to "reclaim excellence" and recognize that excellence *and* equality could be realized only if schools were organized "for the steady and unswerving pursuit of learning" (pp. 32–33).

No article, poll, or manifesto, however, captured public attention more completely than did the U.S. Department of Education's 1983 report, *A Nation at Risk*. Apocalyptic in tone, this report, which was prepared by the National Commission on Excellence in Education (NCEE), focused on a host of indicators, all of which revealed a profound crisis in public education, with problems of the high schools receiving the lion's share of attention. These problems included exceptionally low rankings by American students in international comparisons of student achievement; high rates of functional illiteracy among 17-year-olds, with rates for minorities running as high as 40% of the age group; declines over the past 26 years in the average achievement of high school students on standardized tests; the "virtually unbroken decline from 1963 to 1980" of SAT scores, with average verbal scores dropping "over 50 points and average mathematics scores drop[ping] nearly 40 points"; dramatic declines in "both the number and proportion of students demonstrating superior achievement on the SATs (i.e., those with scores of 650 or higher)"; consistent declines in College Board achievement test scores in such areas as physics and English; the failure of many 17-year-olds to master "higher order" thinking skills; the "steady decline in science achievement scores of U.S. 17-year-olds, as measured by the national assessments of science in 1969, 1973, and 1977"; the increase in remedial courses in basic skills such as mathematics and English offered in 4-year colleges, industry, and the military (NCEE, 1983, pp. 8–9).

While scholars and the media already had identified many of these problems, the solution offered by the NCEE marked an important change in the nature of the policy debates about American high schools. Specifically, the commission called for an end to or at least a severe limitation of curricular differentiation and the system of electives that sustained it. Decrying the "cafeteria-style" curriculum in which students could get a large portion (in some cases 50% or more) of their credits for graduation through such courses as physical and health education, work experience outside of school, remedial courses, and personal service and development courses such as training for adulthood, bachelor living, and marriage, the commission called for *all* students to take a required set of core academic courses, labeled the "Five New Basics." The commission urged states and local districts to mandate that, at a minimum, all students seeking a diploma take as part of a 4-year high school education: "(*a*) *4 years of English;* (*b*) *3 years of mathematics;* (*c*) *3 years of science;* (*d*) *3 years of social studies; and* (*e*) *one-half year of computer science. For the college bound, 2 years of foreign language in high school are strongly recommended in addition to those taken earlier"* (p. 24; emphasis in original).

Although the commission did not mention the report of the Committee of Ten, from a historical perspective perhaps the most important aspect of *A Nation at Risk* was its resurrection of the three main ideas that had defined that earlier document. Like the Committee of Ten, the NCEE supported the idea that all high school students should follow essentially the same *academically* oriented program regardless of their future plans. In addition, the commission shared the committee's assumption that some courses, specifically academic courses, were inherently more important than others for high school students. Finally, *A Nation at Risk* reanimated the idea that equality of educational opportunity meant that all students should have access to the same high-quality programs, in other words, that "identical" education was indeed the true definition of equal education.

As we have described in previous chapters, such ideas had not been absent from earlier debates about American high schools, but until the 1980s educational leaders had successfully kept them from influencing policy and practice. *A Nation at Risk*, however, restored their legitimacy and focused the national media spotlight on them. For the rest of the decade, the arguments presented in *A Nation at Risk* became central to debates about the American high school.

A Nation at Risk was soon joined by a series of reports that supported the NCEE's general assessment that American education was in trouble. Some of these reports also offered similar policy recommendations (Stedman & Jordan, 1986). Beyond their criticism of American education, these reports were notable for the fact that several of them were directed or authored by such prominent educationists as John Goodlad, then dean of the Graduate School of Education at the University of California at Los Angeles, and Theodore Sizer, former dean of the Graduate School of Education at Harvard. For our purposes, the most important of these reports were Ernest Boyer's (1983) study of high schools conducted for the Carnegie Foundation, the studies that reported on Sizer's "A Study of High Schools" series, and Goodlad's *A Place Called School* (1984).

Beginning from the premise that the American high school is "adrift," lacking a "clear and vital mission" (1983, p. 63), Boyer's report provided even more evidence of the institution's failures than did *A Nation at Risk*. Whether in terms of international comparisons of student achievement, standardized test score declines, or the consistent failure to serve Black and Hispanic students, Boyer concluded that the comprehensive high school was a "troubled institution" (p. 9). Like the Conant and Silberman reports, also commissioned by the Carnegie Foundation, Boyer's report called for renewing and revitalizing the comprehensive high school rather than abolishing it. But unlike those earlier authors, Boyer challenged several key aspects of what had been conventional educational wisdom about high schools. Specifically, Boyer argued that one academic requirement, the mastery of English, should have priority over all other subject areas and that all students should follow a core program composed mainly of academic subjects. This core curriculum should amount to "two-thirds of the total units required for high school graduation" (p. 303). While these recommendations did not amount to a thorough repudiation of differentiation, they did mark an important change in curricular emphasis, especially when viewed in comparison to the guidelines offered by the earlier reports supported by the Carnegie Foundation. In stark contrast to Conant and Silberman, Boyer called for narrowing the function of the high school and mandating more academic coursework for *all* students.

The three books that reported the findings of "A Study of High Schools" (Hampel, 1986; Powell, Farrar, & Cohen, 1985; Sizer, 1984) made similar points. However, these works, particularly the study by Powell, Farrar, and Cohen, provided a particularly comprehensive and nuanced portrait of American secondary education. Powell, Farrar, and Cohen demonstrated how the simultaneous commitments to enrolling all 14–17-year-olds, reducing the dropout rate, keeping students happy, and maximizing their coursetaking choices had created an institution in which the vast majority of students wandered through the high school as if it were a shopping mall, picking courses that were attractively packaged but rarely were designed to challenge them intellectually. In such institutions, they wrote, "Learning is not discounted or unvalued, but it is profoundly voluntary" (p. 4).

Central to the operation of this educational mall were "treaties" or "bargains" in which educators and students tacitly agreed about the level of difficulty and expectations in various classes. Thus, in some of the mall's "specialty shops," such as advanced placement courses, students were committed to mastering difficult material, but in most other courses the treaties rested on teachers making few educational demands on the students in exchange for acceptable classroom behavior (see also Sedlak, Pullian, & Wheeler, 1986; Cusick, 1983). Not surprisingly, such institutions promoted mediocrity, with student choice rather than academic excellence being the dominant value. Powell, Farrar, and Cohen (1985) note, "The idea that serious mastery is possible and necessary for most Americans is simply not widely shared" (p. 6). "A Study of High Schools" called for renewed emphasis on traditional subject matter (although redesigned into broad integrated areas of learning); demanded that all students master such intellectual processes as reasoning, expression, and interpreting data; and called for students to demonstrate their mastery of these processes before advancing.

If Powell, Farrar, and Cohen produced the most nuanced analysis of how American high schools promoted mediocrity, John Goodlad (1984) provided the most trenchant critique of how tracking shortchanged students in the lower tracks and how the practice exacerbated social and racial inequalities. Drawing on the work of a team of researchers who intensively studied 38 schools, Goodlad declared simply, "The findings from the classes studied revealed significant differences in curricular content, instructional procedures, and elements of the student–teacher relationship" (p. 152). He argued that virtually every aspect of the educational environment—including teachers' expectations for student performance, the types of class discussions, and even the willingness of teachers to use humor with students—was shaped by track placement and that "these differences favored the upper tracks." Specifically, "practices supported in the literature as most advantageous were perceived most frequently in the upper tracks and least frequently in the lower; and practices associated negatively with student satisfaction and achievement were perceived most and least frequently in the lower and upper tracks respectively" (p. 155). Finally, Goodlad and his fellow researchers found clear evidence that minority and economically disadvantaged students consistently were placed in lower tracks, while Whites were placed with equal consistency in higher tracks. Goodlad concluded that in order to correct this problem, schools should move toward heterogeneous groupings of students and the implementation of "a common core of studies which students cannot escape through electives, even though the proposed electives purport to be in the same domain of knowledge" (p. 297).

The unprecedented appearance of so many major studies challenging curricular differentiation shook the intellectual foundations of the modern American high school. Combined with other, sophisticated studies conducted by historians and sociologists of education, it appeared that the theoretical ground that supported comprehensive high schools was undergoing a profound shift. Like Goodlad's work, many of these historical and sociological studies concentrated on the impact of curriculum differentiation on minorities and women. All told, these studies amounted to the most serious scholarly attack ever launched at the Progressive idea that equality of educational opportunity could best be achieved by providing different programs to students of diverse abilities and backgrounds. As we have noted, earlier works by such scholars as A. B. Hollingshead (1949) and Patricia Cayo Sexton (1961) had scored the relationship between social class and track placement, but not until the late 1970s and early 1980s did these ideas begin to attract wide scholarly attention.

The earliest attack on the Progressive idea of equality of educational opportunity came from left-wing, "revisionist" historians who argued that such Progressive Era reforms as the elite takeover of urban school boards, the use of culturally biased IQ tests, and the implementation of differentiated curricula belied claims about equality of educational opportunity. Rather than producing greater social and educational equality, these historians argued, these reforms had produced schools in which curricular inequality paralleled and reproduced the existing inequality in society (Bowles & Gintis, 1976; Katz, 1973; Spring, 1973; Tyack, 1974). As we have noted in Chapters 2 and 3, these historians were mistaken in several of their assumptions about the relationship between the expansion of vocational education, the enrollment of large numbers of working-class students in high school, and the degree to which school officials were able to impose their will on students' curricular choices; and in any case, they did not condemn outright the concept of the differentiated high school. Nevertheless, they were unquestionably right in highlighting the unequal and fundamentally undemocratic aspects of curricular differentiation as it was practiced. Moreover, their work encouraged scholars from other disciplines, such as Goodlad, to explore the current effects of tracking on minorities, young women, and the poor.

Throughout the 1980s, a number of educational sociologists did just that, producing an increasingly detailed series of studies that substantiated the claim that tracking exacerbated educational inequality. Jeannie Oakes (1985), who worked with Goodlad on *A Place Called School*, conducted one of the best known of these studies, an examination of the tracking and placement patterns in 25 junior and senior high schools that enrolled almost 14,000 students. Oakes found that tracking unquestionably "subverted" the ideal of equality and that "those students who seem to have the least of everything in their lives most often get less at school as well" (p. 4).[1] In almost every aspect of the high school enterprise—such as time spent on instruction, course content, and students' attitudes about themselves—Oakes found that curricular differentiation worsened educational inequality. She wrote:

> Students bring differences with them to school. Schools, most specifically through counselors and teachers, respond to these differences. Those responses are such that the initial differences between students are likely to widen. Students seen as different are separated into different classes and then provided with vastly different kinds of knowledge and with markedly different opportunities to learn. It is in these ways that schools exacerbate the differences among the students who attend them. And it is through tracking that these educational differences are most blatantly carried out. (pp. 111–112)

Oakes summed up her finding in terms similar to other critics of American secondary education: "In short, we cannot have educational excellence until we have educational equality" (p. xiv).

In 1990, Oakes re-examined this issue through an extensive review of the literature on tracking and curricular differentiation conducted for the National

Science Foundation and the RAND corporation. Focusing on science and mathematics, Oakes (1990a) found substantial evidence that tracking works "to the academic detriment of secondary school students who are placed in low-ability or non-college preparatory groups" (pp. 47–48), which consequently works against minority students who are concentrated in these less advantageous tracks. Track placement also strongly related to the types of courses available to students, with those in lower tracks having virtually no chance of taking higher-level classes. Lack of opportunities to take higher-level classes translated into poorer achievement levels for these students.[2]

Oakes cited studies that were part of a rapidly expanding body of work that consistently found a relationship between tracking and educational and social inequality. These studies were conducted by some of the most distinguished educational researchers in the nation (e.g., Gamoran & Berends, 1987; Gamoran, Nystrand, Berends, & Lefore, 1995), and their importance cannot be overestimated. They were unquestionably the best researched and, above all, most widely publicized attacks on the idea that curricular differentiation encouraged greater educational equality, the idea that we have argued dominated curricular planning for most of the twentieth century. Equally important was the fact that many of the scholars attacking this idea were faculty members in leading schools and colleges of education. That these challenges were coming from educationists themselves indicated the degree to which philosophical uniformity on this issue (once a hallmark of these schools and colleges) was eroding.

But more was at stake here than the erosion of that once monolithic philosophical stance. Since at least the 1920s, educators frequently had allied themselves with "progressive" social and political movements, for example, linking their efforts to get more children into school to the campaign to end child labor or rescue teenagers from the Great Depression. Many of these efforts were strongly supported by organized labor or liberal political organizations. Indeed, by the 1940s in some cities and states these political ties had become quite strong and quite explicit, especially in battles for greater funding and in efforts to keep large numbers of students out of the labor market (Cohen, 1990; Mirel, 1993). These alliances help explain why, for example, leading educators such as Harold Rugg could attack critics of "progressive education," including those who denounced differentiated curricula, as part of a group of reactionaries who also opposed "progressive political initiatives."

Indeed, this taken-for-granted assumption that progressive school reforms (such as trying to keep larger numbers of students in high school) were of a piece with progressive political goals (such as increasing social mobility through education) also helps explain why such critics of the high school as Arthur Bestor were immediately and routinely labeled by educationists as "conservatives." It did not matter that Bestor, for example, was an early and passionate supporter of civil rights, surely a stand that would define someone as a liberal in the 1950s. As

far as educationists were concerned (from the 1950s to the present), the mere fact
that Bestor had criticized the high schools and their effort to hold increasing numbers of students through differentiation and curricular dilution, clearly identified
him as someone who was, at best, a political conservative or, at worst, a fascist
(see Courtis, 1939).

From that perspective, one of the most important aspects of the criticism of
differentiation and tracking that emerged in the 1970s and 1980s was that much
of it came from liberal or left-wing critics who eventually were joined in these
attacks by organized labor (particularly in the person of Albert Shanker), civil
rights, and women's organizations. Indeed, during this period, some civil rights
groups specifically targeted tracking as one of the most powerful mechanisms for
depriving Black children of an equal education (Gursky, 1991). As we noted in
Chapter 5, Black leaders in the 1950s and early 1960s had voiced similar com-
plaints, but in the 1980s these criticisms were reaching a wider audience and were
supported by people and organizations from across a wider spectrum of opinion.

Beyond denouncing tracking, at least one Black leader, John Jacob, president of the Urban League, began advocating an educational program for the African American community that stressed academic excellence as the key to racial
progress. Asking, "What will it take for our children to develop into outstanding
twenty-first century citizens?" Jacob (1992) replied:

> Every African American child should graduate from high school with the ability to
> do calculus.
> Every African American child should be fluent in a foreign language.
> Every African American child should be able to research, organize and write a 25
> page essay on a challenging topic. (p. 13; see also Howard, 1993; Raspberry, 1993)

These are hardly sentiments that would give aid and comfort to the supporters of curricular differentiation. More important, they came from someone whom
educationists had an exceedingly difficult time dismissing as a reactionary. When
Albert Shanker, president of the American Federation of Teachers (and a prominent leader in the American labor movement generally), added his support to efforts to strengthen academic coursetaking, restrict elective choices, and improve
educational standards, it truly appeared that the educational tide was changing (see,
for example, Shanker, 1994a, 1994b). In all, this loss of "political" support for
curricular differentiation from liberal, civil rights, and labor leaders and organizations marked an important change in the nature of the debate on the American
high school.

At the same time that these developments were taking place on the liberal
side of the political spectrum, similar efforts were coalescing among conservatives. Following *A Nation at Risk*, business leaders, for example, became increasingly involved in educational issues, often pushing for higher educational stan-

dards for all students. One commentator noted in the mid-1980s, "[F]or the first time in recent memory major business leaders were identifying education as a key national problem and priority. Chief executive officers from some of the country's major corporations began to involve themselves in coalitions to improve public education, giving of both their time and their influence" (Atkin, quoted in Bunzel, 1985, p. 48). Such groups as the California Business Roundtable and the Minnesota Business Partnership began to play active roles in educational reform, with curricular issues high on their agendas (Kearns & Doyle, 1988).

One of the most prominent business leaders to address educational issues was David Kearns, chairman and chief executive officer of Xerox Corporation. In 1988, in collaboration with Denis Doyle, Kearns published a book highly critical of American education, which noted the "sad fact . . . that not enough is expected of American students. They have it too easy academically" (p. 67). Kearns and Doyle called for a core curriculum for all American high school students that would "require the *flexible term equivalent* of two years of the same foreign language and four years of English, three years of math and history, two years of science, and one year of computer science" (p. 76; emphasis in the original).[3] By the 1990s, such sentiments also inspired organizations like the National Alliance of Business, which campaigned specifically to improve educational standards (Smith, 1996).

These varied efforts by individuals and groups from all points along the political spectrum quickly paid dividends in state legislatures across the nation. Just 3 years after *A Nation at Risk* appeared, 45 states and the District of Columbia had increased their high school graduation requirements, 42 states had increased their math requirements, and 34 had toughened graduation requirements in science (Stedman & Jordan, 1986). Indeed, as Clune and White (1992) noted, "Higher state high school graduation requirements were the most popular policy instrument used for . . . academic upgrading, in the sense of more students taking more challenging academic subjects" (p. 2). These simple legislative changes directly challenged key aspects of the prevailing high school philosophy since they rested on the assumption that all students should follow a fairly similar sequence of required courses and that the number of electives available for students should be reduced. More important, these reforms hit the schools with the force of law, making them potentially the greatest engine for curricular change in almost a century.

As important as such legislation might be, a number of educational and political leaders realized in the 1980s that unless the nation's schools were guided by high-quality, rigorous educational standards (standards that articulated both the content and skills students at various grade levels needed to know), the campaign to improve American education could easily be sidetracked. As we have seen, educators committed to differentiation have been quite adept at subverting efforts to have all students learn the same material by shunting large numbers off into less demanding courses. Increased graduation requirements in mathematics, for example, might just as easily be met by 3 years of business or consumer math as by algebra I, geometry, and algebra II. Thus, some educational and political leaders from both sides of the political spectrum began a highly visible and to some extent successful campaign to produce sets of standards that states and school boards could voluntarily adopt (Ravitch, 1995).

Despite the seemingly broad support for national standards, this effort provoked serious opposition from three quite disparate groups: professional educators, proponents of a form of progressive education that draws on racial and ethnic materials to inspire children's learning, and Protestant fundamentalists. We discuss each of these groups in turn.

Despite the massive outcry about problems with high schools and the calls for tougher academic requirements for all students, many educationists reacted to the criticism as if nothing had changed since the 1950s.[4] They argued, for example, that such "top-down" reform often inspired by people outside the educational establishment would never work—that only through the involvement and commitment of the whole educational profession could the nation's high schools be radically reformed and that the best ideas for reform would come from educators themselves. In other words, they repeated the assertion born in the Progressive Era and refined in the 1960s, that only educational professionals should control such issues as determining curricula.

In addition, professional educators continued to maintain that identical education would lead to greater inequality, that tougher graduation requirements would increase the dropout rate, and that national educational standards would have an adverse effect on poor and minority students. In a widely cited article defending tracking, for example, one educator declared, "[A]n approach that treats all students the same and ignores the real differences among them can guarantee unequal experiences for them all. Treating all students the same is not a formula for equity or excellence" (Nevi, 1987, p. 26). Similarly, in an otherwise favorable review of Oakes's *Keeping Track* (1985), Deborah Meier (1985) argued that as "recommendations for more course requirements, reduced options, more frequent use of standardized tests and stiffer promotion standards are implemented, it has become increasingly difficult to find alternatives to tracking. One of the tragic results of these recommendations has been the rise in both truancy and dropout rates among students who find themselves at the bottom of the schools' achievement (and economic) ladder. Those youngsters have been tracked out of school entirely" (p. 627; see also Russell, 1995).

Educationists leveled virtually the same set of arguments against national educational standards. Opponents of standards (like those who attacked tougher graduation requirements and the reduction of electives) repeated arguments that were nearly a century old and that were virtually unchanged since they were first articulated. There is, for example, a profound sense of déjà vu when Gerald Bracey

(1996a) asks, "Where would one set a standard that would be perceived as credibly high without failing large percentages of students? And what would one do then?" (p. 7; see also Eisner, 1994; Fulk, Mantzicopoulous, & Hirth, 1994).[5] Among many defenders of the status quo, the idea that educators could or even should devise methods and materials that would enable all students (or at least the vast majority of students) to master rigorous high-quality content seems to be as illusive in the 1990s as it was in the 1920s.

Finally, professional educators and their allies argued that substantial increases in educational resources were necessary to carry out any major reform of American education that would improve the performance of most students in U.S. schools (Darling-Hammond, 1991; Howe, 1991; Kaplan, 1991; Kozol, 1991; Lipsitz, 1991). We will examine these arguments in the next section.

The newest arguments directed against efforts to end differentiation through tougher graduation requirements or national standards have come from two groups that are rarely allies in educational or political debates, supporters of educational programs that promote distinct racial and/or ethnic perspectives (e.g., Afrocentrists) and Protestant fundamentalists. Neither group opposes higher standards or more rigorous graduation requirements per se, but both object to state-mandated requirements in large part because of their distrust of governmental action in education generally and their opposition to curricular content found in many standards (especially those that are detailed and highly prescriptive) and in courses required for graduation, such as history or biology. Both groups see state efforts to raise standards as attempts to impose an "alien" philosophy upon their children, Eurocentrism in the one case, and secular humanism on the other (Asante, 1987, 1992; Dow, 1991; Holt, 1992; Larson, 1985; Lee, Lomotey, & Shujoa, 1990; Okutsu, 1989). Nowhere was the opposition of these groups to curriculum reform more visible than in the furor that erupted over the national history standards that both groups vehemently denounced, albeit for very different reasons (Ravitch, 1995).

Both groups have been quite active in stalling or watering down efforts to create strong state standards or in promoting their own curricular agendas in local school districts. Protestant fundamentalists appear to have been more successful in influencing activities at the state level, while those promoting ethnic or race-based education have been more successful in some large urban school systems such as Detroit and Milwaukee. These activities are troubling not only because they threaten prospects for substantial curricular reform in many states and localities but also because they encourage an even more insidious form of differentiation, one blatantly based on race, ethnicity, or religion.

Given such disparate but potent opposition, the fate of the current movement to toughen high school graduation requirements, establish standards, and strengthen academic curricula remains very much in doubt. Indeed, despite the vigorous support from such prominent educational leaders as Albert Shanker and Diane Ravitch, one key element of this movement, the establishment of national educational standards, appears to have stalled, perhaps permanently. We now turn to our analysis of the national, state, and local data to assess the impact that these various reform and counterreform efforts have had on curricula and coursetaking and to speculate on the significance of these efforts for the history of the American high school.

COURSETAKING TRENDS IN THE NATION

The national reports of the 1980s presented a solid consensus that high schools needed to require that all students follow a regimen of challenging, core academic courses. The chief means for bringing this about was expected to be state legislation or local regulation to increase graduation requirements, and the establishment of national educational standards and forms of assessment (National Commission on Excellence in Education, 1983). As we have noted, critics of the reports and policies, particularly those from inside the profession of education, made three arguments against this strategy. First, they argued that such "top-down" reform would never work; that increasing high school graduation requirements and educational expectations generally would increase the dropout rate, and that this would work a disproportionate hardship on minority youth; and that substantial increases in educational resources were necessary to carry out any major reform of American education. Were these concerns justified?

That states should require explicitly that students take particular courses to qualify for a high school diploma was hardly a new idea when legislatures revived its use in the 1980s and 1990s. Legislatures often responded to perceived crises by adopting or changing such requirements. In the nineteenth century, for example, responding to intense lobbying by the Women's Christian Temperance Union, states mandated courses in physiology with special emphasis on the effects of alcohol and tobacco on the human body. In the twentieth century, states began to require physical education and, in the politically unstable years of the Great Depression, economics or civics. But in the 1970s, as concern over falling test scores raised anxieties over educational quality in general, states began to adopt more general requirements in the academic subject fields. If we take 1974 as a baseline year, 40 states had adopted a minimum requirement in English, 42 had established a minimum social studies requirement, and 35 had set requirements in mathematics and science. By 1985, the numbers were 45, 49, and 45, respectively. Eight years later, the lines had become sharper between states with the political will to legislate higher graduation requirements in all the core subjects and states that reverted to or continued a tradition of local determination. Five states, Colorado, Iowa, Massachusetts, Michigan, and Wyoming, had virtually no state-level requirements. Nebraska set a total hours requirement of 200, of which 80 needed to be in core subjects, with the details left to local districts (NCES, 1995).

In addition to this increase in the number of states asserting control over high school graduation requirements, the number of credits or years required in core subjects also rose. Between 1958 and 1980, the national mean requirements for graduation from high school remained flat at 3.4 years of English, 2 years of social studies, and 1.2 years each of mathematics and science. By 1985, the comparable figures were 3.8 years of English, 2.4 years of social studies, 2.2 years of mathematics, and 1.9 years of science; by 1993, while English remained the same, the other three subjects increased an additional 0.2 year each.[6] There were similar increases in the total credit hours required for graduation. In 1980, 42 states had such a requirement. Five years later this had risen to 46 states, 35 of which had either raised the requirement or set it for the first time. The mean units (course/years) required rose from 17.3 in 1980 to 19.2 in 1985 and 19.8 in 1993, while the mode rose from 16 to 20. In a related development, by 1985, 19 states had adopted some type of competency test for graduation and three others had made such a test a local option. By 1993, 22 states had established either different types of diplomas or some kind of endorsement or seal on the diploma to distinguish those students who had performed particularly well or who had taken a more rigorous program of studies (National Center for Education Statistics, 1987).

With all this upward pressure on graduation requirements, one would expect to see some shifts in student coursetaking. Beginning in 1983, the National Center for Education Statistics made a concerted effort to trace such shifts, as well as to collect other evidence of the effectiveness of the 1980s reforms. One of the agency's earliest attempts was a 1983 study that compared course enrollment data estimated from the 1982 *High School and Beyond* study with the 1972–73 U.S. Office of Education (USOE) study by Osterndorf and Horn (West, Diodato, & Sandberg, 1984). The comparison showed just a 2% shift from nonacademic to academic courses, with a 2% increase in the mathematics share accounting for all of this (see Appendix A, Table A.2). In fact, the big gainer in this period was the trade and industry category, which nearly quadrupled enrollments between 1972 and 1982, a time when overall high school enrollments were declining. This was due largely to the growth of regional skills centers throughout the nation, a somewhat belated and perhaps unintended result of the career education movement.

A better indication of changes in patterns of coursetaking after the mid-1970s is a comparison of the subject field distribution of the credits earned by graduates. As we saw in Chapter 5, the earliest available data of this type is a 1958 study carried out by USOE staffers. The most recent data come from a series of studies by Westat, Inc., under contract to the National Center for Education Statistics, of national samples of high school graduates representing the classes of 1982, 1987, 1990, 1992, and 1994. These studies can be compared with the study that Clifford Adelman (1983) prepared for the National Commission on Excellence in Education, analyzing transcript data from graduates of classes between 1976 and 1981 (see Appendix A, Table A.5). Across these six time points, there was a steady rise in the academic share of coursetaking, from 60 to 65%, a figure still well below the 74% academic share in 1958 but one that attained Ernest Boyer's proposed target of a diploma including two-thirds academic subjects. Increases in the enrollment shares of mathematics, science, foreign language, and computers make up these differences, with English actually losing share and social studies staying about even. The vocational fields were the big losers, declining from a combined share of just under 20% to just below 14%. Health and physical education courses also lost course credit share.

Perhaps a better way to see the impact of increases in graduation requirements on coursetaking is to look at the Westat tables (NCES, 1993) reporting the percentages of graduates having completed particular combinations of core requirements (see Appendix A, Table A.6). For example, among the 1982 graduates, only about 30% completed a regimen consisting of 4 years of English, 3 years of social studies, and 2 years each of mathematics and science. Among the 1990 graduates, this rose to two-thirds and by 1994 it was nearly three-quarters. About 13% of the 1982 graduates completed 3 years each of math and science, rising to 40% among the 1990 graduates and to 50% among those of 1994. Looking specifically at the core requirements recommended by *A Nation at Risk*—4 years of English; 3 years each of mathematics, science, and social studies; and one-half year of computers—less than 3% of the 1982 graduates had accomplished this pattern. By 1990, this had risen to more than one-fifth, and among 1994 graduates it was one in four (NCES, 1997).

These gains were particularly impressive among minority graduates. At the level of the most rigorous curriculum reported—4 years of English; 3 years each of social studies, mathematics, and science; 2 years of foreign language; and a half year of computers—the share of Black and Hispanic graduates following this regimen increased from less than 1% in 1982 to 20 and 28% respectively, in 1994, while the share of White graduates increased from 2% to 27%. Of course, since these figures represent only graduates, the increases would not be impressive if they were accompanied by increases in the dropout rates among these minority students. But, dire predictions to the contrary, this has not happened. Over this same period, the dropout rate for Black students actually declined slightly, and the rate for Hispanics has remained high but steady (Mirel & Angus, 1994).

In an attempt to tie coursetaking even more directly to changes in graduation requirements at the state level, Westat compared the percentage of graduates taking certain course regimens in states with more rigorous requirements with that in states with less rigorous ones. For example, in the three states requiring 3 years each of math and science to receive a standard diploma in 1994, 81% of graduates completed such courses, whereas in the other 47 states the percentage was only 47. In 24 states requiring 2 years each of science and math, in addition to 4 years of English and 3 years of social studies,[7] the percentage of graduates completing this pattern of coursework was 84, compared with just 63 in states without such requirements.

While this is an impressive demonstration of the power of top-down reform to bring changes, it is nevertheless clear that the relationship between state requirements and student coursetaking is not necessarily one-to-one. Many students take more academic work than is required for graduation, either by their state or their local district. For another thing, we do not know from these studies what has happened in regard to the coursetaking of those who do not graduate. In addition, there appear to be a certain number of graduates who have not actually met the requirements in their own state. This may be a matter of time lag or lax enforcement, or, far more troubling, it may be a difference between how state departments classify courses and how Westat does it. The question of classification is not trivial. As we know from our case studies, sometimes business math and shop math are counted as meeting graduation requirements in mathematics, sometimes not. It is therefore important to look beyond the distribution of enrollments between subject families and to consider shifts in enrollments within subject families. We can best do this by focusing on what happened in the cases of mathematics and science.

Math and Science in the 1980s

In the decade following the 1972–73 USOE course enrollment study, enrollment rates in both science and mathematics showed sizable gains—a 12% increase in the overall science enrollment rate and a more than 40% increase in mathematics. However, in both fields these increases were concentrated in lower-level courses. The noncollege preparatory mathematics courses showed over three times the gains of the college preparatory sequence, and in science, except for biology, the gains were mostly in general science courses (see Tables 6.1 and 6.2). It appears that prior to *A Nation at Risk*, while the high schools did respond to the public pressure for increased academic coursework, they did so in a time-honored fashion, designing new courses with academic titles geared to students of supposedly middling or low abilities. Over this same period of rising enrollments in science and mathematics, some studies showed a drift from the academic curriculum into the general curriculum (Adelman, 1983). Achievement test scores continued to decline, even for the college-bound student (Raizen & Jones, 1985).

During the period following *A Nation at Risk*, enrollment rates in both science and mathematics continued to increase, but the pattern of these increases was sharply different from previous increases. Science increased at a faster rate than before, while math increased at a slower rate. More striking, however, were the increases in the traditional academic courses—biology, chemistry, and physics; algebra, geometry, trigonometry, and advanced mathematics (NCES, 1997). Moreover, enrollment rates in general science courses seemed to be on the wane.

Table 6.1. Changes in Mathematics Coursetaking in U.S. High Schools, 1972–73 Through 1994

	Percent of 9–12 Enrollment		Percent of Graduates Receiving Credit			
	1972–73	1978–1982[a]	1982	1987	1990	1994
College-preparatory mathematics	40.2	49.8				
Pre-algebra	0.2	4.3	13.5	13.3	19.7	20.9
Elementary algebra	11.2	18.1	67.7	75.8	74.2	76.2
Intermediate algebra	8.3	7.1	31.1	45.3	47.2	56.5
Advanced alg./trig.	4.8	1.9	12.7	11.5	12.9	15.1
Geometry	11.6	11.4	49.5	59.9	64.2	71.4
Trigonometry	1.4	1.6	7.5	11.5	9.9	11.6
Advanced math[b]	2.2	4.3	16.2	26.0	26.0	34.0
Computer math	0.5	1.1	3.1	4.1	2.8	1.9
Non–college preparatory mathematics	15.0	28.2				
General math	13.8	21.7	46.4	38.5	35.9	25.7
Applied math	0.9	3.7	9.0	10.0	9.6	12.4
Consumer math	0.3	2.8	8.1	12.0	11.7	8.3
Total	55.3	77.8				

Sources: 1972–73 and 1978–1982 are derived from West, Diodato, and Sandberg, 1984; 1982, 1987, 1990, and 1994 are derived from National Center for Education Statistics, 1997, tab. 121.

Note: The last four columns include private school students, since it was not possible to adjust the figures at this level of detail.

[a]Based on student cohort of 1978–1982.

[b]Includes analysis, functions, college mathematics, probability and statistics, calculus, and combinations of these.

Certainly much of this change can be attributed to the more rigorous state-mandated graduation requirements that we discussed earlier.[8] However, we believe two other factors were equally, if not more, important. First, reformers in the 1980s, in contrast to many of those of the Sputnik era, appear to have taken seriously the need for greater scientific literacy in the general population. Second, insofar as these reformers also have been concerned with increasing the pool of potential scientists and engineers, they have stressed the need to include women and members of minority groups in that pool. As long as these ideas hold sway, it is unlikely that the nation's high schools will be able to "subvert" or "contain" the reforms as they have in the past, by sharply differentiating between the academic courses made available for bright, college-bound students and the "academic" courses designed for the general track or the perceived low-ability student.

Table 6.2. Changes in Science Coursetaking in U.S. High Schools, 1972–73
Through 1994

	Percent of 9–12 Enrollment		Percent of Graduates Receiving Credit			
	1972 73	1982[a]	1982	1987	1990	1994
General science	8.6	15.1	62.1	61.3	68.1	71.2
Biology	19.5	25.3	76.2	91.6	92.8	99.2
AP/honors biology			11.0	10.9	11.7	13.0
Chemistry	8.6	7.6	35.8	49.4	54.8	63.5
Physics	2.9	1.0	16.2	21.3	23.5	25.2
Chemistry and physics, adv.	0.1	2.3				
Physical science	6.0	8.5	31.2	38.7	41.5	51.3
Earth/space science	4.5	4.9	17.4	16.9	27.4	26.7
Applied science (engineering)	0.8	0.3	1.2	2.7	4.3	4.4
Other	0.2	0.4				
NSF and other special programs	7.2					
Total science	58.4	65.4				

Sources: Same as in Table 6.1.
[a]Based on student cohort of 1978–1982.

In all, the national trends provide strong, clear evidence that top-down reform has worked in terms of changing the nature and direction of high school student coursetaking, even if there are other forces at work. In every instance, the changes have been substantial. Moreover, the tougher graduation requirements have not been accompanied by increases in the dropout rate, a fact that should set to rest the traditional argument that demanding a more rigorous regimen of academic courses inevitably works to the detriment of low-ability students or of poor or minority students. Indeed, the national data indicate that minority students have responded more positively than majority students to the tougher graduation requirements, a fact that is surely among the best educational news in decades.

With these data in mind, we can assess the criticisms that professional educators have set forth about efforts to increase graduation requirements and establish national standards. First, the idea that professional educators will do the best job in determining requirements and standards gets little support from our research. In previous chapters we have seen that as educational professionals gained power over educational policy generally and as teacher power grew in the 1960s and 1970s, curriculum proliferation flourished, both with respect to the numbers of courses offered and to the range of different offerings that were created within subject domains, such as mathematics. For the most part, educational professionals have gotten American high schools into their present difficulties, and those educational leaders who are willing to pursue policies to dramatically change these schools remain a distinct minority. Given their failure to improve the quality of education for most high school students in the past, there seems little reason to believe that more input from professional educators, except perhaps through the media of their disciplined-based national associations, will lead to greatly improved results in the future. We are not saying that their voices should not be heard—indeed teachers are crucial to the successful implementation of reform—but their voices should not take precedence over those of other concerned citizens. In addition, regarding the efficacy of top-down reform, we also find that changes in graduation requirements have been a potent factor in determining what courses high school students take, regardless of whether teachers or other educational professionals have a hand in adopting or approving them.

Second, with respect to the dropout argument, one of the earliest responses to *A Nation at Risk* came from the National Education Association, which launched a multimillion dollar campaign of full-page ads in national magazines warning the country about the increases in dropout rates that surely would follow, a fear that the data indicate was entirely unwarranted. Third, arguments claiming that funding increases are necessary for bringing about substantial improvements in student achievement simply miss the point. The real consequence of such arguments is to consign huge numbers of students, primarily in inner cities, to an inferior education, in essence holding them hostage while educational interest groups engage in political battles that seem nowhere near resolution. Raising graduation requirements and setting standards appear to promote improved educational outcomes. We are not denying that greater equality of educational funding is desirable or that increases in funds for promising programs such as summer learning should not be given strong support (Vinovskis, 1997). Rather, we maintain that tightening graduation requirements and implementing high standards are policies that can be implemented immediately without substantial increases in funds and that these policies can have a positive impact on student achievement. Indeed, the state and local data that we analyze next point even more directly to the need for national educational standards as the centerpiece of major educational reform.

EXCELLENCE REFORM IN MICHIGAN

If the aggregate national data provide considerable evidence that increases in state-mandated graduation requirements have had a pronounced effect on patterns of student coursetaking, what has happened in those states that have failed or chosen not to establish such requirements at the state level? Our Michigan data can serve as the basis for a close examination of changes in coursetaking in one such state. For those interested in the mechanisms of excellence reform, the Michigan experience may hold an important lesson. Beginning in the late 1970s, when other states set or raised high school graduation requirements, Michigan demurred. It is now one of only five states that do not have minimum requirements in the core academic subjects. This is not to say that the national debate over the high school core curriculum did not arise in Michigan, but rather that it took some very strange turns.

The question of high school core curriculum and standards was not a state-level issue in Michigan until the spring of 1983. However, following the publica-tion of *A Nation at Risk*, Michigan responded with a spate of reports of its own. For example, the Michigan Commission on High Schools, established jointly by the State Board of Education and the Michigan Association of Secondary School Principals (including in its ranks teachers, administrators, board members, legislators, and others), issued a report calling for new graduation requirements, including 4 years of English; 3 years of social studies; 2 years each of mathematics and science; 2 years of either a foreign language, fine arts, or vocational education; 1 year of health and physical education; and one-half year of computer training (Michigan Commission on High Schools, 1983). True to Michigan's laissez faire tradition in school management, these standards were to be voluntary for a 4-year period, and only after that period were they to be mandated.[9]

Soon after this report appeared, the Republican caucus in the state legislature supported somewhat more rigorous standards, calling for the immediate adoption of the core curriculum set out in *A Nation at Risk*, a competency test for graduation, an extended school day and year, and a system of state inspection (Michigan State Republican Caucus, 1983). One year later, the state board of education issued its own document. This "blueprint for action" listed one standard for what high schools should be required to offer and another standard for what should be required for graduation, but it also claimed that the state board had no authority to make such standards mandatory and therefore merely recommended that they be included in each school's improvement plan (Michigan State Board of Education, 1984).

Michigan moved beyond debate in 1984 by introducing a state aid incentive program in the 1984–85 School Aid Act. The program offered a $28 per pupil incentive to those districts that would require secondary students to follow a 6-period day and would offer 4 years of English; 3 years each of math, science, and social studies; 2 years of a foreign language, arts, or vocational education (or any combination of these); 1 year of health and/or physical education; and a half year of computer training. That the vast majority of high schools were already meeting these incredibly modest demands seemed to have escaped the notice of the legislature. Worse, this program misidentified the problem.

In its research, the Michigan Department of Education (MDE) focused only on what courses high schools were *offering* rather than on what courses high school students were *taking*. Thus they ignored one of the key findings of the Michigan Commission on High Schools (1983) survey, which showed that only 8% of the state's high schools were *not* offering physics but that in the 92% offering the course, only 18% of the students took it. Thus, by providing incentives for schools to get students to choose courses within broad subject areas rather than requiring *specific* courses, Michigan adopted a 1950s approach to a 1980s problem.[10] This approach, using financial incentives to get schools to do what they were already doing, remained the state's primary reform strategy until 1990 and the passage of Public Act 25. At this point, another odd twist was added to the first.

Under Public Act 25, the legislature empowered the state board of education to develop a "model" core curriculum and to urge school districts to adopt it voluntarily. During the legislative debate and meetings with MDE staff, the concept of a "core curriculum" became distorted beyond all conceivable meaning. Michigan's "recommended" core curriculum, established by the MDE in 1991, included language arts, mathematics and science, "world studies," physical education and health, arts education, technology, aesthetic and cultural awareness, life and personal management, and career and employability skills (Michigan State Board of Education, 1992). In other words, it included just about anything that anyone might want to offer or to study in a high school. In calling this a "model core curriculum," Michigan's state board put its official imprimatur on the shopping mall high school. This version of a core curriculum was strongly supported by the state's largest teachers' union, the Michigan Education Association, largely because if the legislature were actually to mandate it in grades 7–12, as some of its supporters proposed, it would have been the largest job-creation program in the history of the state.

The MDE's "core curriculum" was still in draft form when the supporters of educational quality reform attacked it. The Michigan Business Roundtable (1991), for example, asked the state board "to develop a more ambitious and challenging core curriculum" and to avoid "a compromise document that lowers standards and includes all subject areas." It called for the board to set aside this document and to develop a "much more ambitious plan to build core curriculum frameworks" such as those developed in California and Connecticut (p. 6). When the legislature revisited the debate in the fall of 1993, a majority of representatives sided with this view. In December, the legislature added amendments to the school code that inserted the word "academic" into the phrase "model core curriculum." Moreover, the amendments designated math, science, reading, history, geography, economics, American government, and writing at all levels as subjects in which "desired learning objectives" should be developed; they called for the setting of academic performance standards in math, science, and communication arts consistent with the state board's model curriculum; and finally they mandated that all school districts be required to *offer* the "core academic curriculum" by 1997–98 (*Detroit Free Press*, 4/11/95).

Two fundamental difficulties remained with this approach: It still left the determination of what constitutes a core curriculum in the hands of a state board of education that had already shown itself to be unable to resist the lobbying efforts of curriculum special interest groups, and it continued to put the emphasis on what schools were required to teach rather than on what students were required to take.

Given these checkered, and in many ways misdirected, attempts at educational quality reform, what shifts occurred in student coursetaking? As a state that has failed to put rigorous high school graduation requirements in place, did Michigan deviate substantially from the national pattern described above? Appendix D, Table D.2, presents an array of the percentage distribution of subject field enrollments of Michigan high schools from 1948 to 1990.[11]

The trend data for Michigan suggest that the long-term decline in the academic share of coursetaking discussed in earlier chapters and evident from at least 1924 to 1960 reversed sometime between 1960 and 1972. But as we saw in our previous analysis of curriculum developments in this period, that increase in the academic share may be misleading. In fact, all of the shift is accounted for by a 7% increase in the English share, and thus is probably an artifact of the breaking up of year-long English courses into semester-long courses. From 1972 on, the academic share held steady until the 1980s at about 62%, and then increased quite dramatically. While this trend line is very similar to what happened in the nation as a whole, Michigan showed a higher academic share of coursetaking in 1960 and has remained slightly ahead of the nation in the academic share in the past 2 decades. Further, it has done so without benefit of the kind of state-level mandates that other states have utilized.

To consider the data in more detail, in 1972 Michigan students were ahead of the national average in both math and science. In the 1980s they were still ahead; the share of course enrollments represented by mathematics, science, and foreign language stood at one-third, while in 1972 it was only one-fifth. In the 1960s and 1970s, Michigan high schoolers took more industrial arts and home economics than the national average, while in the 1980s they took less. The combined share of all vocational field enrollments stood at 20% in 1979, but fell to less than 14% in 1990. In the 1970s, Michigan high school students took less physical education than the national average, but were almost exactly at that average in the 1980s, the share of health and physical education enrollments having declined by nearly a third. Art and music enrollment share remained fairly steady throughout.

Clearly, the Michigan experience suggests that strong state-mandated graduation requirements are not the only way to increase academic coursetaking in the nation's high schools. Throughout the 1980s, Michigan's school districts, one by one, strengthened their own graduation requirements without benefit of a state mandate, or even of strong state leadership. It would be impossible to generalize about whether these changes were the result of parent pressure, school board-initiated actions, or the urgings of high school principals (whose national and state organizations were endorsing many of the reforms laid out in *A Nation at Risk*). On the other hand, it is possible, as we will see in the case of Grand Rapids, that the increases in academic coursetaking might actually mask declines in the academic content of academic courses. Without such devices as curriculum frameworks, high schools could, for example, substitute "algebra topics" for algebra. At the time of this writing, Michigan is in the process of developing such frameworks, but the process is proving to be difficult and politically charged. The governor and the most influential voices on the state board are no longer interested in a strong, mandated state core curriculum, believing instead that parental choice and local control are the keys to improved educational quality, and the legislature has capitulated to these shifts in sentiment.

TRENDS IN GRAND RAPIDS: 1975–1990

If increases in graduation requirements and, perhaps, decreases in the number of courses offered in high school can be taken as evidence of an educational quality reform movement, then it is clear that such a movement gained momentum in Grand Rapids after 1975. The Grand Rapids Board of Education began to increase high school graduation requirements in 1978, when they raised the total number of required credits from 160 to 180. Four years later, the board again raised total credits to 200, of which 105 were required subjects and 95 were elective, and in 1985 the board raised the total to 225, of which 150 were required subjects. In 1995, the graduation requirements remained at 225 total credits consisting of 4 years of English (40 credits); 3 years each of mathematics and social studies; 2 years of science, including one life science and one physical science; 2 years of health and physical education; 1 year of either fine and performing arts, a foreign language, or career development and technology; and a half-year each of computer literacy and career planning. Since 1986, passing a competency test also has been a requirement for graduation. These graduation requirements are far more rigorous than those in place in Grand Rapids in either 1913 at the height of Progressive reform or in the 1950s as the nation wrestled with the challenge of Sputnik, and these dramatic increases did not occur because of any changes in state law. Moreover, there is clear evidence that these increases had an impact on the coursetaking patterns of Grand Rapids high school students.

As we saw in Chapter 5, the academic share of coursetaking in Grand Rapids high schools rose in the 1950s, and then remained stable at the 63 to 64% range throughout the next 2 decades. As late as 1980, the academic share of coursetaking in Grand Rapids high schools still stood at 62.5%, slightly lower than in 1971 (see Appendix B, Table B.12). But after the spate of national reports in the early 1980s, a major shift occurred. By 1986 the academic share was over 69%, 2 years later it was over 74%, and by 1990 it topped 75%. All of the academic fields except English, which was already nearly maximized, shared in this expansion, with mathematics enjoying the largest gains. Even the study of foreign language, which fell to an all-time low of 3% of all courses taken in 1980, began to show increases. In contrast, all of the nonacademic fields except the trade and industry category (which was offered largely in the skills centers) suffered losses of enrollment share. Commercial courses continued a decline that had begun as early as 1950; industrial arts and home economics enrollments fell as students with clear vocational objectives left to attend classes at the skills centers. Art and music also fell well below their peak years, and even health and physical education classes lost enrollment share as the closing of the educational park eliminated such popular electives as backpacking and modern dance. Bear in mind that these shifts occurred at a time when total high school enrollment was falling from 6,723 in 1980 to 4,508 in 1990, fewer students than were enrolled in 1957.

Further evidence of a major shift in educational values is found in the sharp reduction in the total number of different course titles offered in the Grand Rapids high schools (see Appendix B, Table B.11). The expansion of course titles that began in the 1950s reached a peak in 1975, when the schools offered 172 distinct courses.[12] Of these, 68 courses were offered only in the educational park or the skills centers, but that still left 104 courses, 54 academic courses and 50 nonacademic courses, offered in some or all of the four comprehensive high schools. After 1985, the board reduced the educational park offerings to four or five vocational courses, and by 1990 the educational park (although not these courses) was eliminated altogether. Partly as a result of this, but also because of significant curriculum revision in the comprehensive high schools, the total number of courses fell to 98 by 1990. The skills centers continued to operate and continued to draw at least a small number of students into a diverse array of vocational training opportunities. About 34 of the offerings were available only in the skills centers, but the enrollment in these courses represented only about 2% of student coursetaking. The comprehensive high schools offered 64 courses, about as many as they had offered in 1920.

The high school inspectors from the University of Michigan gave these changes only guarded approval. Their reports mentioned the shift in philosophy, but were ambivalent toward it. For example, in the 1986 evaluation of Ottawa Hills High School, the inspector observed, "The recently revised diploma requirements demonstrate a heavy academic swing," and then cautioned, "There needs to be close monitoring of the effects of these requirements to be sure that they do improve achievement, that there remains a balanced educational experience for students, and that the practical arts and fine arts are not neglected." Generally, the inspector praised the increased "academic emphasis," but the reports continued to emphasize the need to offer a broad range of programs to "meet the needs of an increasingly diverse student population," code words for the old progressive philosophy (Bureau of Accreditation and School Improvement Studies Archives, folders for Grand Rapids Ottawa Hills High School). Despite Grand Rapids' renewed emphasis on a strong core of academic subjects, the inspectors thought that the city *was* meeting diverse student needs through such programs as the Business Applied Technology (BAT) program, the Tech Prep program, and advanced placement classes.

But if there is considerable evidence of a fundamental and historic shift in Grand Rapids toward emphasizing an academic core program, there is also evidence that the older view—that many students were incapable of such a regimen—continued to exert influence. To see this, we must again consider coursetaking at a somewhat more detailed level, looking at the distribution of enrollments in specific courses within academic subject families. As graduation requirements rose, as the educational park closed, and as curriculum revision took hold in the comprehensive high schools, what sorts of changes in student coursetaking occurred? What specific courses within the academic subject areas gained or lost enrollment?

Table 6.3 presents an array of the distribution of enrollments in certain groupings of courses at specific times during the reform period. In English, for example, all students generally took at least one course every year they were in school. Raising the English requirement for graduation from 3 years to 4 did not affect the total enrollments in English significantly, but since it also became necessary to get a passing grade in 4 years of English, enrollments in reading and remedial English rose. By 1990, a course in speech, called oral communication, became part of the requirements. This had the effect of raising enrollments from 4 to 15%, while lowering enrollments in reading and remedial English proportionately.

In the 1970s, American history was dropped in favor of something called American Life. World history was eliminated altogether as a graduation requirement. Only American Life (2 years) and government (1 semester) were required of all students. By 1986, the board had restored the world history requirement and enrollments rose to more than a quarter of the social studies total. Similarly, U.S. history replaced American Life and drew another quarter of registrations. Government, combined with a 1-semester course in economics, was the third-year requirement, and a 1-semester course in careers, to be taken in senior year, rounded out the social studies requirement. With these changes, the proportion of students taking a social studies class rose above the 100% mark.

Mathematics, however, presents a somewhat different picture and raises serious questions about the effectiveness of the reform. When the board raised the mathematics requirement from 1 year to 2 between 1971 and 1980, the gain in math enrollments was spread fairly evenly across all levels of mathematics courses. Yet when the board raised the requirement to 3 years in 1986 and mathematics enrollments reached a 75% share of students, *all of the gains were in mathematics courses below algebra in difficulty level.* Several new courses—general math, consumer math, math topics, prealgebra, algebra topics, and math essentials—were developed to absorb the increase, presumably because the mathematics faculty felt that many students could not handle algebra and geometry. In fact, by 1990 the mathematics faculty offered more distinct course titles than any other academic

Table 6.3. Percentage Distribution of Enrollments by Course Level Within Subject Field, Grand Rapids High Schools, 1971–72 Through 1990–91

	1971–72	1980–81	1986–87	1990–91
English				
Regular, honors, advanced	87 6	76.5	72.7	72.7
Speech, drama, journalism, etc.	4.8	7.0	3.9	14.7
Reading, remedial English	7.5	16.5	23.3	12.6
Mathematics				
Below algebra	35.4	33.8	55.0	51.0
Algebra and geometry	48.5	48.4	30.1	35.1
Above geometry	16.1	17.8	14.9	13.9
Science				
Below biology	33.3	55.3	44.7	36.5
Biology, chemistry, and physics	53.9	39.7	48.2	54.3
Physiology	12.9	4.9	7.1	9.2
Social studies				
World history	6.0	2.8	26.6	26.2
American life	49.6	62.7		
U.S. history			22.9	24.0
Government	18.9	13.1	12.6	10.6
Careers			17.1	13.7
Other	25.5	21.4	20.8	25.4

Source: Bureau of Accreditation and School Improvement Studies, folders for Grand Rapids public high schools.

area. It may have been that without significant reform of the mathematics curriculum in the preceding grades, it was not possible to place more students in an algebra/geometry/trigonometry/calculus sequence. In any case, this example makes clear that merely raising mathematics requirements without specifying the expected content of courses (or preparing students adequately in elementary and junior high schools) will not produce the intended result.

We see yet another pattern of change in the sciences. In 1971 and 1980, when only 1 year of science was required, it appears that a large majority of students took more than 1 year of science. The main alternatives to the biology/chemistry/physics sequence were earth science and practical science in the ninth and tenth grades, and physiology in the twelfth. But by 1980 there were other titles, and the alternative science courses outdrew the traditional ones by a significant margin. Such titles as emergency medical care, science topics, ecology and life, and agriculture (as a science course) appeared at some of the comprehensive high schools, and the educational park offered astronomy. By 1986, when the graduation requirement was raised to 2 years, school officials offered two distinct sequences— the traditional biology/chemistry/physics sequence, physics having returned to the comprehensive high schools with the closing of the educational park, and another sequence consisting of earth science/physical science/life science. As science enrollments approached 70% of all students, the traditional and alternative sequences drew roughly equal numbers. By 1990, the enrollments in the biology/ chemistry/ physics sequence had pulled ahead of the other grouping by a significant margin.

The alternative science sequence provides evidence that even as they raised graduation requirements, Grand Rapids school leaders still found new ways to differentiate students within the academic subject fields. In addition to the alternative science courses, in English students were tracked into basic, regular, advanced, or honors English, and, as we noted, in mathematics they chose from a host of courses whose attraction was that they were easier than algebra. Tracking was also evident in social studies as "advanced" sections of U.S. history and world history began to appear. Even in the nonacademic fields, there was some evidence of this type of segregation. For example, while students could still take a few courses in such commercial subjects as typing and shorthand, those students who were most serious about training for office work were placed in a block program called the Business Applied Technology program. Similarly, Tech Prep was offered as a block-type program alongside a few traditional industrial arts offerings. Both of these special programs had strong associations with businesses in the community and an emphasis on mentorship.

One other troubling way in which differentiation seemed to increase even as graduation requirements and the academic share of coursetaking rose was the growth of special education and bilingual education programs. In the four Grand Rapids high schools in 1986, special education class enrollments totaled 879 and bilingual education enrollments totaled 334. By 1988, the totals were 1,385 and 375, respectively, and by 1990, they were 1,546 and 562. The combined enrollments in these two types of special classes increased from 1.9% of total course enrollments in 1980 to 8.4% in 1990. Most of the classes designated as one or the other of these were academic classes, that is, classes in English, mathematics, science, or social studies. Special education and bilingual students also were included in nonacademic classes, but not in specifically designated sections of such classes. Because the designated classes were extremely small, the ratio of special teachers to regular staff shifted even more dramatically than did enrollments. At the beginning of the period, one teacher in 12 was a special teacher. By the end of the period, it was one in five.

In summary, while it is clear that a new dedication to higher standards, a more focused curriculum, and an emphasis on basic skills swept through the Grand Rapids high schools after 1980, it also is evident that new ways of differentiating students came into vogue. Teachers of mathematics and science were especially imaginative. When the board raised graduation requirements in their fields, these teachers developed new courses designed to meet the letter of the requirements while ignoring their spirit. In fairness, however, this seems more the case in the early stages of reform than in the later stages. The Grand Rapids case suggests that educators can find many ways to give the appearance of adopting more rigorous graduation requirements by raising the required amounts of academic subjects, yet continue to practice differentiated schooling by finding new ways to differentiate students *within* the academic subject fields. Detroit also presents examples of the difference between appearance and reality in curriculum reform.

TRENDS IN DETROIT

One of the arguments heard most persistently in opposition to the high school curriculum reforms advocated by the national reports of the 1980s was that raising high school graduation requirements or requiring a passing score on a basic skills proficiency test would work a special hardship on minority students. Some critics went so far as to suggest that the purpose of these reforms was to increase the dropout rate and decrease the high school graduation rate of minority young people. Detroit would seem to be an excellent test case of these assertions, first because of the extremely high proportion of minority students in its public schools, and second because, in the absence of a state mandate, the district controlled its own destiny with respect to the conditions of graduation. It chose to do precisely what Grand Rapids did, namely, increase its graduation requirements throughout the 1980s. As late as 1977, the requirements for high school graduation were unchanged from what they had been in 1950—160 total credit hours, consisting of 4 years of English; 2 years of history; 1 year each of government/economics, mathematics, and science; and 2 years of health (see Appendix C, Table C.3). By the fall of 1983 the board had increased the total hours requirement to 200, raised the mathematics requirement to 2 years, lowered the health requirement to 1 semester of physical education and 1 semester of personal health management, and added two new requirements—1 semester of vocational education and 200 clock hours of "out-of-school learning experience." Further, the board established an "endorsed diploma," which required a passing grade on a basic subjects (reading, writing, and mathematics) proficiency test.

There was, however, both more and less to these changes than appears at first glance. At the same time that it raised the total hours requirement to 200, the board raised the amount of credit granted for a host of nonacademic courses from half to full credit. A few double-period vocational courses were even granted double credit. Thus, for students who took substantial numbers of nonacademic courses, there was no real increase in the total credits for graduation. Surely this was a mixed message to send to the students. At the same time that national reports stressed core academic subjects, Detroit indicated that academic subjects were "worth" no more than nonacademic.

Of these changes only the addition of the vocational education requirement is specifically related to circumstances in Detroit. As a part of the final decision in the *Milliken v. Bradley* case, the federal judge overseeing the case ordered the State of Michigan to build five new vocational schools in the city of Detroit. The state appealed this part of the decision, but after the Supreme Court ruled against the state, it provided the funds for the schools, which came on line in the late 1970s. One unintended consequence of the opening of these schools, admission to which was limited to students with good academic records, was the reduction in both offerings and enrollments in the vocational departments of the regular high schools.[13] We speculate that the addition of vocational education as a graduation requirement for all students was motivated by a desire to maintain these enrollment levels.

By 1987, the Detroit board raised the total credit hour requirement to 210 and the science requirement from 1 year to 2, making ninth-grade general science a required course.[14] All other requirements remained the same. By 1995, the board returned to the 200–credit hour requirement and changed the 1-semester vocational education requirement to 2 years in either vocational courses, the arts, or foreign language. A 1-semester course in computer applications also was required. In order to receive an endorsed diploma, students had to pass not only the city's proficiency test but also the state's high school competency test, which went into effect in 1995–96.

In all, this appears to be a mixed picture. Detroit gave the appearance of joining the movement toward a more focused high school curriculum and higher standards, but at the same time it took steps to increase student enrollment in vocational classes and the arts. How did these modest changes in graduation requirements affect student coursetaking?

The ratio of academic to nonacademic course enrollments in Detroit remained virtually unchanged between 1975 and 1983 at 62 to 38% (see Appendix C, Table C.2). In response to the increase in required mathematics, the math share rose from 12 to 15.5%, but this was offset by slightly smaller shares in science, foreign language, and English. On the nonacademic side, despite the opening of the new vocational schools, the total of all vocational enrollments remained virtually the same at just under 20%.

Given Detroit's previous struggles to find forms of mathematics that students could handle, how did educators in Detroit respond to the increase of the math requirement from 1 year to 2? Recall that by 1975, the practice of placing students in business and shop mathematics as a way of getting them through the 1-year requirement had been replaced by offering more sections of general mathematics and prealgebra (see Table 6.4). By 1983, educators developed a new approach.

Table 6.4. Mathematics and Science Course Enrollment and Percentage Distributions, Detroit High Schools, 1975–76, 1983–84, and 1989–90

	1975–76[a]		1983–84[b]		1989–90[c]	
	n	%	*n*	%	*n*	%
Mathematics						
Remedial mathematics					532	1.9
Math competency			5,605	18.2	1,577	5.7
Freshman math			4,856	15.7		
Prealgebra	6,873	22.4				
Basic algebra/geom.					10,996	40.0
Alg./geom./precalc.	17,678	57.7	14,787	47.9	11,783	42.8
Junior math			2,544	8.2		
Refresher math	1,729	5.6	1,726	5.6	1,276	4.8
Business mathematics	3,470	11.3	827	2.7	839	3.0
Shop mathematics	895	2.9	131	0.4	0	
Other					510	1.9
Total	30,645	99.9	25,089	99.9	27,513	100.1
Science						
General science			168	0.9	5,088	15.8
Gen. biol./gen. chem.	5,948	37.7	4,680	25.2	7,006	21.7
Biol./chem./physics	7,010	44.5	10,468	56.2	12,997	40.4
IPS and phys. sci.	1,283	8.1	1,700	9.1	4,148	12.9
Earth science	1,031	6.5	956	5.1	2,007	6.2
Physiology/anatomy	349	2.2	466	2.5	848	2.6
Other	148	0.9	165	0.9	160	0.5
Total	15,769	99.9	18,603	99.9	32,254	100.1

Source: Bureau of Accreditation and School Improvement Studies, folders for Detroit public high schools.

[a]Schools are Cass, Central, Cooley, Denby, Finney, Ford, Kettering, King, Mackenzie, Mumford, Murray–Wright, Northeastern, Northwestern, Osborn, Pershing, Redford, Southeastern, Southwestern, Western (19).

[b]Schools are Cass, Chadsey, Cooley, Denby, Finney, Ford, Kettering, King, Mackenzie, Mumford, Murray–Wright, Northern, Northwestern, Pershing, Redford, Southwestern, and Western (17).

[c]Schools are Central, Chadsey, Cody, Cooley, Denby, Finney, Ford, Kettering, Mackenzie, Mumford, Northern, Northwestern, Osborn, Pershing, Redford, Southeastern, Southwestern, Western (18).

The math curriculum included *4 full years of general mathematics*, consisting of Math Competency 1 and 2, Freshman Math, Junior Math, and Refresher Math. The range of math offerings was described as follows:

> The high school math program is designed for students of varying abilities. Students completing Algebra 1–2, continue with Geometry 1–2. Next in this sequence is Algebra 3–4 and Pre-Calculus 1–2.
>
> Students needing a little additional math before assuming the above should take Freshman Math 1–2 (Pre-Algebra) first.
>
> Students desiring an excellent foundation in mathematics which includes a review of basic skills, business applications, and technical applications should take any, or all, of the following: Math Competency 1–2, 9th grade; Math Competency 3–4, 10th grade; Junior Math 1–2, 11th grade; Refresher Math 1–2, 12th grade. *There are no prerequisites for these classes.* (BASIS Archives, University of Michigan, Osborne High School Course Planning Folder, 1983, n.p.)

The course descriptions for these general math classes all used the phrase, "review of basic skills." When enrollments in freshman math were combined with those in algebra, geometry, and precalculus, the total represented 64% of all math enrollments. *But more than a third of all high school students in Detroit never got beyond general mathematics, even with a 2-year graduation requirement.*

By 1987, with the national "excellence" reform in full swing, the academic share of coursetaking had increased in Detroit to two-thirds, with science and computer training representing most of the increase, but with foreign language showing small gains as well. Vocational fields lost enrollment share, and health and physical education declined slightly. In assessing these changes, the critical question is, What happened in science coursetaking as the requirement was doubled? Not surprisingly, the big increase was in ninth-grade general science, which went from less than 200 enrolled in 1983 to over 5,000 in 1989. The share of science enrollments represented by biology, chemistry, and physics, which was at 56% in 1983, fell to 35% in 1989. Even with the general science enrollments omitted from the calculation, their share was only 42%. Again, the irony is that an increase in graduation requirements in an academic subject in Detroit actually resulted in a reduction in the proportion of students exposed to challenging coursework.

In summary, Detroit does not appear, after all, to be a good test site for the argument that toughening academic standards works a special hardship on minority students. The reason is that Detroit managed to give the appearance of toughening standards without really doing so. It managed to double its graduation requirements in science and math without requiring students to take additional challenging math and science courses. It increased its total credit requirement by one-fourth, but did not expect students to actually complete more courses. Detroit stands as an example of the continuing capacity of educators to maintain the old progressive philosophy of low expectations and demands on students whose abilities and/or past performances suggest that they cannot master challenging subject matter.

SUMMARY

In the 1980s and 1990s, deepening national concern by parents, politicians, and employers over the quality of secondary education, a concern shared by some leading professional educators, combined with a series of highly critical national reports and legislated changes in high school graduation requirements, led to a significant, and we believe historic, shift in the pattern of courses taken by the nation's high school students. The share of high school coursework represented by the academic subjects, particularly mathematics, science, foreign language, and computer training, rose substantially. This reversed a long-term trend of de-emphasizing academic subjects in favor of vocational and personal development subjects that was almost as old as the twentieth century itself. More important, the very idea of the differentiated curriculum, an idea that was absolutely basic to the modern, American, comprehensive high school, came under serious and sustained attack from several quarters for the first time in history.

At the same time, however, the idea of differentiation has shown a quiet resiliency, a fact that is not at all surprising given the idea's long service to professional educators as a defense against the waves of critical assaults unleashed against the schools since the end of World War II. Among many educators the belief persists that many, if not most, high school students are incapable of mastering tough academic courses and need to be tracked into less challenging (but also less useful) regimens of coursework. At the level of local school districts, as evidenced in Grand Rapids and Detroit, educators developed variations of courses within subject domains to meet the letter but not the spirit of new, stiffer graduation requirements. Local boards or other educational policy makers that are not in sympathy with excellence reforms or that continue to believe educational equity means equal time spent in school rather than equal access to the forms knowledge necessary for successful participation in a complicated, high-tech world will find ways to give the appearance of toughening standards without actually doing so.

As encouraging as the recent increases in academic coursetaking by minority students certainly are (indeed we see them as perhaps the most positive development of the entire excellence movement), our findings about the nature of many of the math and science courses that students in Grand Rapids and Detroit are taking give us great cause for concern. Many educators still resist clear mandates to provide all students with opportunities to master rigorous, academic coursework. Playing an educational form of "bait and switch," these educators offer courses with academic titles but unchallenging content. As such, they maintain the structure of split level education that has dominated American secondary education for most of this century and consequently the structure of educational inequality that has been the hallmark of that system.

There appear to be only a small number of policy options that would eliminate such forms of educational malpractice—the establishment of a national curriculum similar to those found in other industrialized or postindustrialized countries or, failing that, the implementation of high-quality national educational standards in every academic subject area, standards that states and local school districts can adopt and enforce. These are the only approaches to educational reform that would ensure that all students had access to the same high-quality material, the only steps that could begin to ensure that *all* students would graduate from high school with the knowledge and skills necessary for meeting the challenges of the rapidly changing world they will inherit. For a variety of cultural and political reasons there is no possibility of creating a national curriculum in the United States. Even more unfortunate, however, are the prospects for the educational standards movement, which, after a very inspiring beginning, appears to have lost its momentum nationally and is bedeviled by dozens of petty battles in various states (Ravitch, 1995). Unless the campaign for national standards can be revitalized, the most exciting and promising opportunity for improving American secondary education in this century will have been squandered. Worse, the old order will triumph once again.

NOTES

1. As we have seen, such an observation was common in the 1930s, but was never connected with the principle of curricular differentiation at that time.

2. Oakes found a somewhat different pattern for girls and young women, who tended to "opt-out" of math and science courses in high school despite good performance in earlier classes.

3. By *flexible term equivalent* Kearns and Doyle meant demonstrated competence in a subject area, not seat-time or credits. It offers a way for students to move through a required curriculum at their own pace, with proof of mastery the only criterion for completing courses.

4. In 1976, for example, one of the mainstays of the educationists' arguments that *enrollments* in academic courses had been rising since the 1950s disappeared as demographic trends caught up with prevailing educational policy. In that year, high school enrollments began to fall for the first time since World War II, and there were enrollment declines in nearly all subject fields.

5. Bracey, who has been one of the most vigorous defenders of the educational status quo, also emerged recently as one of the last defenders of life-adjustment education. In a letter to the editor of the *Atlantic Monthly*, he wrote that life-adjustment education might have been anti-intellectual, "but at least its advocates were trying to cope with 100

percent of the population" (Bracey, 1996b, p. 10). Apparently, Bracey still cannot conceive of the possibility of teaching high-quality, rigorous academic work to the vast majority of high school students.

6. While these increases are significant, it should be borne in mind that in many Asian countries, high school students routinely take 4 years each of language arts, social studies, mathematics, and science. In many cases, they also take 4 years of English or another foreign language.

7. For a list of these states, see NCES (1997, p. A21).

8. Thirty-six states increased requirements in mathematics and thirty-three states increased them in science between 1980 and 1984, mostly prior to the influence of *A Nation at Risk* (Raizen & Jones, 1985).

9. A 1983 survey showed that 80% of Michigan high school principals opposed state-mandated graduation requirements (Michigan Commission on High Schools, 1983).

10. A Michigan Department of Education report claimed that this program was a success, but an analysis by C. Philip Kearney (1986) showed it to be "an exercise in symbolic policymaking."

11. It should be noted that while all of the University of Michigan data are limited to accredited high schools, these schools generally have represented about 95% of the state's high school enrollment.

12. Some might argue that this is an undercount, since we tallied, for example, Spanish 1, 2, 3, and 4 as a single offering.

13. Detroit had an unbending rule that if, by the fourth Friday of each term, enrollments in a given class did not reach a predetermined level, the class would be canceled. With a few students being "creamed off" the regular vocational classes to attend the specialized schools, enrollments in many classes fell below the "cut" point, and those students who did not qualify for transfer were left with few or no vocational classes.

14. In previous years, science had not been taught as a ninth-grade subject and the one-year science requirement was met by taking a science class in 10th, 11th, or 12th grade.

7

Implications for Policy and Practice

WE BEGAN THIS BOOK with two main objectives. First, we wanted to present a new and different interpretation of the modern history of the American high school. Unlike previous historians who have explored that topic, we wanted to base this new interpretation not only on an analysis of the rhetoric of school reform but also on an examination of data on curriculum offerings and student coursetaking. Second, we hoped that this historical approach would contribute to current political and policy discussions about the future of high schools. In this final chapter, we bring these two objectives together, demonstrating where our key findings shed light on some current issues of policy and practice in secondary education.

Our historical analysis has demonstrated that, for the most part, two ideas have guided the professional educators who shaped the development of the public high school in the twentieth century: (1) that equalizing educational opportunity meant offering different courses to different students based on their probable futures, which in turn would equalize the amount of time students spent in public schools; and (2) that most of the steadily increasing number of high school students were incapable of and had no need for serious academic study. Rather than furthering equality, however, these ideas spurred the creation of high schools in which students followed increasingly separate and substantially unequal educational programs.

Indeed, few ideas have been more destructive to equal educational opportunity or to democratic education itself than the two cited above. Despite claims by educators that they were building "democracy's high school," the institutions they created were deeply undemocratic, providing only a small percentage of students with the opportunity to master the knowledge and skills that might lead to power and success in American society. Moreover, because educators increasingly sorted students along class, racial, and gender lines, the differentiated curriculum served to exacerbate rather than ameliorate the deepest divisions in American society. The introduction of intelligence testing compounded these problems by providing a supposedly scientific rationale for differentiation (and the social stratification it encouraged) and by strengthening the belief that only a small number of students could master and profit from a rigorous, academic program.

These ideas also inspired an educational version of Gresham's law in which bad curriculum ultimately drove out good. Our analysis of American secondary education has uncovered numerous examples of reforms introduced to accommodate students of supposedly low ability (e.g., the life-adjustment movement, the reduction of graduation requirements, the increasing use of electives) that gradually became features of high school programs for all students. By the middle of the twentieth century, education aimed at the lowest common denominator had become the norm in America's high schools. In short, the differentiated high school curriculum fulfilled few if any of the grand goals that its advocates claimed, and the problems it has created far outweigh its alleged benefits.

Even if one were to grant that the structure of the American economy and the requirements for political and civic participation in the first half of the twentieth century made differentiated secondary education a rational choice, in the latter half of the century, the emergence of the United States as a world power, the globalization of the economy, and the dawn of the information age all signaled the need for a fundamental rethinking of this philosophy. Yet such rethinking is precisely what educational leaders failed to do as they defended their vision in the face of the Great Depression, World War II, the cold war, Sputnik, and the upheavals of the 1960s. Only in the late 1970s did challenges to differentiation begin to have an impact. Arising from a broad spectrum of opinion, new critics of the educational status quo began a quiet revolution that by the 1980s had contributed to substantial changes in educational policy, curriculum, and coursetaking. In the past 2 decades, we have seen historically unprecedented changes in patterns of student coursetaking that have moved us closer to equality of educational opportunity and toward greater democracy in education than ever before.

That said, we still have a long way to go. The goal of providing all young people access to the same kinds of rigorous, challenging, and empowering educational programs remains elusive. In order to realize the kind of democratic education we envision, a number of steps still need to be taken. Some of these steps relate to policy questions that are outside the scope of this book, including greater equalization of funding of schools in impoverished urban and rural areas, the expansion and improvement of preschool programs, and the introduction of summer learning and tutoring programs for low-achieving youngsters. But as necessary as we believe these structural changes to be, they are not sufficient for ensuring the kinds of educational change that will provide truly equal education for all American students.

Our research leads us to several specific reform proposals that we believe can contribute substantially to the improvement of American education. First, if we are to seriously address the problems that differentiation has produced, we need to move steadily toward even more rigorous and demanding high school graduation requirements. While many states have raised their graduation requirements, few have adopted what the authors of *A Nation at Risk* termed the New Basics,

namely, 4 years of English; 3 years each of mathematics, science, and social studies; 2 years of a foreign language; and a half-year of computer training.[1] This is
clearly a necessary first step but one that will require a real display of will from
political and educational leaders in every state. Since few states may be able to
muster that political will alone, we believe that continued pressure from national
leaders is vital to move us in that direction.[2]

Second, as we have seen, raising graduation requirements does little good if
schools are permitted to respond with the educational version of "bait and switch"
in which courses with academic titles simply mask watered-down content. For
this reason, national content standards such as those that have been developed in
civics, history, music, and to some extent mathematics, and detailed curriculum
frameworks like those adopted in some states, are a necessary concomitant to higher
graduation requirements.

Of course, setting high academic standards for high school courses demands
that equally high standards and expectations become the norm in the elementary
and middle schools. Many features of education in the pre–high school grades
sustain a system of low expectations—social promotion, ability grouping, how
teachers allocate time during the school day, and the use of criterion-referenced
tests in statewide testing programs designed to measure minimum competencies.
As a consequence of such policies and practices, many students enter high school
lacking not only the skills and knowledge necessary for success but also with the
belief that there is little need to put forth effort to master challenging material.
National standards in reading and mathematics and a national examination system, such as those advocated by President Clinton, would be a step in the right
direction.

In addition, these changes can succeed only if the educators who are responsible for teaching academic material are well prepared themselves in the content
areas. Standards-based curriculum reform depends on the depth of knowledge that
educators have of subject matter. Unfortunately, recent surveys have found that
39.5% of science teachers, 34% of math teachers, and 25% of English teachers are
not well prepared, having neither a major or a minor in the subjects they are teaching (Ravitch, 1998; U.S. Department of Education, 1997). Frankly, we cannot
imagine any major improvements in student achievement if this situation persists.
On the surface, correcting this problem by tightening certification standards and
hiring practices appears to be relatively simple. However, during a period in which
teacher shortages loom (as they do particularly in urban school systems), taking
such action demands concerted efforts by both political and educational leaders.

Third, educational policy makers must demand that our schools, particularly
our high schools, focus on their academic mission above all other considerations.
The idea that key academic subjects have higher priority than other subjects and
activities must prevail. This does not mean that students should not have some

electives, that activities such as school newspapers or drama clubs should be eliminated, or that vocational courses should be immediately scrapped. Rather, a New Basics high school in which students take all the graduation requirements listed above during a 6-period day would still leave almost 25% of instructional time for courses and activities in non-Basics classes.[3]

Such a focus on academic subjects will not, as supporters of vocational education contend, leave large numbers of noncollege-bound students poorly prepared for the working world. Such arguments falsely assume that a solid core of academically rigorous courses could not also be part of a career-oriented high school program. Other industrialized countries have been able to balance these objectives; we can as well. Moreover, this argument misses the most fundamental aspect of modern economic life, namely, that in a high-tech, information-rich world, the best vocational preparation is academic.

Fourth, professional educators, professors in schools and colleges of education, and classroom teachers must begin working diligently on methods and materials that will enable all students to master challenging coursework. One of the most widely repeated educational clichés today is that all children can learn. The question we pose to our colleagues is whether they believe that all children can learn the same challenging material. As we have seen, for most of the twentieth century, education professors generally have replied to that question with an emphatic no. We are convinced that that assumption is wrong. Nevertheless, we recognize that simply offering rigorous and challenging courses without addressing the question of how to make such coursework accessible to a diverse body of students is both foolish and naive.

Children come to school with diverse abilities, backgrounds, talents, and problems. They learn different things at different rates and at different times in their development. Given that, schools emphasizing high academic standards will succeed only if educational professionals create developmentally appropriate, challenging course materials and methods for all students on every grade level. Much of the failure of modern American education lies in our avoiding the formidable task of discovering how to teach difficult subjects in ways that are both accessible to young people and yet true to the complexity and richness of the material. Such efforts are central to ending the culture of low expectations that differentiation has created in American schools.

Differentiation has survived so long in part because it made the process of teaching and learning so simple for teachers and students alike. Teachers put forth little effort developing methods and materials for the vast majority of students because educators assumed these students didn't need and wouldn't master much of the material anyway. These students responded with equally little effort because so little was expected of them. Everyone drifted on an easy sea of blissful ignorance. That drifting must end.

It is long past time for educational professionals to stop selling students short and to begin using their skills and talent to give all American children an equal and equally good education. Over 30 years ago, Jerome Bruner declared that "any subject can be taught effectively in some intellectually honest form to any child at any stage of development" (Bruner, 1960, p. 33). Bruner's vision remains a goal for which all educators should strive, perhaps the most important and worthiest goal the profession has before it.

NOTES

1. As rigorous as this program of studies might be for American students, it is still a few notches short of the "world-class standards" in place in the educational systems of Asia and parts of Europe.

2. Certainly, numerous critics will challenge this recommendation by arguing that any strengthening of graduation requirements will have an adverse effect on children of low ability. This is, of course, the same argument that professional educators have been using for most of the twentieth century. It is no more true now than it was in 1920 (see Mirel & Angus, 1994).

3. We believe that courses such as physical education and keyboarding should not necessarily meet 5 days per week nor should these classes and such activities as working on the school newspaper receive academic credit.

Summary Data, United States

Table A.1. Enrollment for Grades 9–12, Population Aged 14–17, and High School Graduates by Gender (in thousands), United States, 1889–90 Through 1993–94

	Enrollment			Pop. Aged 14–17		Graduates		
	Total	Public	Private	Total	% Enrolled	Boys	Girls	Percent of Population Aged 17
1889–90	298	203	95	5,355	5.6	19	25	3.5
1899–1900	630	519	111	6,152	10.2	38	57	6.4
1909–10	1,032	915	117	7,220	14.3	64	93	8.8
1919–20	2,414	2,200	214	7,736	31.2	124	188	16.8
1929–30	4,741	4,399	341	9,341	50.7	300	367	29.0
1939–40	7,059	6,601	458	9,720	72.6	579	643	50.8
1943–44	6,031	5,585	446	9,449	63.8	424	595	42.3
1949–50	6,397	5,725	672	8,405	76.1	571	629	59.0
1959–60	9,306	8,271	1,035	11,155	83.4	895	963	69.5
1969–70	14,337	13,037	1,300[a]	15,549	92.2	1,430	1,459	76.9
1975–76	15,604	14,304	1,300[a]	17,125	91.1	1,552	1,596	73.7
1979–80	14,916	13,616	1,300[a]	16,610	89.8	1,491	1,552	71.4
1989–90	12,583	11,390	1,193[a]	13,496	93.2	2,588		74.2
1993–94	13,152	11,961	1,191[a]	13,802	95.3	2,479		71.5

Source: National Center for Education Statistics, 1995, Tabs. 55, 98.
[a]Estimated.

203

Table A.2. Percentage Distribution of Subject Field Enrollments in Public Secondary Schools for Grades 9-12, United States, 1914-15 Through 1981-82

Subject Field	1914-15	1921-22	1927-28	1933-34	1948-49	1960-61	1972-73	1981-82
English	22.6	17.0	19.1	18.6	18.4	17.9	20.1	19.9
Foreign language	14.5	11.9	9.5	6.9	4.0	4.3	3.9	3.3
Mathematics	15.2	13.9	12.8	11.1	9.8	9.9	9.2	11.2
Science	13.0	13.9	10.6	10.1	9.7	9.3	10.0	9.4
Social studies	13.3	16.7	15.2	15.5	17.4	15.6	16.2	16.9
Computer training								0.4
Commercial	4.3	11.1	11.4	11.3	10.5	8.9	6.8	6.7
Industrial arts	2.4	2.3	4.0	3.5	3.7	3.7	4.2	3.4
Household arts	2.5	3.1	3.3	3.3	4.3	3.6	3.5	3.4
Trade and industry			0.6	0.7	1.2	0.7	0.5	2.3
Agriculture	1.4	1.1	0.7	0.7	1.2	1.0	0.4	0.5
Health and phys. ed.[a]	—	—	4.9	11.5	12.4	15.9	17.5	15.9
Music	6.2	5.5	5.2	5.0	5.4	6.6	4.7	3.1
Art	4.5	3.2	2.3	1.7	1.6	2.5	3.0	3.5
Other		0.4	0.4	0.2	0.4	0.2	0.2	—
Total academic	78.7	73.4	67.2	62.2	59.3	57.0	59.4	61.1
Total nonacademic	21.3	26.6	32.8	37.9	40.7	43.0	40.7	39.0
Registrations/student	5.05	4.62	5.02	5.09	5.61	6.42	7.00	6.97

Sources: Recoded and adapted from U.S. Bureau of Education, 1915, 1926; U.S. Office of Education, 1930, 1938, 1951; Wright, 1965; Osterndorf & Horn, 1976; West, Diodato, & Sandberg, 1984.

[a]Includes Safety, Driver's Training, and ROTC.

Table A.3. Subject Field Enrollments (in thousands) in Public Secondary Schools for Grades 9–12, United States, 1914–15 Through 1981–82

Subject Field	1914–15	1921–22	1927–28	1933–34	1948–49	1960–61	1972–73	1981–82
Total 9–12 enrollment	1,167	2,157	2,897	4,497	5,399	8,219	13,438	12,661
English	1,332	1,694	2,776	4,266	5,576	9,438	18,911	17,716
Foreign language	857	1,185	1,377	1,575	1,200	2,293	3,659	2,953
Mathematics	896	1,387	1,859	2,532	2,958	5,224	8,608	9,850
Science	766	1,388	1,534	2,308	2,944	4,908	9,414	8,278
Social studies	786	1,665	2,213	3,540	5,265	8,226	15,224	15,008
Computer training								344
Commercial	251	1,104	1,656	2,588	3,194	4,706	6,410	5,874
Industrial arts	140	226	285	798	1,127	1,944	3,921	2,980
Household arts	150	308	477	750	1,305	1,901	3,249	3,024
Trade and industry			92	158	369	365	484	1,874
Agriculture	84	110	106	159	364	505	346	420
Health and phys. ed.	—	—	713	2,625	3,747	8,395	16,460	14,057
Music	367	545	754	1,149	1,625	3,473	4,461	2,733
Art	267	318	340	394	486	1,335	2,795	3,061
Other		38	62	38	124	91	103	80

Sources: Same as Table A.2.

Table A.4. Percentage of High School Students (Grades 9–12) Enrolled in Subject Fields, United States, 1914–15 Through 1981–82

Subject Field	1914–15	1921–22	1927–28	1933–34	1948–49	1960–61	1972–73	1981–82
English	114.2	78.6	95.8	94.9	103.3	114.8	140.7	139.0
Foreign language	73.5	55.0	47.5	35.0	22.2	27.9	27.2	23.3
Mathematics	76.9	64.4	64.2	56.3	54.8	63.6	64.1	77.8
Science	65.7	64.4	53.0	51.3	54.5	59.7	70.1	65.4
Social studies	67.4	77.2	76.4	78.8	97.5	100.1	113.6	118.0
Computer training								2.7
Commercial	21.5	51.2	57.2	57.6	59.2	57.3	47.7	46.4
Industrial arts	12.6	10.5	20.2	17.8	20.9	23.6	29.2	23.5
Household arts	12.9	14.3	16.5	16.7	24.2	23.4	23.1	23.9
Trade and industry			3.2	3.5	6.8	4.4	3.6	15.7
Agriculture	7.2	5.1	3.7	3.5	6.7	6.1	2.6	3.3
Health and phys. ed.	—	—	24.6	58.4	69.4	102.1	122.5	111.0
Music	31.5	25.3	26.0	25.5	30.1	42.3	33.2	21.6
Art	22.9	14.7	11.7	8.6	9.0	16.2	20.8	24.2
Other		1.7	2.1	0.9	2.3	1.1	0.8	1.5

Sources: Same as Table A.2.

Table A.5. Percentage Distribution of Credits Earned by High School Graduates by Subject Field, United States, 1958–1987

Subject Field	1958	1969	1973	1976–81	1982	1987
English	24.2	20.3	18.4	18.8	17.9	17.5
Foreign language	6.0	5.8	4.8	3.6	4.9	6.3
Mathematics	12.7	12.7	10.6	11.5	12.0	12.9
Science	11.7	11.2	12.1	10.6	10.3	11.3
Social studies	18.9	16.5	16.5	15.4	14.6	14.5
Computer science	0.0	0.0	0.0	0.0	0.5	1.7
Commercial	8.5	7.3	7.7	8.5	4.1	3.4
Industrial arts	3.2	1.9	0.7	2.1	6.1	5.0
Home economics	4.0	1.3	3.8	2.6	4.8	4.0
Trade and industry	0.4	5.2	5.4	5.3	3.1	2.7
Agriculture	0.7	0.7	0.5	0.7	0.8	0.7
Health and phys. ed.	4.4	9.1	11.6	10.5	9.1	8.6
Music	2.3	2.5	4.6	3.3	6.5	6.2
Art	1.1	1.9	3.2	1.6		
Other	2.1	4.1	0.1	5.0	5.4	5.1
Total academic	73.5	65.5	62.4	59.9	60.2	64.2
Total nonacademic	26.7	33.5	37.7	39.6	39.9	35.7
Average credits per graduate	15.54	—	—	—	21.23	23.01

Sources: Adapted by the authors from Greer & Harbeck, 1962; Adelman, 1983; Osterndorf & Horn, 1976; Westat, Inc., 1992.

Table A.6. Coursetaking Patterns Among High School Graduates by Race/Ethnicity, United States, 1982 and 1994

	All	White	African American	Hispanic	Asian Pacific
1982					
4 yrs. English; 3 yrs. social studies; 2 yrs. mathematics, science	31.5	32.5	31.7	25.2	34.3
4 yrs. English; 3 yrs. social studies; 3 yrs. mathematics, science	14.0	15.5	11.6	6.5	21.3
4 yrs. English; 3 yrs. social studies; 3 yrs. mathematics, science; ½ yr. computer training	2.9	3.4	1.3	0.9	6.6
4 yrs. English; 3 yrs. social studies; 3 yrs. mathematics, science; 2 yrs. foreign language; ½ yr. computer training	2.0	2.4	.9	0.6	5.6
1994					
4 yrs. English; 3 yrs. social studies; 2 yrs. mathematics, science	74.6	75.5	76.7	77.5	73.1
4 yrs. English; 3 yrs. social studies; 3 yrs. mathematics, science	49.8	52.7	45.0	41.2	56.1
4 yrs. English; 3 yrs. social studies; 3 yrs. mathematics, science; ½ yr. computer training	32.0	33.5	28.2	31.1	40.2
4 yrs. English; 3 yrs. social studies; 3 yrs. mathematics, science; 2 yrs. foreign language; ½ yr. computer training	25.3	26.5	19.5	27.7	36.3

Source: National Center for Education Statistics, 1997, Tabs. 11, 13.

APPENDIX B

Summary Data, Grand Rapids

Table B.1. Enrollment by High School for Grades 9–12, Grand Rapids, 1885–1990

	Central	Creston	Ottawa Hills	South	Union	Junior High	Other	Total	Vocational FT	PT	Grand Total
1900	950				191		24	1,165			1,165
1905	966				223			1,189			1,189
1910	1,221				230			1,451			1,451
1915	1,192				412	288		1,892			1,892
1920	909			899	746	504	23	3,082	45	350	3,477
1925	1,123	305		1,386	1,231	384	54	4,483	205	795	5,483
1930[a]	633	514	569	883	1,016			3,615	497	612	4,724
1935[a]	831	669	769	1,031	1,294			4,593	916	281	5,790
1940[a]	712	788	775	1,072	1,265			4,612	905	97	5,614
1945[a]	716	748	626	887	1,011			3,988	Closed		3,988
1950[a]	553	798	556	845	864						3,526
1960[a]	687	1,059	822	943	1,117						4,628
1964[a]	838	1,253	1,338	971	1,112						5,512
1971[a]	1,839	1,596	1,726	Closed	1,832						6,941
1975[a]	1,666	1,481	1,790		1,612						6,549
1980	1,573	1,824	1,671		1,655						6,723
1986	1,009	1,272	1,317		1,310						4,908
1988	1,131	1,067	1,057		1,278						4,533
1990	950	955	1,136		1,331						4,508

Sources: Bureau of Accreditation and School Improvement Studies, folders for Grand Rapids public high schools; Grand Rapids Board of Education, *Annual Reports*.

Note: The figures represent the average number enrolled throughout the year.
[a]Enrollment for grades 10–12.

Table B.2. Permits Issued and Continuation School Enrollments, Grand Rapids Public Schools, 1919–20 Through 1935–36

	Permits Issued							Continuation School Enrollments			Certificates of Age
	To Work in Industry		Farm or Domestic	For Illness	To Help at Home	To Work Outside School Hours	Renewals	FT	PT	Exemptions	
	At 15	At 16									
1919–20	460		40	77	115	1,573	—	45	350	—	160
1920–21	437		22	53	85	386	471	69	454	—	39
1921–22	737		29	63	93	385	333	156	731	—	13
1922–23	271	580	18	63	105	739	517	133	688	142	15
1923–24	267	517	24	60	67	743	484	180	811	162	198
1924–25	229	512	24	59	50	660	400	205	795	206	210
1925–26	229	678	18	55	48	1,047	501	310	788	271	511
1926–27	206	484	39	144	53	837	503	346	679	236	440
1927–28	157	483	85	149	39	626	585	349	660	150	540
1928–29	153	665	86	163	36	797	812	363	680	234	827
1929–30	125	398	61	187	28	492	644	497	612	141	617
1930–31	30	150	60	102	22	182	64	808	488	83	286
1931–32	9	94	29	155	9	139	25	1,177	358	62	190
1932–33	8	64	19	109	14	111	7	1,340	341	30	110
1933–34	5	54	37	141	12	49	10	893	303	19	225
1934–35	1	64	28	127	14	43	4	916	281	20	129
1935–36	6	82	33	101	15	170	11	889	227	27	323

Source: Grand Rapids Board of Education, *Annual Reports*, 1919–20 to 1935–36.

Note: Continuation school enrollment represents the average number enrolled throughout the year.

Table B.3. High School Graduation Requirements in Credit Hours, Grand Rapids High Schools, 1904–1990

	1904	1906	1914	1923	1929	1931	1953	1967	1977	1983	1990
English	28	32	30	30	30	30	30	40	40	40	40
Review grammar	4	4									
Social studies						10					
History	20	20	10	10	20						
Civics				5			5	5			
Government									5	5	5
American history (12th grade)					10	10	10	10	10	10	10
World history							10	10	10	10	10
Economics							5	5	5	5	5
Mathematics			20	10		10	10	10	10	10	30
Algebra	15	15									
Plane geometry	10	10									
Science			10	5	5	10	10	10	10	10	30
Physics	12.5	12.5									
Another science	10	12.5									
General science				5	5						
Vocational subjects			10	10	10	10				5	10
Phys. ed. and hygiene				8	8	8	20	20	20	10	10
Subtotal	99.5	106	80	83	88	88	100	110	110	105	150
Electives	50.5	44	70	75	76	80	60	50	50	95	75
Total credit hours	150	150	150	158	164	168	160	160	160	200	225

Source: Grand Rapids Board of Education, Annual Reports.

Notes: The review grammar requirement could be omitted by those taking a foreign language. State law required phys. ed. for 2 periods per week each semester until 1946, when the requirement was reduced to 2 years.

Table B.4. Percentage Distribution of Parental Occupations of Ninth-Grade Cohorts, Grand Rapids, 1900–1940

	Cohort							
	1900 (n = 125)	1910 (n = 171)	1920 (n = 279)	1930 (n = 289)	1935 (n = 294)	1940 (n = 286)
Professionals	13	12	6	7	2	7
Managers, proprietors, officials	10	7	13	8	7	4
Small business	17	14	13	8	10	5
Clerical and sales	20	22	27	22	20	18
Total white collar	60	55	59	45	39	35
Skilled workers	29	30	28	24	21	22
Semiskilled workers	4	6	6	20	26	28
Unskilled workers	7	10	8	11	14	15
Total blue collar	40	45	41	55	61	65

Sources: Student transcripts, Grand Rapids high schools; Grand Rapids City Directories, 1895–1945.

Table B.5. Mean Number of Semesters Taken in Each Subject Field, Grand Rapids High Schools, 1900–1940

Subject Field	Cohort					
	1900	1910	1920	1930	1935	1940
English	6.1	8.7	6.1	7.0	7.2	7.2
Foreign language	4.3	3.6	2.5	2.2	1.9	1.5
Math	5.4	5.2	4.2	4.7	4.1	4.3
Science	4.8	2.1	3.2	3.5	3.3	3.3
History & social studies	4.2	3.5	3.8	4.9	5.3	5.0
Commercial	1.6	2.3	3.1	3.0	3.4	2.9
Industrial arts	0.0	1.1	1.2	1.0	1.0	1.1
Home economics	0.0	0.5	1.4	1.5	1.7	1.3
Trade and industry				1.2	1.0	1.8
Health & phys. ed.				6.3	6.7	6.5
Music	0.1	0.4	0.7	1.8	1.7	1.6
Art	2.1	1.0	0.8	0.6	0.6	0.7
Other				1.0	0.9	0.8
Total	27.3	28.4	29.7	38.8	38.8	38.0

Source: Student transcripts, Grand Rapids high schools.

Table B.6. Percentage Distribution of Number of Semesters of Each Subject Taken, Grand Rapids High Schools, 1900–1940

	Cohort					
	1900	1910	1920	1930	1935	1940
English						
6 sems. or less	56	18	50	30	29	29
More than 6 sems.	44	82	50	70	71	71
Foreign language						
None	29	34	39	43	51	60
4 sems. or less	30	28	40	41	35	30
More than 4 sems.	41	37	21	16	14	11
Science						
4 sems. or less	50	85	77	74	78	77
More than 4 sems.	50	15	23	26	22	23
Math						
4 sems. or less	35	43	59	50	64	57
More than 4 sems.	65	57	41	50	36	43
History & social studies						
4 sems. or less	72	73	64	39	27	28
More than 4 sems.	28	27	36	61	73	72
Commercial						
None						
All students	69	60				
Girls			33	34	27	20
Boys			41	44	36	57
4 sems. or less						
All students	13	19				
Girls			36	24	30	33
Boys			39	44	39	35
More than 4 sems.						
All students	18	21				
Girls			31	42	43	48
Boys			20	12	25	9
Industrial arts (boys)						
None	100	28	35	57	50	49
1 or 2 sems.		20	23	30	17	18
More than 2 sems.		51	42	28	32	33
Home economics (girls)						
None	100	68	36	27	32	30
1 or 2 sems.		16	26	22	17	21
More than 2 sems.		16	38	51	52	49

(Continued)

Table B.6. *Continued*

	Cohort					
	1900	1910	1920	1930	1935	1940
Trade and industry (boys)						
None				44	48	34
1 or 2 sems.				21	17	15
More than 2 sems.				36	35	51
Music						
None	91	85	75	60	62	63
1 or 2 sems.	9	8	16	11	12	13
More than 2 sems.		7	9	29	26	25
Art						
None	12	73	75	81	82	80
1 or 2 sems.	55	12	14	9	8	11
More than 2 sems.	33	15	11	10	10	10

Table B.7. Average Grade in Subject Field by Gender, Grand Rapids High Schools, 1900–1940

| | Cohort | | | | | | | | | | |
| | 1900 | | 1910 | | 1920 | | 1930 | | 1935 | | 1940 | |
	Boys	Girls	Boys	Girls	Boys	Girls	Boys	Girls	Boys	Girls	Boys	Girls
English	1.4	1.6	[1.3	1.5]**	[1.3	1.9]***	[1.5	1.9]***	[1.7	2.0]***	[1.6	2.1]***
Foreign language	1.3	1.4	[1.2	1.5]**	1.7	1.9	[1.5	1.9]*	1.9	2.1	2.0	2.3
Mathematics	1.6	1.6	1.4	1.4	[1.5	1.9]**	[1.7	1.9]*	1.9	2.0	1.7	2.2
Science	1.7	1.7	1.7	1.7	[1.6	2.0]**	1.8	1.6	2.0	2.2	1.9	2.2
History	1.6	1.5	1.3	1.5	[1.6	2.0]**	1.8	1.8	1.8	1.9	2.0	2.1
Commercial	1.7	2.0	1.7	1.7	[2.1	2.4]*						
Vocational	1.8	1.8	1.8	1.9	2.1	2.3	2.3	2.1*	2.2	2.2	2.3	2.3
Arts	1.8	1.8	1.8	2.0	2.6	2.8	2.7	2.6	[2.8	3.2]***	[2.7	3.3]***
Ninth-grade academic subjects	1.6	1.6	1.4	1.6	[1.5	1.8]***	1.6	1.9*	1.7	2.0*	[1.7	2.1]***

Note: A = 4.0

Differences between bracketed pairs are significant: *p < .05. **p < .01. *** p < .001.

216

Table B.8. Mean Semesters Taken in Each Subject Field by Gender, Grand Rapids High Schools, 1900–1940

	Cohort											
	1900		1910		1920		1930		1935		1940	
	Boys	Girls	Boys	Girls	Boys	Girls	Boys	Girls	Boys	Girls	Boys	Girls
English	6.1	6.0	8.4	8.9	6.2	6.1	[7.0	7.4]*	7.0	7.4	7.1	7.3
Foreign language	3.8	4.6	[3.0	4.1]*	2.4	2.6	2.2	2.3	1.9	2.1	[1.2	1.8]*
Mathematics	[5.8	5.1]**	[5.6	4.8]**	[4.6	3.9]**	[5.4	4.3]***	[4.6	3.6]***	[4.8	3.7]***
Science	[5.3	4.5]*	[3.0	4.1]*	2.4	2.6	2.2	2.3	3.4	3.1	[1.9	2.2]*
History & social studies	4.1	4.3	3.1	3.8	3.9	3.7	4.9	4.9	5.4	5.1		
Commercial	1.8	1.4	2.0	2.5	[2.4	3.7]**	[1.8	4.2]***	[2.5	4.1]***	[4.6	5.4]**
Industrial arts			2.3	0.2]***	[2.5	0.0]***	[4.2	0.2]***			[1.4	4.6]***
Home economics			0.1	0.9]***	[0.7	2.1]***	[0.2	2.7]***				
Music	0.1	0.1	2.4	1.1]***	3.2	2.2	[4.4	3.1]***	1.9	1.6	1.5	1.6
Art	2.1	2.1	0.4	1.5]***	0.7	0.8	[0.3	0.9]***	[0.3	0.8]**	0.6	0.8

Differences between bracketed pairs are significant: *$p < .05$. **$p < .01$. ***$p < .001$.

Table B.9. Mean Semesters Taken in Each Subject Field by White Collar and Blue Collar Students, Grand Rapids High Schools, 1900–1940

	Cohort											
	1900		1910		1920		1930		1935		1940	
	White Collar	Blue Collar	White Collar	Blue Collar	White Collar	Blue Collar	White Collar	Blue Collar	White Collar	Blue Collar	White Collar	Blue Collar
English	6.3	5.7	8.4	8.9	6.1	6.3	7.3	7.0	7.4	7.1	7.1	7.3
Foreign language	4.2	3.9	4.0	3.4	[3.0	1.9]***	[3.1	1.8]***	[2.8	1.3]***	[2.1	1.0]***
Mathematics	5.3	5.4	5.2	5.0	4.2	4.4	4.7	4.8	3.9	4.0	4.4	4.3
Science	4.8	4.7	2.6	2.4	3.1	3.4	3.6	3.7	3.4	3.3	3.6	3.2
History & social studies	4.1	4.2	3.6	3.1	4.0	3.5	[5.2	4.6]*	5.7	5.0*	5.0	5.0
Commercial	1.5	2.1	[1.5	2.8]*	[2.5	4.0]**	2.9	3.1	3.4	3.5	[3.7	2.2]***
Industrial arts			1.1	1.2	1.2	1.2	[0.5	1.3]**	[0.7	1.2]*	0.8	1.2
Home economics			0.6	0.4	1.5	1.5	1.3	1.6	[1.2	2.0]**	[1.2	1.9]**
Trade and industry							1.0	1.3	0.8	1.2	1.0	1.4
Music	0.1	0.1	[0.3	0.7]*	0.9	0.6	[2.3	1.4]**	1.7	1.8	[2.1	1.4]*
Art	2.0	2.2	1.2	0.8	0.9	0.7	0.5	0.7	0.8	0.5	0.5	0.8
Vocational[a]			1.7	1.6	2.7	2.7	[2.8	4.2]***	[2.7	4.4]***	[3.0	4.5]**

[a]Combines household arts, industrial arts, and trade and industry.
Differences between bracketed pairs are significant: *p < .05. **p < .01. ***p < .001.

Table B.10. Percentage Distribution by Inferred Course of Study, Grand Rapids High Schools, 1920–1940

| | \multicolumn{16}{c}{Cohort} | | | | | | | | | | | | | | |
| | 1920 | | | | 1930 | | | | 1935 | | | | 1940 | | | |
	A	C	V	G	A	C	V	G	A	C	V	G	A	C	V	G
Girls	33	25	5	38	30	35	9	26	25	33	12	30	22	42	10	27
Boys	32	16	13	39	36	9	25	30	24	22	19	35	18	9	34	39
White collar	40	13	8	40	45	22	8	25	36	23	9	32	30	22	10	38
Blue collar	26	31	9	34	28	21	23	28	15	34	19	32	12	23	32	33
White collar girls	42	15	5	37	31	39	6	24	42	29	6	24	37	37	0	26
Blue collar girls	22	40	6	33	33	33	9	26	12	38	15	35	13	41	16	30
White collar boys	35	11	11	44	57	7	9	27	29	17	13	42	24	11	17	48
Blue collar boys	31	20	13	36	22	9	38	31	19	28	24	29	12	8	45	35
All	32	21	9	39	33	22	17	28	24	26	17	33	20	23	23	34

Note: A = Academic, more than 4 semesters of foreign language and more than 3 semesters of mathematics; C = Commercial, more than 6 semesters of commercial subjects; V = Vocational, more than 6 semesters of industrial arts, trade and industry, home economics, or a combination of these; G = General, all others.

Table B.11. Number of Different Course Titles Offered by Subject Field, Grand Rapids Public High Schools, Fall Semesters, 1900–1990

	1900	1910	1920	1930	1940	1950	1960	1971	1975	1990
English	2	3	3	7	8	8	10	19	19	7
Foreign language	4	4	3	4	4	3	4	7	6	4
Mathematics	6	7	7	8	8	7	9	12	16	11
Science	8	6	6	9	7	5	6	7	14	8
Social studies	4	4	6	8	12	7	8	14	24	8
Total academic courses	26	24	25	36	39	30	37	59	79	38
Commercial	3	5	10	10	8	8	8	13	12	8
Industrial arts	0	3	6	11	10	7	9	12	11	9
Home economics	0	3	5	8	7	4	5	8	7	3
Trade and industry	0	0	7	8	10	0	4	26	34	33
Health and phys. ed.	0	2	3	3	4	2	3	7	8	4
Music	0	5	7	5	7	5	6	7	12	4
Art	1	5	5	5	2	1	4	7	9	2
Total nonacademic courses	4	23	43	50	48	27	39	80	93	63
Total courses	30	47	68	86	87	57	76	139	172	101

Sources: Grand Rapids Board of Education, *Semester Grade Reports*; Bureau of Accreditation and School Improvement Studies, folders for Grand Rapids public high schools.

Table B.12. Percentage Distribution of Enrollments in Subject Fields, Grand Rapids Public High Schools, 1950–51 Through 1990–91

	1950–51	1957–58	1960–61	1964–65	1971–72	1980–81	1986–87	1988–89	1990–91
English	20.1	21.0	20.2	21.1	20.3	19.5	18.1	20.1	20.3
Foreign language	3.6	4.5	5.9	6.2	4.8	3.0	3.3	3.8	3.5
Mathematics	5.7	9.4	8.6	8.5	9.9	11.1	13.9	14.8	16.3
Science	10.9	12.2	11.3	10.6	11.5	11.8	12.8	13.2	13.2
Social studies	20.2	17.3	17.2	16.2	18.1	16.8	19.6	19.5	19.7
Computer training						0.3	2.5	2.7	2.5
Commercial	11.6	10.3	8.2	10.1	7.6	6.3	5.3	3.4	4.2
Industrial arts	8.1	6.6	7.5	5.4	5.6	4.7	2.6	2.6	2.3
Home economics	3.3	4.0	3.4	3.4	3.3	3.6	1.5	0.5	0.2
Trade & industry		0.2	0.3	0.4	1.7	2.8	2.3	2.9	2.1
Health & phys. ed.	9.6	9.2	8.8	10.9	9.8	13.3	14.7	11.4	11.5
Music	5.2	3.9	4.4	4.6	4.1	3.4	2.7	2.9	2.6
Art	1.8	1.5	1.9	2.5	3.0	3.3	1.5	2.0	1.5
Other	0	0	0	0	0.2	0.2	0	0	0
Total academic	60.4	64.4	63.2	62.6	64.6	62.5	69.4	74.2	75.5
Total nonacademic	39.6	35.7	36.8	37.3	35.3	37.5	30.6	25.8	24.5
Total 9–12 enrollment (N)	3,526	4,590	4,628	5,512	7,300	6,723	4,908	4,722	4,508

Source: Bureau of Accreditation and School Improvement Studies, folders for Grand Rapids public high schools.

Summary Data, Detroit

Table C.1. Percentage Distribution of Course Sections by Subject Field, Detroit Comprehensive High Schools, 1928–29 Through 1966–67

Subject Field	1928–29	1939–40	1944–45	1956–57[a]	1966–67
English	23.3	22.9	21.8	24.2	23.3
Foreign language	12.9	5.9	6.6	5.1	6.1
Mathematics	17.0	12.2	11.7	12.2	10.4
Science	8.5	9.8	11.0	10.7	12.7
Social studies	14.5	17.9	14.3	16.5	14.8
Commercial	12.7	16.4	18.5	16.5	18.2
Industrial arts	4.4	7.2	8.0	7.7	6.9
Home economics	3.8	5.1	5.3	4.7	4.9
Music and art	2.7	2.8	2.7	2.5	2.7
Total academic	76.2	68.7	65.4	68.7	67.3
Total nonacademic	23.6	31.5	34.5	31.4	32.7

Sources: Mirel & Angus, 1986; Detroit Board of Education, 1958b, p. 363.
[a]Derived from student registrations, rather than numbers of course sections.

Table C.2. Percentage Distribution of Student Enrollments in Subject Fields, Detroit Comprehensive High Schools, 1956–57 Through 1989–90

Subject Field	1956–57	1961–62	1966–67	1975–76	1983–84	1989–90
English	20.2	19.5	20.4	20.5	19.7	18.0
Foreign language	4.3	5.0	4.6	3.9	3.1	4.0
Mathematics	10.2	9.3	8.6	12.1	15.5	14.0
Science	8.9	11.2	11.0	10.2	9.6	13.0
Social studies	13.9	12.7	13.3	15.1	14.9	14.9
Computer training				0.1	0.6	2.9
Commercial	13.8	13.3	15.1	10.3	7.8	8.0
Industrial arts	6.4	7.3	5.1	4.9	3.6	2.2
Home economics	3.9	3.8	3.5	4.2	3.9	3.7
Trade & industry					3.5	3.0
Health & phys. ed.	12.2	12.0	12.7	12.6	13.3	12.1
Music	4.0	3.4	3.4	3.3	2.4	2.1
Art	2.1	2.4	2.3	2.5	2.2	2.1
Other	0	0	0	0.3	0	0.1
Total academic	57.5	57.7	57.9	61.9	63.4	66.8
Total nonacademic	42.5	43.5	42.1	38.1	36.7	33.2

Source: Bureau of Accreditation and School Improvement Studies, folders for Detroit public high schools.

223

Table C.3. High School Graduation Requirements, Detroit, 1952–53 Through 1988–89

	1952–53	1957–58	1966–67	1976–77	1983–84	1988–89
English	3 yrs.	4 yrs.	4 yrs.	4 yrs.	4 yrs.	4 yrs.
History						
American	1 yr.	1 yr.	1 yr.	1 yr.	1 yr.	1 yr.
World	1 yr.	1 yr.	1 yr.	1 yr.	1 yr.	1 yr.
Social Studies						
Civics	1 sem.	1 sem.				
Government	1 sem.	1 sem.	1 sem.	1 sem.	1 sem.	1 sem.
Economics	1 sem.	1 sem.	1 sem.	1 sem.	1 sem.	1 sem.
Mathematics	1 yr.	1 yr.	1 yr.	1 yr.	2 yrs.	2 yrs.
Science	1 yr. (in 10–12)	1 yr.[c]	1 yr. (in 10–12)	1 yr. (in 10–12)	1 yr. (in 10–12)	2 yrs. (9–12)
Health & phys. ed.	2 yrs. health	2 yrs. health	2 yrs. health	2 yrs. health	1 sem. PE / 1 sem. PHM[a] / 1 sem.	1 sem. PE / 1 sem. PHM / 1 sem.
Vocational education						
Total credit hours	160 credit hrs.[b]	160 credit hrs.[b]	160 credit hrs.[b]	160 credit hrs.[b]	200 credit hrs.[b]	210 credit hrs.[b]
Other	40 hours in one subject, 30 in another, 20 in a third	Same as 1952–53	Same as 1952–53	Same as 1952–53	Proficiency exam in reading, writing, mathematics for endorsed diploma; 200 hours of out-of-class learning	Same as 1983–84

[a]Personal health management.

[b]Most classes that met 5 days per week for 2 semesters were granted 10 of these hours of credit. Some classes were granted half credit. By 1983, all formerly half-credit courses received full credit and a few industrial arts courses received double credit.

[c]Biology, chemistry, physics, or physical science.

Summary Data, Michigan

Table D.1. Percentage Distribution of Enrollment by Subject Field, Michigan High Schools, 1924–25 Through 1948–49

Subject Field	1924–25[a]	1927–28[b]	1929–30[a]	1933–34[b]	1934–35[c]	1939–40[c]	1944–45[c]	1948–49[c]
English	21.8	20.8	21.2	18.9	19.7	19.2	18.8	17.1
Foreign language	12.5	8.2	9.4	5.3	6.3	4.0	3.8	3.0
Mathematics	14.3	13.4	12.2	10.7	9.2	8.7	10.6	8.1
Science	9.7	10.3	8.9	9.6	9.5	9.5	9.4	7.8
Social studies	14.4	15.0	12.9	15.9	15.6	15.3	15.0	16.4
Commercial	12.8	13.3	15.1	13.6	14.8	14.2	12.4	11.3
Industrial arts	3.8	4.0	4.0	5.4	4.7	6.3	6.3	7.5
Home economics	2.2	3.2	2.8	3.7	3.2	4.1	3.9	4.2
Agriculture	0.6	0.7	0.6	0.7	1.0	0.8	0.7	0.8
Health & phys. ed.		5.1	5.4	9.3	8.8	9.1	11.6	14.2
Music	6.1	4.4	6.2	5.2	5.9	6.2	5.4	6.2
Art	1.6	1.4	1.3	1.4	1.2	1.7	1.5	3.2
Other		0.3		0.4	0.2	0.9	0.5	0.2
Total	100.0	100.0	100.0	100.1	100.1	100.0	99.9	100.0
Total academic	72.7	67.7	64.6	60.4	60.3	56.7	57.6	52.4
Total nonacademic	27.3	32.4	35.4	39.7	39.8	43.3	42.3	47.6
Number of schools	556	—	595	590	534	509	565	—
Total enrollment	123,259	—	108,176	191,031	185,194	229,146	216,560	304,120

Sources: University of Michigan, Bureau of Cooperation with Educational Institutions; U.S. Office of Education, 1930, 1938, 1951.
[a]Accredited high schools only.
[b]All public high schools.
[c]Accredited public high schools.

Table D.2. Percentage Distribution of Enrollment by Subject Field, Michigan High Schools, 1948–49 Through 1990–91

Subject Field	1948–49[a]	1960–61[a]	1972–73[a]	1979–80[b]	1984–85[b]	1987–88[b]	1990–91[b]
English	17.1	15.1	22.1	19.4	19.1	19.0	18.4
Foreign language	3.0	4.4	2.5	3.5	5.2	5.5	5.6
Mathematics	8.1	10.7	8.7	12.5	15.3	14.8	14.2
Science	7.8	6.3	9.8	10.2	11.7	12.2	13.0
Social studies	16.4	18.2	18.9	16.3	14.7	15.4	15.1
Computer training				0.2	0.9	1.0	1.8
Commercial	11.3	8.9	8.2	8.7	8.1	7.7	6.1
Industrial arts	7.5	5.6	5.6	5.7	5.0	4.5	3.4
Home economics	4.2	4.2	4.4	3.2	2.5	2.5	2.2
Trade & industry				2.1	1.6	1.5	1.9
Agriculture	0.8	0.7	0.2	0.2	0.2	0.1	0.1
Health & phys. ed.	14.2	14.5	12.9	10.3	8.7	8.7	8.8
Music	6.2	7.1	2.3	3.7	3.5	3.6	3.3
Art	3.2	3.0	3.1	3.1	2.5	2.7	2.6
Religion & ethics		1.0	1.0	0.4	0.4	0.4	1.1
Other	0.2	0.3	0.3	0.5	0.6	0.6	2.3
Total academic	52.4	54.7	62.0	62.1	66.9	67.9	68.1
Total nonacademic	47.6	45.1	38.0	37.9	33.1	32.3	31.8

Sources: U.S. Office of Education, 1951; Wright, 1965; Osterndorf & Horn, 1976; Bureau of Accreditation and School Improvement Studies, Electronic accreditation files, University of Michigan.

Note: Percentages for some years do not total 100 due to rounding.

[a]All public high schools

[b]Accredited high schools, public and private.

Summary Data, Selected States and Cities

Table E.1. Percentage Distribution of High School Population by Occupation of Father, Comparison of Nine Studies, 1910–1932

Occupational Group	26 Small New England H.S. 1910–1914 (n = 628)	Wilmington, DE 1918 (n = 820)	Elyria, OH 1918 (n = 590)	Four Cities[a] 1920 (n = 1,726)	Wisconsin 1923 (n = 1,968)	Pennsylvania 1928 (n = 27,219)	Eight Small MI Cities 1930 (n = 2,748)	Two Cities[b] 1931 (n = 1,786)	11 Southern Cities 1932 (n = 2,059)
Proprietors	12	17	7	20	11	15	5	20	17
Professionals	5	6	9	9	5	7	2	9	8
Managerial	8	15	11	17	7	12	10	13	8
Commercial	3	10	3	10	6	6	7	10	15
Clerical	1	4	5	6	2	5	2	5	4
Total white collar	29	52	35	62	31	45	26	57	52
Agricultural	38	5	20	2	29	9	11		4
Artisan/proprietor	5	2	3	4	3		2		3
Skilled trades	14	26	25	21	14	24	26	23	10
Transportation	4	7	6	5	4	6	9	7	10
Public service	4	3		2	1	1	2	3	9
Personal service	1		3	1	1	1	2	3	
Miners, lumbermen, fishermen	1				1	5	5	2	
Common labor	5	4	1	1	9	6	4	5	2
Total blue collar	72	47	58	35	62	52	61	43	40
Unknown			8	3	6	4	13		8

Sources: Mueller, 1929, p. 340; U.S. Bureau of Education, 1918a, 1918b; Counts, 1922; Uhl, 1925, p. 215, 217; Moore, 1933, p. 14; Dear, 1933, p. 591; Kefauver, Noll, & Drake, 1933; Jordan, 1933, pp. 48–49.
[a]Seattle, St. Louis, Bridgeport, Mt. Vernon.
[b]Seattle, Bridgeport.

Table E.2. Percentage Distribution of Occupational Background of High School Students, St. Louis, 1860–1920

Occupational Group	1860 (n = 387)	1870 (n = 391)	1875 (n = 1,287)	1880 (n = 943)	1885 (n = 949)	1890 (n = 1,468)	1895 (n = 1,967)	1920 (n = 7,537)
Professionals	6	13	12	12	15	10	11	9
Merchants and manufacturers	29	25	26	28	26	23	24	38
Agents, clerks, & public officials	13	17	12	19	20	23	26	19
Tavern and hotel keepers	1	1	3					
Total white collar	49	56	52	60	62	57	62	66
Mechanics	8	18	17	14	15	13	12	23
Semiskilled workers	7	3	3	2	3	2	2	5
Laborers and domestics	7	3	3	4	2	2	3	2
Total blue collar	22	24	24	20	20	18	18	31
Farmers	5	4	3	2	2			
Unclassified	24	16	21	17	16	25	20	3

Sources: St. Louis Board of Education; Counts, 1922.

Notes: Percentages for 1880 do not total 100 due to rounding.
"Occupational Background" is defined as father's occupation.

Table E.3. Occupational Background of Three Ninth Grade Cohorts, Rochester, New York, 1924–25, 1927–28, and 1930–31

| | Cohort | | | | | | | |
| | 1924–25 | | 1927–28 | | 1930–31 | | Total | |
Occupation of Parent	n	%	n	%	n	%	n	%
Proprietors or								
managers (large)	79	8.7	106	8.1	118	5.3	303	6.8
Professionals	90	10.0	79	6.0	102	4.6	271	6.1
Proprietors or								
managers (small)	135	15.0	200	15.2	285	12.8	620	14.0
Clerical and sales	105	11.6	139	10.6	150	6.7	394	8.9
White collar	409	45.3	524	39.9	655	29.4	1,588	35.8
Skilled trades	192	21.3	312	23.7	564	25.4	1,068	24.1
Semiskilled workers	191	21.2	306	23.3	589	26.5	1,086	24.5
Public service	50	5.5	51	3.9	106	4.8	207	4.7
Personal service	22	2.4	37	2.8	73	3.3	132	3.0
Unskilled workers	39	4.3	84	6.4	236	10.6	359	8.1
Blue collar	494	54.7	790	60.1	1,568	70.6	2,852	64.4
Total	903		1,314		2,223		4,440	

Source: Rand, 1937.
Note: Total percentages do not total 100 due to rounding.

Table E.4. Nativity and Graduation Rate by Nativity of Three Ninth Grade Cohorts
(Interviewed Sample), Rochester, New York, 1924–25, 1927–28, and 1930–31

| Nativity of Parents | Cohort | | | | | | Graduation Rate (%) |
| | 1924–25 | | 1927–28 | | 1930–31 | | |
	n	%	n	%	n	%	
U.S.	571	55.1	742	48.1	1,134	45.6	60.9
English	43	4.2	42	2.7	56	2.3	59.6
Canadian	13	1.3	16	1.0	17	0.7	52.2
German	62	6.0	72	4.7	78	3.1	50.0
Italian	82	7.9	253	16.4	534	21.5	38.4
Polish	32	3.1	60	3.9	120	4.8	41.0
Russian	85	8.2	112	7.3	117	4.7	59.9
Other	54	5.2	89	5.8	192	7.7	50.1
Mixed	94	9.1	156	10.1	240	9.6	60.4
Total	1,036		1,542		2,488		

Source: Rand, 1937.
Note: Percentages for 1924–25 do not total 100 due to rounding.

Table E.5. Educational Statistics of Three Ninth Grade Cohorts (Interviewed Sample), Rochester, New York, 1924–25, 1927–28, and 1930–31

	Cohort					
	1924–25		1927–28		1930–31	
	n	%	n	%	n	%
Gender						
Boys	603	49.2	848	47.2	1,298	49.7
Girls	625	50.8	949	52.8	1,315	50.3
Years completed						
1 or less	361	29.4	528	29.4	552	21.1
2	139	11.3	164	9.1	365	14.0
3	80	6.5	93	5.2	192	7.3
graduated	648	52.8	1,012	56.3	1,504	57.6
Boys	315	48.6	483	47.7	712	47.3
Girls	333	51.4	529	52.3	792	52.7
Postgraduates	19	1.5	71	4.0	199	7.6
grads attending college	209	32.3	229	22.6	226	15.0
Course of study						
College preparatory	565	46.0	675	37.6	947	36.2
Boys	294	23.9	375	20.9	518	19.8
Girls	271	22.1	300	16.7	429	16.4
Commercial	190	15.5	447	24.9	758	29.0
Boys	37	3.0	64	3.6	175	6.7
Girls	153	12.5	383	21.3	583	22.3
Vocational	109	7.7	212	11.9	500	19.1
Industrial arts	43	2.3	73	4.1	267	10.2
Home economics	6	0.5	21	1.2	82	3.1
Technical (boys)	60	4.9	118	6.6	151	5.8
None declared	364	29.7	463	25.7	407	15.6
Boys	169	13.8	218	12.1	187	7.2
Girls	195	15.9	245	13.6	220	8.4
Percent taking at least one course in						
English		97.9		97.7		99.3
Foreign language		59.0		50.8		46.7
Mathematics		79.1		72.9		80.6
Science		92.7		95.8		98.1
History		63.5		63.0		63.7
Practical arts		30.1		28.9		35.2

Table E.6. Grade Point Averages of Selected Groups of Students, Rochester, New York, 1924–1931

| Group | Ninth Grade Cohort | | |
	1924–25	1927–28	1930–31
Interviewed sample	1.79	1.77	1.78
1 year or less	1.48	1.50	1.47
Graduates	2.05	1.98	2.07
Boys	1.77	1.78	1.72
Girls	1.86	1.76	1.83
College preparatory	1.99	2.06	2.18
Commercial	1.75	1.56	1.67
Industrial arts/home economics	1.76	1.77	1.59
Technical	1.63	1.43	1.13
No course declared	1.52	1.65	1.45
Transcript sample			
In English	1.78	1.80	1.76
In mathematics	1.72	1.79	1.72
In science	1.94	1.86	1.85
In history	1.90	1.92	1.92
In foreign languages	1.61	1.74	1.76
In practical arts	2.40	2.42	2.43

Table E.7. Educational Statistics of Three Ninth Grade Cohorts (Transcript Sample), Rochester, New York, 1924–25, 1927–28, and 1930–31

	Class Cohort					
	1924–25		1927–28		1930–31	
	n	%	n	%	n	%
Gender						
Boys	1,050	52.2	1,222	47.3	1,900	49.1
Girls	962	47.8	1,364	52.7	1,972	50.9
Years completed						
1 or less	692	34.4	921	35.6	1,167	30.1
2	234	11.6	242	9.4	547	14.1
3	138	6.9	127	4.9	300	7.7
4 or more	929	47.1	1,296	50.1	1,858	48.0
Graduated	925	46.0	1,290	49.9	1,840	47.5
Boys	461	43.9	620	50.7	830	43.7
Girls	464	48.2	670	49.1	1,010	51.2
Course of study						
College preparatory	810	40.3	917	35.4	1,124	29.0
Boys	435	21.6	479	18.5	584	15.1
Girls	375	18.6	438	16.9	540	13.9
Commercial	304					
Boys	66	3.3	80	3.1	165	4.3
Girls	238	11.8	467	18.1	763	19.7
Vocational	175					
Industrial arts	75	3.7	101	3.9	377	9.7
Home economics	11	0.5	30	1.2	109	2.8
Technical (boys)	92	4.6	180	7.0	197	5.1
No course	709					
Boys	380	18.9	381	14.7	575	14.9
Girls	329	16.4	427	16.5	558	14.4
Course of study, graduates						
College preparatory	672	72.7	778	60.3	958	52.2
Commercial	164	17.7	339	26.3	579	31.5
Vocational	31	3.3	76	5.9	198	10.8
Technical	21	2.3	59	4.6	48	2.6
Fine arts	9	1.0	1	0.1	2	0.1
No course	31	3.3	37	2.9	55	3.0

Source: Same as Table E.3.

Note: Average age on leaving high school was 16.9 years for the 1924–25 cohort, 17.0 years for the 1927–28 cohort, and 17.2 years for the 1930–31 cohort.

References

Adelman, Clifford. 1983. Devaluation, diffusion, and the college connection: A study of high school transcripts, 1964–1981. Paper prepared for the National Commission on Excellence in Education, ERIC ED #228-244.

Adler, Mortimer. 1939. The crisis in contemporary education. *The Social Frontier* 5: 140–145.

———. 1982. *The Paideia proposal.* New York: Macmillan.

Advisory Committee on Education. 1938. *Report of the committee.* Washington, DC: GPO.

American Association of School Administrators. 1938. *Youth education today.* Washington, DC: The Association.

American Historical Association, Commission on the Social Studies. 1934. *Conclusions and recommendations of the commission.* New York: Charles Scribner's Sons.

American Youth Commission. 1942. *Youth and the future: The general report of the American Youth Commission.* Washington, DC: American Council on Education.

Anderson, James D. 1988. *The education of blacks in the South, 1880–1935.* Chapel Hill: University of North Carolina Press.

Angus, David L. 1965. The dropout problem: An interpretive history. Ph.D. diss., Ohio State University.

———. 1981. A note on the occupational backgrounds of public high school students prior to 1940. *Journal of the Midwest History of Education Society* 9:158–83.

———. 1982. The politics of progressive school reform: Grand Rapids, 1900–1910. *Michigan Academician* 14:239–58.

———. 1988. Conflict, class, and the nineteenth century public high school in the cities of the Midwest. *Curriculum Inquiry* 18 (1): 7–31.

———. 1991. The media, Black leadership, and the university in the post-Sputnik curriculum debate. *Journal of the Midwest History of Education Society* 19:1–17.

———. 1993. The Committee of Ten and the professionalization of curriculum planning. Paper presented at a symposium on the one hundredth anniversary of the Report of the Committee of Ten, History of Education Society, Chicago.

Angus, David L., and Jeffrey E. Mirel. 1993. Equality, curriculum, and the decline of the academic ideal: Detroit, 1930–68. *History of Education Quarterly* 33:177–206.

———. 1994. "The high school question": Class, politics and the founding of the nineteenth century American high school. Paper presented to the American Educational Research Association, New Orleans.

Asante, Molefi K. 1987. *The Afrocentric idea*. Philadelphia: Temple University Press.

————. 1992. Afrocentric curriculum. *Educational Leadership* 49:28–31.

Bailey, Larry J., and Ronald W. Stadt. 1973. *Career education: New approaches to human development*. Bloomington, IL: McKnight Publishing Co.

Beals, Melba Pattillo. 1994. *Warriors don't cry*. New York: Washington Square Press.

Bedell, Earl L., and Walter R. Gleason. 1943. Detroit public schools in the war effort. *Industrial Arts and Vocational Education* 32:86.

Bell, Bernard Iddings. 1949. *Crisis in education: A challenge to American complacency*. New York: McGraw-Hill.

Bell, Howard M. 1938. *Youth tell their story*. Washington, DC: American Council on Education.

————. 1940. *Matching youth and jobs*. Washington, DC: American Council on Education.

Bestor, Arthur. [1953] 1985. *Educational wastelands: The retreat from learning in our public schools*. Chicago: University of Illinois Press.

Bobbitt, Franklin. 1915. *What the schools teach and might teach*. Cleveland: Survey Committee of the Cleveland Foundation.

————. 1918. *The curriculum*. Boston: Houghton Mifflin Co.

————. 1924. *How to make a curriculum*. Boston: Houghton Mifflin Co.

Bowles, Samuel, and Herbert Gintis. 1976. *Schooling in capitalist America*. New York: Basic Books.

Boyer, Ernest L. 1983. *High school: A report on secondary education in America*. New York: Harper and Row.

Bracey, Gerald W. 1996a. International comparisons and the condition of American education. *Educational Researcher* 25:5–11.

————. 1996b. What should children learn? *The Atlantic Monthly* 277:10.

Bradley, Raymond J. 1929. The American high-school program of studies. Ph.D. diss., University of Minnesota.

Briggs, Thomas H. 1920. *The junior high school*. Boston: Houghton Mifflin Co.

————. 1926. *Curriculum problems*. New York: Macmillan.

————. 1931. *The great investment: Secondary education in a democracy*. Cambridge: Harvard University Press.

Broome, Edwin Cornelius. 1903. *A historical and critical discussion of college admission requirements*. New York: Macmillan.

Brown, John Franklin. 1909. *The American high school*. New York: Macmillan.

Brown, Kenneth E. 1953. *Mathematics in public high schools*. U.S. Office of Education Bulletin 1953, no. 5. Washington, DC: GPO.

Brown, Kenneth E., & Ellsworth S. Obourn. 1957. Offerings and enrollments in science and mathematics in public high schools. U.S. Office of Education Pamphlet no. 120. Washington, DC: GPO.

Bruner, Jerome. 1960. *The process of education*. Cambridge: Harvard University Press.

Bunzel, John H., ed. 1985. *Challenge to American schools: The case for standards and values*. New York: Oxford University Press.

Bureau of Accreditation and School Improvement Studies. Archives. Bentley Historical Library, University of Michigan, Ann Arbor.

————. Electronic accreditation files. University of Michigan, Ann Arbor.

Burrell, Jeanette, and R. H. Eckelberry. 1934. The high school question before the courts in the post-Civil-War period. *School Review* 42:255–65, 333–45, 606–14, 662–75.

Butterfield, E. W. 1934. The new fifty per cent. *Junior-Senior High School Clearinghouse* 8:265–72.

Calguire, Joseph A., Jr. 1975. Union township schools and the depression. *New Jersey History* 113:115–26.

Callahan, Raymond E. 1962. *Education and the cult of efficiency; A study of the social forces that have shaped the administration of the public schools.* Chicago: University of Chicago Press.

Cameron, E. M. 1940. Personal standards course for high school girls. *Practical Home Economics* 18:24–27.

Center for Statewide Educational Assessment. 1973. *State educational assessment programs, 1973 revision.* Princeton, NJ: Educational Testing Service.

Chamberlain, John. 1939. Our jobless youth: A warning. *Survey Graphic* 28:579–81.

Chancellor, William Estabrook. 1908. *Our schools: Their administration and supervision,* rev. ed. Boston: D. C. Heath and Co.

Charters, Werrett Wallace. 1923. *Curriculum construction.* New York: Macmillan.

Church, Robert L., and Michael Sedlak. 1976. *Education in the United States: An interpretive history.* New York: Free Press.

Clifford, Geraldine, and James Guthrie. 1988. *Ed school: A brief for professional education.* Chicago: University of Chicago Press.

Clune, William H., and Paula A. White. 1992. Education reform in the trenches: Increasing academic course taking in high schools with lower achieving students in states with higher graduation requirements. *Educational Evaluation and Policy Analysis* 14:2–20.

Cohen, Ronald D. 1990. *Children of the mill: Schooling and society in Gary, Indiana, 1906–1960.* Bloomington: Indiana University Press.

Commission on the Reorganization of Secondary Education. 1918. *Cardinal principles of secondary education.* Bureau of Education Bulletin 1918, no. 35. Washington, DC: GPO.

Committee on the Orientation of Secondary Education. 1934. *Issues of secondary education.* Washington, DC: Department of Secondary School Principals of the National Education Association.

Comptroller General of the United States. 1973. *Evaluation of the Office of Economic Opportunity's performance contracting experiment.* Washington, DC: GPO.

Conant, James B. 1940. Education for a classless society: The Jeffersonian tradition. *Atlantic Monthly* 169:593–602.

———. 1959. *The American high school today.* New York: McGraw-Hill.

Counts, George S. 1922. *The selective character of American secondary education,* Supplementary Education Monographs, no. 19. Chicago: University of Chicago School of Education.

———. 1926. *The senior high school curriculum.* Chicago: University of Chicago Press.

Courtis, Stuart A. 1939. The fascist menace in education. *University of Michigan School of Education Bulletin,* January, 51–53.

Cremin, Lawrence A. 1961. *The transformation of the school.* New York: Alfred A. Knopf.

———. 1988. *American education: The metropolitan experience, 1876–1980.* New York: Harper and Row.

CRSE. See Commission on the Reorganization of Secondary Education.

Cubberly, Ellwood Patterson. 1919. *Public education in the United States: A study and interpretation of American educational history.* Boston: Houghton Mifflin Co.

Cusik, Philip A. 1983. *The egalitarian ideal and the American high school.* New York: Longmans.

Darling-Hammond, Linda. 1991. See *Voices from the field,* 15–16.

David, Paul T. 1942. *Barriers to youth employment.* Washington, DC: American Council on Education.

Davis Vocational and Technical High School. 1933. *Student's Handbook, 1933–1934.* Grand Rapids: The Board.

Davis, Allison, and John Dollard. 1940. *Children of bondage: The personality development of Negro youth in the urban South.* Washington, DC.: American Youth Commission.

Davis, Calvin O. 1914. *High school courses of study: A constructive study applied to New York City.* Yonkers, NY: World Book Co.

———. 1920. *The accredited secondary schools of the North Central Association.* U.S. Bureau of Education Bulletin 1919, no. 45. Washington, DC: GPO.

———. 1925. *Our secondary schools.* Ann Arbor, MI: North Central Association.

———. 1927. *Our evolving high school curriculum.* Yonkers, NY: World Book Co.

———. 1945. *A history of the North Central Association.* Ann Arbor, MI: North Central Association.

Davis, Jesse B. 1912. Vocational and moral guidance thru English composition in the high school. In *Proceedings of the National Education Association,* 713–18. Chicago: University of Chicago Press.

———. 1914. *Vocational and moral guidance.* Boston: Ginn and Co.

———. 1916. Educational guidance thru the high-school library. In *Proceedings of the National Education Association,* 553–54. Chicago: University of Chicago Press.

———. 1956. *The saga of a schoolmaster: An autobiography.* Boston: Boston University Press.

Dear, Ernest R. 1933. Distribution and persistence according to paternal occupations represented in the secondary schools in Michigan. *Journal of Educational Research* 26:585–92.

Detroit Board of Education. *Annual reports.* 1856–1900.

———. *Proceedings.* 1900–1960.

Detroit Board of Education, Citizens' Advisory Commission on School Needs. 1958a. *Consultants' report on the curriculum.* Detroit: The Board.

———. 1958b. *Findings and recommendations.* Detroit: The Board.

Detroit Commission on Community Relations. Papers. Table IV, Box 17, Folder: Detroit Board of Education, Inter-racial/Inter-cultural Program, 1946–47. Archives of Labor History and Urban Affairs, Walter P. Reuther Library, Wayne State University, Detroit, MI.

Detroit High School Study Commission. 1968. *The report of the Detroit high school study commission.* Detroit: Board of Education.

Detroit Public School Staff. 1943. *Frank Cody: A realist in education.* New York: Macmillan.

Detroit Public Schools. 1938. *Semester grade reports.* Typescript.

Detroit Public Schools, Department of Guidance and Placement, High school war service inventory, November, 1943. Detroit Federation of Teachers Papers, Box 3, Mayor's

Committee on Youth Problems Folder. Archives of Labor History and Urban Affairs, Walter P. Reuther Library, Wayne State University, Detroit, MI.

Dionne, E. J., Jr 1991. *Why Americans hate politics*. New York: Simon and Schuster.

Douglass, Harl R., ed. 1947. *The high school curriculum*. New York: Ronald Press.

Dow, Peter B. 1991. *Schoolhouse politics: Lessons from the Sputnik era*. Cambridge: Harvard University Press.

Du Bois, W. E. B. [1903] 1982. *The souls of black folk*. New York: New American Library.

Educational Policies Commission. 1937. *The unique function of education in American democracy*. Washington, DC: National Education Association.

Educational Policies Commission. 1938a. *The economic basis of education*. Washington, DC: National Education Association. Typescript.

———. 1938b. *The purposes of education in American democracy*. Washington, DC: National Education Association.

———. 1941. *The Civilian Conservation Corps, the National Youth Administration and the public schools*. Washington, DC: National Education Association.

———. 1944. *Education for All American youth*. Washington, DC: National Education Association.

———. 1956. *Manpower in education*. Washington, DC: National Education Association.

Eisner, Elliot W. 1994. Do American schools need standards? *School Administrator* 51:8–15.

Fass, Paula S. 1989. *Outside in: Minorities and the transformation of American education*. New York: Oxford University Press.

Featherstone, Joseph. 1971. *Schools where children learn*. New York: Liveright.

Feingold, Gustave. 1934. The basic function of secondary education. *School and Society* 40:825–32.

Flack, Bruce Clayton. 1969. The work of the American Youth Commission, 1935–1942. Ph.D. diss., Ohio State University.

Franklin, Barry M. 1982. The social efficiency movement reconsidered: Curriculum change in Minneapolis, 1917–1950. *Curriculum Inquiry* 12:9–33.

Frazier, E. Franklin. 1940. *Negro youth at the crossways: Their personality devlopment in the middle states*. Washington, DC: American Youth Commission.

Fulk, Barbara M., Panayota Y. Mantzicopoulous, and Marilyn A. Hirth. 1994. Arguments against national performance standards. *Educational Forum* 58:365–73.

Fuller, Bruce. 1983. Youth job structure and school enrollment, 1890–1920. *Sociology of Education* 56:145–56.

Gaiser, Paul F. 1923. Occupation representation in high school. *Educational Administration and Supervision* 9:537–45.

Gamble, Joseph N. 1931. The place of natural science in programs of high-school graduates. *School Review* 39:177–85.

Gamoran, Adam, and Mark Berends. 1987. The effects of stratification in secondary schools: Synthesis of survey and ethnographic research. *Review of Educational Research* 57:415–35.

Gamoran, Adam, Martin Nystrand, Mark Berends, and Paul C. LePore. 1995. An organizational analysis of the effects of ability groupings. *American Educational Research Journal* 32:687–715.

Gitlin, Todd. 1987. *The sixties: Years of hope, days of rage*. New York: Bantam Books.

Goodlad, John I. 1984. *A place called school: Prospects for the future.* New York: McGraw-Hill.

Goodman, Paul. 1960. *Growing up absurd: Problems of youth in the organized society.* New York: Vintage Books.

——. 1966. *Compulsory mis-education and the community of scholars.* New York: Vintage Books.

Goss, Dwight. 1906. *History of Grand Rapids and its industries.* Vol. 1. Chicago: C. F. Cooper and Co.

Graham, Hugh Davis. 1984. *The uncertain triumph: Federal education policy in the Kennedy and Johnson years.* Chapel Hill: University of North Carolina Press.

Grand Rapids Board of Education. 1890–1945. *Annual reports.*

——. 1894–1914. *Proceedings.*

Grand Rapids Civic Club. 1903–1906. *Live Issues in Kent County.* Civic Affairs Supplements nos. 1–4.

GRAR. See Grand Rapids Board of Education, *Annual reports.*

GRP. See Grand Rapids Board of Education, *Proceedings.*

Greer, Edith S., and Richard M. Harbeck. 1962. *What high school pupils study: A national survey of the scholastic performance of pupils of various abilities,* U.S. Office of Education Bulletin 1962, no. 10. Washington, DC: GPO.

Greeson, William A. 1914. Substitution of work of vocational or prevocational character in the upper grades. In *Proceedings of the National Education Association,* pp. 426–28. Chicago: University of Chicago Press.

Greet, Robert L. 1972. The Plainfield school system in the depression: 1930–1937. *New Jersey History* 110:69–82.

Gregory, Karl D. 1967. The walkout: Symptom of dying inner city schools. *New University Thought* 5 (3): 29–54.

Grinnell, John Erle. 1935. The rise of the North Central Association. *North Central Association Quarterly* 9:468–95; 10:365–82, 469–526.

Gross, Ronald. 1971. From innovations to alternatives: A decade of change in education. *Phi Delta Kappan* 53 (September): 22–24.

Grubb, W. Norton, and Marvin Lazerson. 1982. Education and the labor market: Recycling the youth problem. In *Work, Youth and Schooling,* ed. Harvey Kantor and David Tyack, 110–41. Stanford, CA: Stanford University Press.

Gursky, Daniel. 1991. After the reign of Dick and Jane. *Teacher* 2:23–29.

Hampel, Robert. 1986. *The last little citadel: American high schools since 1940.* Boston: Houghton Mifflin Co.

Hand, Harold C. 1958. A scholar's devil theory. *The High School Journal* 41:270–97.

Hanus, Paul H. 1904. *A modern school.* New York: Macmillan.

——. 1908. *Beginnings in industrial education and other educational discussions.* Boston: Houghton Mifflin Co.

——. 1913. *School efficiency: A constructive study applied to New York City.* Yonkers, NY: World Book Co.

Hawkins, Hugh. 1972. *Between Harvard and America: The educational leadership of Charles W. Eliot.* New York: Oxford University Press.

Henry, Nelson B. 1947. The shifting problem of youth unemployment. *School Review* 55:7–9.

Herbst, Jurgen. 1996. *The once and future school: Three hundred and fifty years of American secondary education*. New York: Routledge.

Herr, Edwin I. 1976. *The emerging history of career education: A summary view*. Washington, DC: National Advisory Council on Career Education.

Hershberg, James G. 1993. *James B. Conant: Harvard to Hiroshima and the making of the nuclear age*. New York: Alfred A. Knopf.

Hofstadter, Richard. 1963. *Anti-intellectualism in American life*. New York: Alfred A. Knopf.

Hollingshead, A. B. 1949. *Elmstown's youth: The impact of social classes on adolescents*. New York: John Wiley and Sons.

Holt, Kenneth C. 1992. A rationale for creating African-American immersion schools. *Educational Leadership* 49:18.

Homel, Michael W. 1984. *Down from equality: Black Chicagoans and the public schools, 1920–41*. Chicago: University of Illinois Press.

Horn, Ernest. 1937. *Methods of instruction in the social studies*. New York: Charles Scribner's Sons.

Howard, Jeff P. 1993. The third movement: Developing black children for the 21st century. In *The state of black America 1993*, ed. Billy J. Tidwell, 11–34. New York: National Urban League.

Howe, Harold, II. 1991. See *Voices from the field*, 26–27.

Hoyt, Kenneth B. 1974. *An introduction to career education: A policy paper of the U.S. Office of Education*. Washington, DC: GPO.

———. 1976. *Refining the career education concept*. Washington, DC: GPO.

———. 1977. *Refining the career education concept. Part II*. Washington, DC: GPO.

Inglis, Alexander. 1918. *Principles of secondary education*. Boston: Houghton Mifflin Co.

———. 1924. Secondary education. In *Twenty-five years of American education*, ed. Isaac Kandel, 249–69. New York: Teachers College Press.

Jacob, John E. 1992. Keynote speech to the National Urban League, July 26. Typescript.

Jarrett, Vernon. 1979. When schools had a mission. *Chicago Tribune*, September 23, sec. 2, p. 6.

Johns, Ray. 1938. *En route to maturity*. Detroit: Board of Education.

Johnston, Charles Hughes, ed. 1912. *High school education*. New York: Charles Scribner and Sons.

Jordan, Floyd. 1933. *The social composition of the secondary schools of the southern states*. George Peabody Contributions to Education, no. 108. Nashville, TN: George Peabody College of Education.

Judd, Charles H. 1918a. *Introduction to the scientific study of education*. Boston: Ginn and Co.

———. 1918b. *The evolution of a democratic school system*. Boston: Houghton Mifflin Co.

———. 1941. Federal relations with secondary school administrators. *North Central Association Quarterly* 15:312–329.

———. 1942. The real youth problem. *School and Society* 55:29–33.

Kandel, Isaac L. 1930. *History of secondary education: A study in the development of liberal education*. Boston: Houghton Mifflin Co.

Kantor, Harvey A. 1988. *Learning to earn: School, work, and vocational reform in California, 1880–1930*. Madison: University of Wisconsin Press.

Kaplan, George. 1991. See *Voices from the field*, 11–12.

Karpinos, Bernard. 1941. *The socio-economic and employment status of urban youth in the United States, 1935–36*. Public Health Bulletin, no. 273. Washington, DC: GPO.

Katz, Michael B. 1968. *The irony of early school reform: Educational innovation in mid-nineteenth century Massachusetts*. Cambridge: Harvard University Press.

———. 1971. *Class, bureaucracy, and schools: The illusion of educational change in America*. New York: Praeger.

———. ed. 1973. *Education in American history: Readings on the social issues*. New York: Praeger.

Kearney, C. Philip. 1986. Michigan's state aid incentive and educational reform: An exercise in symbolic policymaking? *Secondary Education Today* 27 (4): 36–46.

Kearns, David T., and Denis P. Doyle. 1988. *Winning the brain race: A bold plan to make our schools competitive*. San Francisco: ICS Press.

Kefauver, Grayson N., Victor H. Noll, and C. Elwood Drake. 1933. *The secondary school population*. U.S. Office of Education Bulletin 1932, no. 17. Washington, DC: GPO.

King, Martin Luther, Jr. 1967. *Where do we go from here? Chaos or community*. New York: Harper and Row.

Kirp, David. 1982. Education. *The New Republic* 186 (March 31): 31–33.

Kliebard, Herbert M. 1986. *The struggle for the American curriculum, 1893–1958*. New York: Routledge.

Kluger, Richard. 1975. *Simple justice*. New York: Alfred A. Knopf.

Knight, Edgar. 1953. *Fifty years of American education*. New York: Ronald Press.

Kohl, Herbert R. 1969. *The open classroom*. New York: Vintage Books.

Kozol, Jonathan. 1967. *Death at an early age*. Boston: Houghton Mifflin Co.

———. 1972. *Free schools*. Boston: Houghton Mifflin Co.

———. 1975. *The night is dark and I am far from home*. Boston: Houghton Mifflin Co.

———. 1991. *Savage inequalities: Children in America's schools*. New York: Crown Publications.

Kritek, William J., and Delbert K. Clear. 1993. Teachers and principals in the Milwaukee public schools. In *Seeds of crisis: Public schooling in Milwaukee since 1920*, ed. John L. Rury and Frank A Cassell, 145–92. Madison: University of Wisconsin Press.

Krug, Edward A. 1960. *The secondary curriculum*. New York: Harper and Row.

———. 1964. *The shaping of the American high school, 1880–1920*. Vol. 1. Madison: University of Wisconsin Press.

———. 1972. *The shaping of the American high school, 1920–1941*. Vol. 2. Madison: University of Wisconsin Press.

Labaree, David F. 1988. *The making of an American high school*. New Haven: Yale University Press.

Larson, Edward J. 1985. *Trial and error: The American controversy over creation and evolution*. New York: Oxford University Press.

Lasch, Christopher. 1995. *The revolt of the elites and the betrayal of democracy*. New York: W. W. Norton and Co.

Latimer, John F. 1958. *What's happened to our high schools?* Washington, DC: Public Affairs Press.

Lawson, Douglas E. 1940. *Curriculum development in city-school systems.* Chicago: University of Chicago Press.

Leach, Kent. 1957. Letter to Harlan Hatcher. Harlan Hatcher Papers, Box 19, Folder 9–12, Michigan Historical Collections. Bentley Historical Library, University of Michigan, Ann Arbor.

Lederer, Muriel. 1976. *The guide to career education.* New York: Quadrangle/New York Times Book Co.

Lee, Carol D., Kofi Lomotey, and Mwalimu Shujaa. 1990. How shall we sing our sacred songs in a strange land?: The dilemma of double consciousness and the complexities of African-centered pedagogy. *Journal of Education* 172 (2): 45–58.

Lewis, William D. 1914. *Democracy's high school.* Boston: Houghton Mifflin Co.

Lide, Edwin S. 1931. The social composition of the secondary-school population in Oklahoma. *School Review* 39:350–60.

Lipsitz, Joan. 1991. See *Voices from the field,* 36–37.

Loomis, Arthur K., Edwin S. Lide, and B. Lamar Johnson. 1933. *The program of studies.* National Survey of Secondary Education, U.S. Bureau of Education Bulletin 1932, no. 17, Monograph no. 19. Washington, DC: GPO.

Lowitt, Richard, and Maurine Beasley, eds. 1981. *One third of a nation: Lorena Hickok reports on the great depression.* Urbana: University of Illinois Press.

Lydens, Z. Z., ed. 1966. *The story of Grand Rapids.* Grand Rapids, MI: Kregel Publications.

Lynd, Albert. 1953. *Quackery in the public schools.* Boston: Little, Brown and Co.

Lynd, Robert S., and Helen Merrell Lynd. 1937. *Middletown in transition: A study in cultural conflicts.* New York: Harcourt Brace Jovanovich.

Maehr, Martin L., and Jane M. Maehr. 1996. Schools aren't as good as they used to be: They never were. *Educational Researcher* 25:21–24.

Margo, Robert A. 1990. *Race and schooling in the south, 1880–1950: An economic history.* Chicago: University of Chicago Press.

Matusow, Allen J. 1984. *The unraveling of America: A history of liberalism in the 1960s.* New York: Harper and Row.

Maxwell, G. L., and Francis T. Spaulding. 1941. *The relationship of the federal government to the education of youth of secondary-school age.* Washington, DC: National Association of Secondary-School Principals.

McKelvey, Blake. 1961. *Rochester: An emerging metropolis, 1925–1961.* Rochester, NY: Christopher Press.

Mecklenburger, James A. 1972. *Performance contracting—1969–1971.* Worthington, OH: Charles A. Jones.

Meier, Deborah. 1985. The wrong track. *The Nation* 240:626–30.

Merritt, Ella Arvillo, and Floy Hendricks. 1945. The trend of child labor, 1940–1944. *Monthly Labor Review* 60:756–75.

Michigan Business Roundtable. 1991. *Education excellence: An agenda for education reform in Michigan.* Freeland, MI: The Roundtable.

Michigan Commission on High Schools. 1983. *Striving for excellence: Strengthening secondary education in Michigan.* Lansing: The Commission.

Michigan State Board of Education. 1984. *Better education for Michigan: A blueprint for action*. Lansing: The Board.

———. 1992. *Position statement on core curriculum and the state model core curriculum outcomes*. Lansing: The Board.

Michigan State Republican Caucus. 1983. *Excellence in education: A Republican action plan for the 80's*. Lansing: The Caucus.

Minehan, Thomas. 1934. *Boy and girl tramps of America*. New York: Farrar and Rinehart.

Mirel, Jeffrey E. 1981. The matter of means: The campaign and election for the New York Free Academy. *Journal of the Midwest History of Education Society* 9:134–57.

———. 1984. Politics and public education in the great depression: Detroit, 1929–1939. Ph.D. diss., University of Michigan.

———. 1993. *The rise and fall of an urban school system: Detroit, 1907–81*. Ann Arbor: University of Michigan Press.

Mirel, Jeffrey E., and David L. Angus. 1985. Youth, work, and schooling in the great depression. *Journal of Early Adolescence* 5:489–504.

———. 1986. The rising tide of custodialism: Enrollment increases and curriculum reform in Detroit, 1928–1940. *Issues in Education* 4:101–20.

———. 1994. High standards for all. *American Educator* 18 (6): 4–9, 40–42.

Moehlman, Arthur. 1922. *Public education in Detroit*. Bloomington, IN: Public School Publishing Company.

Moore, Margaret Whiteside. 1933. *A study of young high school graduates*. Contributions to Education, no. 583. New York: Teachers College, Columbia University.

Mueller, A. D. 1929. A vocational and socio-educational survey of graduates and non-graduates of small high schools of New England. *Genetic Psychology Monographs* 6:340.

National Center for Education Statistics. 1987. *Digest of education statistics*. Washington, DC: GPO.

———. 1988. *Digest of education statistics*. Washington, DC: GPO.

———. 1992. *International mathematics and science assessments: What have we learned?* Washington, DC: U.S. Department of Education.

———. 1993. *The 1990 high school transcript study tabulations: Comparative data on credits earned and demographics for 1990, 1987, and 1982 high school graduates*. Washington, DC: U.S. Department of Education.

———. 1995. *Digest of education statistics*. Washington, DC: GPO.

———. 1997. *The 1994 high school transcript study tabulations: Comparative data on credits earned and demographics for 1994, 1990, 1987, and 1982 high school graduates*. Washington, DC: U.S. Department of Education.

National Commission on Excellence in Education. 1983. *A nation at risk: The imperative for educational reform*. Washington, DC: GPO.

National Commission on the Reform of Secondary Education. 1973. *The reform of secondary education: A report to the public and the profession*. New York: McGraw-Hill.

National Education Association. 1892–1944. *Proceedings and addresses*. Chicago: University of Chicago Press; Washington, DC: National Education Association.

———. 1894. *Report of the Committee of Ten on secondary school studies*. New York: American Book Co.

National Education Association, Department of Superintendence. 1936. *The social studies curriculum*. Washington, DC: National Education Association.

National Youth Administration. 1944. *Final report of the National Youth Administration, fiscal years 1936–1943.* Washington, DC: GPO.

NEA. See National Education Association.

Nevi, Charles. 1987. In defense of tracking, *Educational Leadership* 44 (March): 24–26.

Oakes, Jeannie. 1985. *Keeping track: How schools structure inequality.* New Haven: Yale University Press.

————. 1990. *Lost talent: The underparticipation of women, minorities, and disabled persons in science.* Santa Monica, CA: RAND Corporation.

Okutsu, James K. 1989. "Pedagogic hegemonicide" and the Asian American student. *Amerasia* 15:233–42.

Osterman, Paul. 1979. Education and labor markets at the turn of the century. *Politics and Society* 9:103–22.

Osterndorf, Logan C., and Paul J. Horn. 1976. *Course offerings, enrollments, and curriculum practices in public secondary schools, 1972–73.* Washington, DC: GPO.

Perlmann, Joel. 1988. *Ethnic differences: Schooling and social structure among the Irish, Italians, Jews, and Blacks in an American city, 1880–1935.* Cambridge: Cambridge University Press.

Phillips, Roy G. 1971. A study of equal opportunity in the construction trades apprenticeship training program sponsored by the pipefitting industry of metropolitan Detroit within the Detroit Public Schools. Ph.D. diss., University of Michigan.

Pitsch, Mark. 1994. With students' aid, Clinton signs Goals 2000. *Education Week* 13 (April 6), 1, 21.

Plath, Paul. 1996. Admiral Hyman G. Rickover on education. *Journal of the Midwest History of Education Society* 23:76–80.

Polenberg, Richard. 1980. One nation divisible: Class, race, and ethnicity in the United States since 1938. New York: Viking Press.

Postman, Neil, and Charles Weingarten. 1969. *Teaching as a subversive activity.* New York: Delta Books.

Powell, Arthur G. 1980. *The uncertain profession: Harvard and the search for educational authority.* Cambridge: Harvard University Press.

Powell, Arthur G., Eleanor Farrar, and David K. Cohen. 1985. *The shopping mall high school.* Boston: Houghton Mifflin Co.

Powers, Jane Bernard. 1992. *The "girl" question in education: Vocational education for young women in the progressive era.* London: Falmer.

Preskill, Stephen. 1984. Raking from the rubbish: Charles W. Eliot, James B. Conant and the public schools. Ph.D. diss., University of Illinois.

Prosser, Charles A. 1939. *Secondary education and life.* Cambridge: Harvard University Press.

Rainey, Homer P. 1938. *How fare American youth?* New York: D. Appleton-Century.

Raizen, Senta A., and Lyle V. Jones, eds. 1985. *Indicators of precollege education in science and mathematics: A preliminary review.* Washington, DC: National Academy Press.

Rand, Harold S. 1937. *A study of the economic and social status of 8,470 former students of Rochester high schools.* Rochester, NY: Civic Committee on Unemployment. Typescript.

Raspberry, William. 1993. Getting smart is key to 3rd movement in black progress. *Chicago Tribune,* August 9, 13.

Ravitch, Diane. 1974. *The great school wars*. New York: Basic Books.

———. 1983. *The troubled crusade*. New York: Basic Books.

———. 1995. *National standards and assessment in American education*. Washington, DC: Brookings Institution.

———. 1998. Putting teachers to the test. *Washington Post*, February 25, A17.

Rawick, George P. 1957. The new deal and youth: The Civilian Conservation Corps, the National Youth Administration, and the American Youth Congress. Ph.D. diss., University of Wisconsin.

Reese, William. 1995. *The origins of the American high school*. New Haven: Yale University Press.

Reeves, Floyd W. 1942. *Education for today and tomorrow*. Cambridge: Harvard University Press.

Rickover, Hyman G. 1959. *Education and freedom*. New York: Dutton.

———. 1962. *Education for all children: What we can learn from England*. Washington, DC: GPO.

Rivet, Byron J. 1934. Curriculum revision in Detroit high schools. *North Central Association Quarterly* 8:502–5.

———. 1937. Curriculum revision in Detroit. *North Central Association Quarterly* 11:453–56.

Rochester (NY) Board of Education. 1923, 1928. *Annual Reports*.

Roessel, Fred Paul. 1941. Comparative mental ability of high school pupils in three Minnesota towns in 1920 and in 1934. In *Minnesota Studies in Articulation*, ed. Melvin E. Haggerty, 122–28. Minneapolis: University of Minnesota Committee on Educational Research.

Roszak, Theodore. 1969. *The making of a counter culture; reflections on the technocratic society and its youthful opposition*. Garden City, NY: Doubleday.

Rubin, Jerry. 1970. *Do it: Scenarios of the revolution*. New York: Simon and Schuster.

Rudy, Willis. 1965. *Schools in an age of mass culture: An exploration of selected themes in the history of twentieth-century American education*. Englewood Cliffs, NJ: Prentice-Hall.

Rugg, Harold O., ed. [1926] 1969. *Curriculum-making, past and present*. Twenty-sixth Yearbook of the National Society for the Study of Education. New York: Arno Press.

———. 1931. *Culture and education in America*. New York: Harcourt, Brace.

———. 1947. *Foundations for American education*. New York: World Book Co.

Rummell, Frances V. 1950. *High school: What's in it for me?* U.S. Office of Education pamphlet. Washington, DC: GPO.

Rury, John L. 1991. *Education and women's work*. Albany: State University of New York Press.

Russell, James Earl. 1922. *The trend in American education*. New York: American Book Co.

Russell, James Earl, and Frederick G. Bonser. 1914. *Industrial education*. New York: Teachers College Press.

Russell, John Dale, and Charles H. Judd. 1940. *The American educational system*. Boston: Houghton Mifflin Co.

Russell, Ron. 1995. Educators say tougher standards may backfire. *Detroit News*, May 11, B1.

St. Louis Board of Education. 1860–1896. *Annual Reports.*

Salmond, John A. 1967. *The Civilian Conservation Corps, 1933–1942: A new deal case study.* Durham, NC: Duke University Press.

Schlesinger, Arthur M., Jr. 1958. *The coming of the new deal.* Boston: Houghton Mifflin Co.

Schwarz, Jordan A. 1981. *The speculator: Bernard M. Baruch in Washington, 1917–1965.* Chapel Hill: University of North Carolina Press.

———. 1993. *The new dealers: Power politics in the age of Roosevelt.* New York: Alfred A. Knopf.

Scott, C. Winfield, Clyde M. Hill, and Hobart W. Burns. 1959. *The great debate: Our schools in crisis.* Englewood Cliffs, NJ: Prentice-Hall.

Seattle Public Schools. 1919–1920, 1924–25, 1929–30. *Superintendent's annual reports.* Seattle: Seattle Public Schools.

———. 1940. *A decade of school history, 1930–1940.* Seattle: Seattle Public Schools.

Sedlak, Michael W., Diane Pullian, and Christopher Wheeler. 1986. *Selling students short: Classroom bargains and academic reform in the American high school.* New York: Teachers College Press.

Seidman, Joel. 1953. *American labor from defense to reconversion.* Chicago: University of Chicago Press.

Sexton, Patricia Cayo. 1961. *Education and income.* New York: Viking Press.

Shanker, Albert. 1994a. Standards and equity. *New York Times*, April 3, E7.

———. 1994b. A major accomplishment. *New York Times*, April 24, E7.

Shattuck, Marquis, and Walter Barnes. 1936. The situation as regards English. In *Ninth yearbook of the Department of Supervisors and Directors of Instruction.* Washington, DC: National Education Association.

Siddle Walker, Vanessa. 1996. *Their highest potential: An African American school community in the segregated South.* Chapel Hill: University of North Carolina Press.

Silberman, Charles E. 1970. *Crisis in the classroom: The remaking of American education.* New York: Random House.

Sizer, Theodore R. 1964. *Secondary schools at the turn of the century.* New Haven: Yale University Press.

———. 1984. *Horace's compromise.* Boston: Houghton Mifflin Co.

Smith, Frank Webster. 1916. *The high school: A study of origins and tendencies.* New York: Sturgis and Walton.

Smith, Gilbert E. 1982. *The limits of reform: Politics and federal aid to education, 1937–1950.* New York: Garland.

Smith, Mortimer. 1949. *And madly teach: A layman looks at public school education.* Chicago: Henry Regnery.

———, ed. 1956. *The public schools in crisis: Some critical essays.* Chicago: Henry Regnery.

Smith, Nelson. 1996. *Standards mean business.* Washington, DC: National Alliance of Business.

Snedden, David. 1917. *Problems of secondary education.* Boston: Houghton Mifflin Co.

———. 1922. *Civic education: Sociological foundations and courses.* Yonkers, NY: World Book Co.

———. 1927. *What's wrong with American education?* Philadelphia: Lippincott.

Spring, Joel H. 1972. *Education and the rise of the corporate state.* Boston: Beacon Press.

———. 1973. Education as a form of social control. In *Roots of crisis: American education in the twentieth century*, ed. Clarence Karier, Paul C. Violas, and Joel H. Spring, 30–39. Chicago: Rand McNally.

———. 1976. *The sorting machine: National educational policy since 1945*. New York: David McKay.

Stedman, James B., and K. Forbis Jordan. 1986. *Education reform reports: Content and impact*. Report No. 86-56 EPW. Washington, DC: Congressional Research Service.

Stolee, Michael. 1993. The Milwaukee desegregation case. In *Seeds of crisis: Public schooling in Milwaukee since 1920*, ed. John L. Rury and Frank A. Cassell, 229–68. Madison: University of Wisconsin Press.

Stout, John Elbert. 1921. *The development of high school curricula in the north central states from 1860 to 1918*. Supplementary Educational Monographs, no. 3. Chicago: University of Chicago Press.

Stuart, Mary. 1936. In business education. In *Proceedings of the National Education Association*, 349–50. Washington, DC: The Association.

Stutsman, Rachel. 1935. *What of youth today?* Detroit: Detroit Board of Education.

Swan, Annalyn, and Ellie McGrath. 1977. High schools under fire. *Time* 110 (November 14): 62–75.

Teicher, Barry James. 1977. James Bryant Conant and "The American High School Today." Ph.D. diss., University of Wisconsin-Madison.

Thayer, Vivian T., Caroline Zachry, and Ruth Kotinsky. 1939. A new education for youth. *Progressive Education* 16:398–409.

Thorndike, E. L. 1908. *Elimination of pupils from school*. U.S. Bureau of Education Bulletin 1907, no. 4. Washington, DC: GPO.

Tildsley, John H. 1936. *The mounting waste of the American secondary schools*. Cambridge: Harvard University Press.

Tozer, Steven E., Paul C. Violas, and Guy B. Senese. 1993. *School and society: Historical and contemporary perspectives*. New York: McGraw-Hill.

Trattner, Walter I. 1970. *Crusade for the children: A history of the national child labor committee and child labor reform in America*. Chicago: Quadrangle Books.

Tryon, Rolla M. 1935. *The social sciences as school subjects*. New York: Scribner.

Ture, Kwame [Stokely Carmichael], and Charles V. Hamilton. [1967] 1992. *Black Power: The politics of liberation*. New York: Vintage Books.

Tyack, David. 1974. *The one best system: A history of American urban education*. Cambridge: Harvard University Press.

Tyack, David, and Elizabeth Hansot. 1982. *Managers of virtue: Public school leadership in America, 1820–1980*. New York: Basic Books.

———. 1990. *Learning together: A history of coeducation in American public schools*. New Haven: Yale University Press.

Tyack, David, Robert Lowe, and Elisabeth Hansot. 1984. *Public schools in hard times: The great depression and recent years*. Cambridge: Harvard University Press.

Ueda, Reed. 1987. *Avenues to adulthood*. Cambridge: Cambridge University Press.

Uhl, Willis L. 1925. *Principles of secondary education: A textbook for students of education*. New York: Silver Burdett.

U.S. Bureau of the Census. 1943a. *Characteristics of the population, 1940*. Vol. 2. Washington, DC: GPO.

————. 1943b. *Statistical abstract of the United States, 1942*. Washington, DC: GPO.

————. 1953. *Characteristics of the population, 1950*. Vol. 2, part 1. Washington, DC: GPO.

U.S. Bureau of Education. 1902. *Report of the Commissioner of Education*. Vol. 2. Washington DC: GPO.

————. 1908. *Report of the Commissioner of Education*. Vol. 2. Washington, DC: GPO.

————. 1911. *Report of the Commissioner of Education*. Vol. 2. Washington, DC: GPO.

————. 1912. *Public and private high schools*. Bulletin 1912, no. 22. Washington, DC: GPO.

————. 1915. *Report of the Commissioner of Education for 1914–15*. Washington, DC: GPO.

————. 1917a. *Report of the Commissioner of Education for 1915–16*. Washington, DC: GPO.

————. 1917b. *Report of the Commissioner of Education for 1916–17*. Washington, DC: GPO.

————. 1918a. *Educational survey of Elyria, Ohio*. Bulletin 1918, no. 15. Washington, DC: GPO.

————. 1918b. *Industrial education in Wilmington, Delaware*. Bulletin 1918, no. 25. Washington, DC: GPO.

————. 1918c. *Report of the Commissioner of Education for 1917–18*. Washington, DC: GPO.

————. 1926. *Statistics of public high schools, 1923–1924*. Bulletin 1925, no. 40. Washington, DC: GPO.

U.S. Congress. 1974. Public Law 93-380, sec. 406. 20 USC 1865.

U.S. Department of Education. 1997. *America's teachers: Profile of a profession*. Washington, DC: GPO.

————. 1991. *America 2000: An education strategy*. Washington, DC: The Department.

U.S. Department of Labor, Children's Bureau. 1933. *Child labor: Facts and figures*. Washington, DC: GPO.

U.S. Office of Education. 1930. *Biennial survey of education, 1926–1928*. Bulletin 1930, no. 16. Washington, DC: GPO.

————. 1938. *Offerings and registrations in high-school subjects*. Bulletin 1938, no. 6. Washington, DC: GPO.

————. 1951. *Biennial Survey of Education, 1948–50*. Washington, DC: GPO.

————. 1956. *Offerings and enrollments in science and mathematics in public high schools*. Pamphlet no. 120. Washington, DC: GPO.

————. 1964. *Digest of educational statistics*. Bulletin 1964, no. 18. Washington, DC: GPO.

————. 1965. *Digest of educational statistics*. Bulletin 1965, no. 4. Washington, DC: GPO.

University of Michigan, Bureau of Cooperation with Educational Institutions. 1935, 1936, 1940, 1945. *Annual Reports*.

USBE. See U.S. Bureau of Education.

USOE. See U.S. Office of Education.

Van Dyke, George E. 1931. Trends in the development of the high-school offering. *School Review* 39:657–64, 737–47.

Vinovskis, Maris A. 1995. *Education, society and economic opportunity*. New Haven: Yale University Press.

———. 1997. The development and effectiveness of compensatory educational programs. In *Giving better, giving smarter: Working papers of the National Commission on Philanthropy and Civic Renewal*, ed. John W. Barry and Bruno V. Manno, 169–92. Washington, DC: The Commission.

Violas, Paul C. 1978. *The training of the urban working class*. Chicago: Rand McNally.

Voices from the field: 30 expert opinions on America 2000, the Bush administration strategy to "reinvent" America's schools. Washington, DC: William T. Grant Foundation and Institute for Educational Leadership.

Wales, John N. 1962. *Schools of democracy: An Englishman's impressions of secondary education in the American Middle-West*. East Lansing: Michigan State University Press.

Walters, Pamela Barnhouse. 1984. Occupational and labor market effects on secondary and postsecondary educational expansion in the United States: 1922–1979. *American Sociological Review* 49:659–71.

Warner, W. Lloyd, Robert Havighurst, and Martin Loeb. 1944. *Who shall be educated?* New York: Harper and Brothers.

Webster, Joan M. 1973. The flash-in-the-pan: Simmered down or whatever happened to performance contracting in Grand Rapids? *Michigan Association of School Boards Journal* 20 (6): 19–21, 26.

Weiss, Iris R. 1978. *Report of the 1977 national survey of science, mathematics, and social studies education*. Research Triangle Park, NC: Center for Educational Research and Evaluation.

West, Jerry, Louis Diodato, and Nancy Sandberg. 1984. *A trend study of high school offerings and enrollments: 1972–73—1981–82*. Washington, DC: National Center for Education Statistics.

Westat, Inc. 1992. *The 1990 high school transcript study tabulations*. Report to the National Center for Education Statistics. Typescript.

Wilkerson, Doxie A. 1939. *Special problems of Negro education*. Washington, DC: GPO.

Williams, Dennis A., Vincent Coppola, Lucy Howard, Janet Huck, Patricia King, Christopher Ma, and Sylvester Monroe. 1981. Why public schools fail. *Newsweek* 97 (April 20): 62–65.

Williams, Stephen. 1986. From polemics to practice: IQ testing and tracking in the Detroit public schools and their relationship to the national debate. Ph.D. diss., University of Michigan.

Wisconsin. 1892. *Biennial report of the superintendent of public instruction*.

Wolf, Eleanor P. 1981. *Trial and error: The Detroit school segregation case*. Detroit: Wayne State University Press.

Wright, Grace S. 1965. *Subject offerings and enrollments in public secondary schools*. Washington, DC: GPO.

Zeitlan, Harry. 1958. Federal relations in American education, 1933–1943: A study of new deal efforts and innovations. Ph.D. diss., Columbia University.

Zilversmit, Arthur. 1993. *Changing schools: Progressive education theory and practice, 1930–1960*. Chicago: University of Chicago Press.

Index

251

About the Authors

David Angus is Professor of Educational History and Policy at the University of Michigan in Ann Arbor. He has published numerous studies utilizing quantitative methods in educational history over a career spanning thirty years. Recently he has carried out several studies of education and human resource development in East and Southeast Asia and served as chairperson of the Fifth International Conference on Chinese Education for the Twenty-First Century.

Jeffrey Mirel is Professor of Educational Studies and Director of the Division of Educational Studies at Emory University, Atlanta, Georgia. His first book, *The Rise and Fall of an Urban School System: Detroit 1907–81*, won the 1995 Outstanding Book Award from the American Educational Research Association and the 1995 Outstanding Book Award from the History of Education Society.